The
Compassionate
Samaritan

The Compassionate Samaritan:

The Life of
Lyndon Baines Johnson

Philip Reed Rulon

Nelson-Hall nh Chicago

LIBRARY OF CONGRESS CATALOGING IN PUBLICATION DATA

Rulon, Philip Reed.
  The compassionate Samaritan.

  Bibliography: p.
  Includes index.
  1. Johnson, Lyndon B. (Lyndon Baines), 1908–1973.
2. United States—Politics and government—1963–
1969. 3. Presidents—United States—Biography.
I. Title.
E847.R8   973.923′092′4 [B]   81–210
ISBN 0–88229–306–0 (cloth)   AACR2
ISBN 0–88229–787–2 (paper)

10   9   8   7   6   5   4   3   2   1

To

Annette Catherine Rulon

for

"the times of our lives"

Contents

Foreword   ix
Preface   xi
1. First-Born   3
2. Young Lyndon   23
3. Learning to Be a Bureaucrat   43
4. Roosevelt's Lieutenant   65
5. Grassroots and Heel Leather   87
6. A Master of Congress   107
7. Our Battlefield Is the Classroom   129
8. In the Shadow of the New Frontier   149
9. The Education Establishment   173
10. The Great Society   197
11. A Wellspring of Education   223
12. A Distant Utopia   247
13. The Cross of Leadership   277
14. Dust to Dust   301
Notes   313
Bibliography   331
Index   339

Foreword

I am delighted that Professor Rulon has written this enlightening and extensively researched book on Lyndon Johnson's unique role in the enactment of significant federal legislation in the field of education.

Education and health were deep common bonds shared by President John F. Kennedy and President Lyndon B. Johnson. These two political leaders from such different backgrounds had a strong and common dedication to extending and effectively implementing a creative and constructive role for the federal government in these two fields.

Professor Rulon has painstakingly researched the origins and development of Lyndon Johnson's compelling support for education as administrator, legislator, majority leader, president and ex-president. In my opinion, the fascinating story of Lyndon Johnson's role in federal educational policy is part of a larger picture of how the Kennedy and Johnson administrations were able to fashion a political partnership in formulating and implementing a remarkable legislative program in a number of fields of domestic policy. The entire picture of developments in social policy during the 1960s has not yet been painted. Moreover, the long-range implications of these developments are not yet known. But Professor Rulon's study will be one valuable source which future authors can consult when they write the definitive history of federal educational ideas and developments during the fifty years from 1950 to the year 2000.

My role as Assistant Secretary of Health, Education, and Welfare for Legislation (1961–1965) was to work closely with Ted Sorensen, President Kennedy's policy coordinator, to help in drafting the Kennedy educational proposals and to assist in the legislative process in the Congress to obtain passage of the legislation. Later I worked closely with Douglass Cater, President Johnson's educational policy coordinator, in the development and implementation of education legislation as Under Secretary of H.E.W. (1965–67), and Secretary (1968–69). From this first-hand vantage point I can attest to the importance which President Kennedy, President Johnson, and their staffs gave to education as a central element of their domestic policy.

Professor Rulon's book indicates not only the origins and historical evolution of ideas of a president; it also shows how dedication to the cause of education can be carried out through the political process. I hope it will be widely read and carefully studied. It contains a message of vital significance to the political process, to education, and to the future of our nation.

Wilbur J. Cohen

Sid W. Richardson Professor
of Public Affairs
Lyndon B. Johnson School
of Public Affairs
The University of Texas at Austin

October, 1980

Preface

More than a decade has passed since Lyndon Baines Johnson faded from the political limelight. Without a doubt, he was a unique individual with a complex personality, a man fully as interesting as the public offices he held and the times in which he lived. Few contemporaries understood the thirty-sixth president of the United States, and, with one or two exceptions, the literature published before and after his death has done little to shed light on the mysteries which still surround him. He remains praised by the few and damned by the many in spite of noteworthy accomplishments. Those who support his record see no blemishes and those who oppose find only warts and wrinkles. Neither view results in a realistic portrait. In addition, during Johnson's lifetime, the American people and their institutions underwent an extensive transformation; and, simultaneously, the balance of power in the world shifted considerably, most notably from West to East. The maturation of colonial entities into independent nations also tilted the old international scales. The first seven decades of the twentieth century, therefore, are virtually unprecedented in history. All of these things—the man, the most powerful office in the world, and sweeping new departures at home and abroad—constitute a biographer's dream. In the case of this book, the setting was intriguing enough to launch a

literary voyage of nearly two thousand days and what often
seemed twice as many nights. A simple question motivated:
"What forces shaped and colored the actions and thought of
Lyndon B. Johnson and how, in turn, did he affect the age
that produced him?"

Politics has never been a major interest of mine, but I hold
one belief in common with Lyndon B. Johnson. Education is
an integral part of the life of a democratic nation, and it is not
often given proper credit for the influence it wields. Moreover,
both of us subscribe to the statement of Thomas Jefferson, "If
a nation expects to be ignorant and free, in a state of civilization, it expects what never was and never will be." Indeed, it
would have been most difficult to resist researching and
writing about a man who wanted to make education an elemental component of foreign policy construction and the basis
for reform in America. LBJ was the first national politician to
place education as subordinate to nothing else. It is even possible to say that he put politics as a subheading under education, because electioneering—at its best—is a form of education, seeking to focus attention on important questions and to
sway opinion from one position to another. His social scheme,
labeled the Great Society, proposed to use teaching and learning in addition to legislation to ensure equal justice, to provide
equal opportunity, and to increase the gross national product
so that a larger economic pie could be split by all, regardless of
age, color, creed, or national origin. And even though few
understood at the time, as president of the United States
Johnson also wanted to champion humane programs in Southeast Asia to increase the literacy rate, lengthen life expectancy,
and help people to eat and be better clothed.

Lyndon Johnson is not the only American to believe that
education could reshape society at home and make the
United States a model nation for others to emulate. The idea is
as old as New England and the first settlers. The Puritans of
Massachusetts Bay, for example, held similar views: they
taught reading and writing so that the people could fashion

covenants directly with their God, and their letters and diaries often employed the phrase "city on the hill" to refer to their civilization. Such ideas reached their zenith in the 1830s when various individuals and groups in America came to believe that men and women could reach perfection on earth. Schools, especially, were thought to be the major force for Good, and to advance the cause of education was to be on the side of Right. Such thoughts remained in the countryside after dying out elsewhere, and Johnson, who was educated in an isolated rural pocket of Texas, learned them a century later as if they were new. A frontier birth and childhood generated strength in his convictions. Subsequently, he placed education high on his agenda as teacher, as bureaucrat, as director of the Texas National Youth Administration, as congressman, as senator, as the majority leader of the Senate, as vice-president, as president of the United States, and as a plain citizen in his waning years.

The life of the architect of the Great Society deserves to be detailed in print by one who does not have a personal bias. It is also important that his story be told now and that it be put into the perspective of the present because the nation, perhaps for the first time in its existence, is questioning the worth of public education. Almost all prior generations had faith that the educational system could solve problems and assist the citizenry in pursuit of life, liberty, and happiness. Lyndon Baines Johnson, however, did not see his educational heavenly city completed in his lifetime: his position on Vietnam, his phobia of the press, and the high cost of his health, education, and welfare programs alienated the majority from him and his goals. Then, too, he had image problems; he supported television and was fascinated by it, but he never learned to master the camera. His style, not his substance, offended a large segment of the intellectual community. He even found that he had to battle disloyalty within his administration as well as without.

Now, however, the mood of the public is beginning to

change, and the moment is at hand when the public can begin to recognize the services rendered to them by Johnson in almost four decades as a civil servant. Much of the goodwill achieved in the 1950s and lost in the 1960s should now be regained.

For assistance on this journey into the past, I am indebted to many people. Harry Middleton and Charles Corkran and their staff at the Lyndon B. Johnson Library in Austin, Texas, assisted with the research. The Lyndon B. Johnson Foundation extended funding at a key time in the development of this project. Charles E. Little, dean of the College of Arts and Science at Northern Arizona University, provided me with encouragement. John Wickman, Charles Curtiss, and Alan Kenyon of the Dwight D. Eisenhower Library in Abilene, Kansas, were instrumental in pointing out the rich resources of presidential libraries. Joan Howard, who worked in Abilene and Austin, prepared several detailed manuscript bibliographies in advance of visits. The late Philip Brooks of the Harry S. Truman Library proved a patient and resourceful tutor.

Malcolm Campbell, professor of education at Bowling Green State University in Bowling Green, Ohio, kindly involved himself in the study from beginning to end. Wilbur Cohen, former secretary of Health, Education, and Welfare, saved me from embarrassing errors. Sharon C. Crowley and Stephen Street offered valuable editorial comments. Others, particularly people at the LBJ State Park in Stonewall, the Boyhood Home in Johnson City, and at Cotulla, Pearsall, and Houston, Texas, took time from their busy schedules at inopportune moments to gather relevant data. Gordon Ring, associate director of the East-West center in Honolulu, and Dick Hiser, formerly with the Department of English at the University of Hawaii, loaned documents that would not have been available elsewhere. Nobody could have been more fortunate in choice of research assistants, for Elizabeth Bischoff, Diana Lubick, and Carl Marshall were totally unselfish in the hours they spent locating lost bits and pieces of information. Maryanna Thomas transformed scribbles into neat typewritten prose. And finally, my wife, Annette, whose debt is acknowledged elsewhere, made this project as much hers as mine. This manuscript could not have been completed without her wise counsel and unfailing support.

All errors of fact or judgment, however, remain solely the responsibility of the author.

This administration is going to be a compassionate administration. We believe in the Golden Rule of doing unto others as you would have them do unto you.

—Lyndon Baines Johnson, 1964

CHAPTER ONE

First-Born

"May this ancestral history be of interest as a record of the lives that have gone into the making of your life, afford you fuller understanding of the traits of mind and heart which are your inheritance, and inspire you to greater heights."
—Rebekah Baines Johnson, 1954

T O MOST OF his contemporaries, Lyndon Baines Johnson loomed larger than life. His huge, gangly frame alone often caused him to be singled out. Those closest to him marveled at his unceasing amount of energy, and likewise, his enthusiasm often seemed to have no limits. Visitors to whatever office he occupied at any given time frequently left his door commenting on his extraordinary grasp of detail and the manner in which he could reduce a complex problem to its elemental components. Few individuals, past or present, have known the inner workings of the United States Congress better than the man who served as the thirty-sixth president.

Johnson had his faults, too. And these as well as his virtues were magnified beyond ordinary limits. His sharp tongue could sear flesh when the occasion demanded. His stubbornness was legendary: once he had made a decision, neither devils nor angels could change his mind. His penchant for secrecy seemed childlike to some, while his earthy manners and language often appeared out of place in the high councils of the land. Lyndon Johnson, then, was not superhuman; he did not come from another world. Thus, we must employ conventional measurements to understand the construction of this individual, who, as president, wanted to make education the basis for reform in America as well as in distant lands. Despite his faults and unpolished edges, his compassion was extended to all, regardless of rank or station.

The character of Lyndon Johnson evolved from the two factors that govern all life—environment and heredity. His style and thought were rooted in rural Texas, in the family trees of his mother and father, and in the educational institutions he attended from 1912 to 1930. The union of these three things produced a unique American who touched the lives of many people here and abroad in the more than three generations granted him. Johnson believed in the impact of environment and did not quarrel with those who felt he was tied to the land of his birth. He once told a prominent television news broadcaster that "there is something about the land that is helpful, that gives you an understanding of economics, gives you an understanding of humanity, and gives you a vision and an appreciation of other countries and civilizations."[1] He loved no place more than the gentle rolling hills which grace the countryside from Austin to Fredericksburg and from Fredericksburg to San Antonio, Texas. These hills left an indelible imprint on their most famous son. And images of its live oak, bluebonnets, and the winding Pedernales frequently provided respite when he needed momentarily to erase the present.

In central Texas, human habitation was no less diverse than the flora and the fauna. The peoples and the cultures there left a lasting influence on Johnson. During his formative years, stories still abounded of the courageous Comanches who held the Spanish at bay and succumbed only when Moses Austin and his Missourians migrated in the 1830s to what would soon be called the Lone Star state. More Anglos, especially

Germans and Mormons, moved to Texas just prior and subsequent to the formation of a separate nation. Then came the refugees of the Civil War as well as Scalawags and Carpetbaggers who lusted for wealth and power. All these new arrivals brought cultural baggage that affected churches, schools, and other social and political institutions. This post–Civil War migration produced permanent homes, pushing back the "herds of white-tailed deer, flocks of wild turkeys, bison, longhorn cattle, armadillos, cottontails, jackrabbits, quail, and scissortail flycatchers."[2] The rudiments of modern civilization had arrived by the time of Lyndon Johnson's birth in 1908. But the spirit of the frontier still hovered over the land and the ghosts of the past still rattled chains to frighten proponents of change.

In many ways, the hill country of Texas is a world unto itself, having remained in the age of homespun substantially longer than many adjacent communities. Then, too, this strip of land is a buffer between the ranches of the West and the farms of the East; sometimes it simply does not seem to fit into the state which encompasses it. Many travelers who lighted in this region did so on grounds of expediency rather than choice. Either their pockets were empty or their bodies sagged from exhaustion. These people found life in their locality hard and desolate. One pilgrim wrote that the road from Austin

> soon starts to rise into regular low hills scattered with slender, bent and scrawny trees. The topsoil was poor and stony. There are few animals and fewer people. The horizon is vast and endless, and the sun comes bearing down from an enormous sky. There are caves full of bats. There are vultures and vicious diamondback rattlesnakes. The region is subject to droughts and floods. It is one of the hardest parts of the United States. It is unrelenting country.[3]

Central Texas, as well as much of the arid West, began its journey into the twentieth century as a debtor organism. Both inventions and ideas had to be borrowed from other places to make the people and the place productive. Survival itself demanded most of the hours ticked away by the clock. There was little leisure for thinking.

Many of those hardy souls who planted human roots in the hill country could think only of escape. Most money, hard or soft, was encumbered. The lack of modern transportation spawned isolation, and isolation bred loneliness and inertia. More than a few were caught in a cultural and economic trap. Only the school system offered a method of unloosing the springs that held them fast. Education, Texans believed, could assist the children of both the ranch and farm to make the transition from country to city, from agriculture to industry, and from old-time religion to science. In short, the classroom offered hope for the coming generation. Teachers, therefore, were respected, books were sacred, and schoolhouses served as social and intellectual centers—the hub of community life. Many an early-day Texan would have shouted a loud amen to hear Lyndon Johnson recall, "I almost didn't get my college education and I know how much difference a full education makes. For me it was a passport out of poverty."[4]

The education paradigm permeating rural Texas at the opening of the current century bore a relationship to the ideas of the pre–Civil War Utopians. The New England Transcendentalists, among others, thought that men and women could be perfected while on earth. This era saw Horace Mann champion free public schools for the masses, and social architects soon hypothesized that the classroom could become the major instrument for solving social problems as well as for transmitting the cultural heritage. The aftershock of rapid industrialism caused some social philosophers to reverse their opinion about what could reasonably be expected from education. In the hill country, however, modern communications came late. To its inhabitants schooling remained a window to the future. The only question was whether a person would use his or her diploma to teach, to preach, or to politick. The forebears of Lyndon Johnson attempted all three, leaving the youngster unclear as to which path to trod.

Family line is important: the arrangement of our genes predestines us to an unknown extent. It is also significant to note the chronological sequence in which one is born. The people of Texas measured their wealth in land during this period, and it was not uncommon for them to follow the practice of primogeniture, meaning that the eldest son would inherit the estate. Rebekah Baines Johnson, the mother of Lyndon, firmly believed that the initial child born into a family was special. She wrote of her husband that he had been the "fifth child and first son."[5] Of herself, she added, "I was fortunate in being the first-born of my parents, a happy circumstance of superior advantage."[6] Rebekah and her husband Samuel Ealy Johnson, Jr., would love all of their five children, but each hungered for the arrival of the first male heir. Their feelings were intensified by the fact that by frontier standards they were old before giving birth to offspring. He was nearly thirty, and she was only four years younger, when Lyndon arrived on the scene. The long wait increased their desire for someone to carry the Johnson name to starry heights. Rebekah, for example, stated in the dedication of her *Family Album*: "To Lyndon, my beloved son, in whom I find the best of all who have gone before."[7] (The dedicatee also possessed some of the family's worst traits. But a doting mother never thought to include that which would not flatter.)

What were the hopes for the first-born son of Sam and Rebekah? Some insight can be obtained by surveying their genealogies and by briefly examining their lives prior to marriage. The family trees of both were first-generation Texan or nearly so. The paternal line of Lyndon included Jesse Thomas Johnson (his great-grandfather), Samuel Ealy Johnson, Sr. (grandfather), and Samuel Ealy Johnson, Jr. (father). All of these men possessed leadership qualities, but their individual and collective promise remained largely unfulfilled. Gold and glory eluded them, partly because of the times and partly because of their own flaws.

Little information is available on Jesse Thomas Johnson. He is known to have lived in Georgia prior to migrating to Texas.

Jesse farmed in Henry County and twice was elected sheriff. His marriage to Lucy Webb Barnett produced ten children. Rebekah Johnson's *Family Album* states that Jesse was energetic, public spirited, devoted to family, and interested in politics, his town, and his church. He and Lucy must have had much of mutual interest to discuss, for her father, Robert Holmes Bunton, was a member of the landed aristocracy in Tennessee and Kentucky who liked to share his views on politics and government with his family. The Jesse Johnson clan were citizens in the best sense of the word, and this attitude set the tone for succeeding generations. The Johnsons supported home, family, and church and were keen observers of state and national events.

Samuel Ealy Johnson, Sr., Lyndon's paternal grandfather, came to Texas in 1846 with his parents, Jesse and Lucy Johnson. He was their last child and had been born in rural Alabama. Sam Ealy was orphaned at an early age. He subsequently purchased land in Gillespie County, Texas, to raise cattle and he organized cattle drives from this region to Abilene, Kansas, over the Chisholm Trail. Samuel served with distinction in the Civil War, and this conflict increased his desire to plant permanent roots when peace finally returned to the Confederacy. He usually attended a Baptist or Christian church. Later, he aligned himself with the Christadelphian sect. His final years were spent along the banks of the Pedernales River. It was here that Lyndon Johnson became acquainted with his grandfather. The long, snowy-white beard and thick mane of Sam Ealy, Sr., were an impressive sight to behold, and he told stories of the Civil War and of Indians, cowboys, and cattle drives, between gifts of fruit and candy. Sam consciously or unconsciously perpetuated thoughts that were vanishing from the scene elsewhere. His legacy to his grandson included familiarity with the "code of the West" and a macho philosophy.

Grandfather Sam married Eliza Bunton on December 11, 1867. She had moved to Texas some seventeen years before, residing in Lockhart in Caldwell County. She brought beauty and poise to the Johnson line. Those who knew Eliza well commented on her personal charm and her sparkling conversation. Much of the latter centered upon members of her family, such as Governor Desha of Kentucky and John W. Breckinridge. Mary Desha, another relative, achieved national prominence as a co-founder of the Daughters of the American Revolution. Two others had signed the Texas Declaration of Independence and that state's constitution. Frontier life, however, severely taxed the health of Eliza, and she suffered a stroke the year that Woodrow Wilson became president of the United States. She died on the eve of World War I. The sight of this paralyzed woman frightened little Lyndon so badly that later he developed a nocturnal fear of losing his own mobility.

Samuel Ealy Johnson, Junior, was born on October 11, 1877, the same year that the last of the Confederate states were readmitted to the federal union. He was a precocious child, one endowed with quick native intelligence. He had a deep and abiding love for people that often made him the center of attention at community gatherings. He spent his formative years ranching and farming, and he attended school in the slack work periods. In off-hours he picked up extra money for his educational expenses by doing odd jobs and barbering. Sam would have liked to be a lawyer, but he settled upon training to teach. Final preparations for his certificate were made in Marfa, Texas, at the home of Uncle Lucius Bunton. Sam often placed dried fruit and pepsin beside his books to sweeten a stomach that often turned sour in times of adversity. He passed his examination for a credential, and in later years Sam recalled with pleasure that he scored one hundred percent on state and national history examinations.

From 1896 to 1898, Sam Johnson taught school. The first year he instructed at the White Oak school near Sandy and the second at the Rocky school near Hye. Existing documents indicate that Sam enjoyed the classroom, but he was too remote from the model of Washington Irving's Ichabod Crane to relish "boarding round" and suffering seasonal unemployment. He brought this phase of his career to a speedy end, deciding instead to occupy the home where his parents had started housekeeping. He remained close to the land for the rest of his life, though he did from time to time hold other positions. "Uncle Sam," as some of his friends called him, served twelve years in the state legislature of Texas, winning his first seat in 1904. In Austin he became acquainted with many of the state's leading lawyers and legislators and became intimately acquainted with individuals such as Sam Rayburn and Wright Patman, who went on to secure national reputations.

Sam's dozen years in the legislature abounded with service to the common man. He was instrumental in passing the Alamo Purchase Bill, a measure that preserved the most sacred of Texas shrines, located in the heart of the city of San Antonio. His World War I speech on tolerance was remarkable for the day. The German-Americans of nearby Fredericksburg never forgot his kind words: Sam spoke on their behalf when American emotions and passions began to supersede the bounds of common decency and brotherhood.

But for the most part, Representative Johnson gained satisfaction from securing pensions for soldiers and widows and from supporting measures that aided subsistence farmers and ranchers to overcome disastrous acts of nature. Sam Johnson had the ability to advance higher in politics, but he opted to remain close to his home, friends, and neighbors.

The San Francisco earthquake of 1906 devastated Sam's cotton holdings that were stored there, leaving him mired in debt. He turned to real estate to reverse his fortunes. According to his wife, he always arranged his transactions to the satisfaction of both buyer and seller. The ventures, however, were seldom profitable to the agent. His desire to serve the public continued, and in 1930 he accepted a new office, inspector of the Motor Bus Division of the Railroad Commission. Five years later, bad health—a heart condition—and

subsequent depression dictated a slower lifestyle. In his
waning years, Sam discussed politics with all who would stop
on his porch to listen. He gardened, too. And sometimes he
sought escape from economic reversals and his impending
death through drink. The family moved Sam to Lyndon's
home just prior to his death in San Antonio. There he found
comfort and peace before laying down the heavy burdens of a
lifetime.

The family tree of Rebekah Baines Johnson is at least as
significant as the paternal lineage, especially those members to
be reviewed here: the Reverend Thomas Baines (Rebekah's
great-grandfather), George Wilson Baines, Sr. (grandfather),
and Joseph Wilson Baines, Jr. (father). The Reverend Thomas
Baines was born on July 4, 1787, in North Carolina. He
married a young Scottish girl, Mary McCoy. Thomas was the
pastor of many rural churches, all of which were located south
of what would become the Mason-Dixon line. In addition to
preaching, he attempted to form independent churches into
associations. His career was terminated by death at the age of
fifty. His three sons and a daughter all outlived him. Of the
Reverend Baines, Rebekah, his great-granddaughter, wrote:
"He was a serious, consecrated student, a tireless worker, an
idealist who translated his dreams into deeds."[8] His father had
been a clergyman, too, migrating to the United States from
Scotland. Thomas is the person who changed the spelling of
the family name from Bains to Baines. Both the Johnsons and
the Baineses believed that names created an image and that
just the right one had to be selected.

Rebekah's grandfather, the Reverend George W. Baines,
Sr., had an illustrious career. He graduated from the University of Alabama in Tuscaloosa, earning some of his tuition by
teaching school. Shortly afterwards, he embarked upon a
ministry that would make him a distinguished member of the
Baptist church. He organized congregations in Arkansas and
served in the state legislature from November 1842 to February
1843. He sojourned briefly in Louisiana where, among other

accomplishments, he acted as a local superintendent of schools. But it was in Texas that he achieved widespread recognition. His church called upon Brother Baines for a variety of community, state, and national services. Of his maternal grandfather's accomplishments, the two most cited by Lyndon Johnson were the conversion of General Sam Houston to Christianity and the period George spent as the second president of Baylor University. The Reverend Baines married Melissa Ann Butler, who bore him ten children.

Joseph Wilson Baines, Jr., did not follow his father and grandfather into the ministry. He was born in Bienville Parish, Louisiana, in 1846. He accompanied his family to Texas at an early age. After completing his basic education, he taught school for three years. Then in 1869 he married Ruth Ament Huffman, forming a union that resulted in one son and two daughters. Joseph Baines and his daughter Rebekah developed an unusually close relationship, one fully approved of by Mother Huffman. Both father and daughter were cultured people who sought refuge from the world of harsh realities in literature and the arts.

In 1870, Joseph Baines was admitted to the Texas bar. He established initial offices in Blanco and McKinney and, at the latter site, purchased a newspaper called the *Advocate*. Most readers regarded it as an effective organ of the Democratic party. From 1873 to 1877, Baines accepted an appointment as secretary of state of Texas under Governor John Ireland. Later, the family moved from Austin to Fredericksburg, where the citizens promptly elected their new resident to the state legislature.

Joseph and Rebekah shared mutual interests in journalism and politics. Rebekah met her future husband on a newspaper assignment. She was asked to write a story about a young politician in Gillespie County. Her interview was with Sam Ealy Johnson, Jr., who had just replaced her father in the legislature. She lost her heart immediately. The two spent many of their dates listening to political speeches, such as those given by Senators Joe Bailey and Charlie Culbertson as well as by the three-time candidate for the national presidency, William Jennings Bryan.

Joseph Wilson Baines, Jr., died less than a year before Sam and Rebekah were married. His health was never good, and his family grieved deeply for him after he was buried in Fredericksburg in November 1906. Rebekah idolized her dead father. In her *Family Album* she wrote: "This was the first sorrow of my life, and it required all my determination and strength of will to adjust myself to life without my father, who had been the dominant force in my life as well as my adored parent, revered mentor, and most interesting companion."⁹

The union with Sam was an attempt to put a man with high ambition back into her life. But unfortunately for Rebekah, her husband did not aspire to be anything more than a state politician, so her dreams for her father and husband had to wait and be transferred when she had given birth to a son.

These, then, are the immediate roots of Lyndon Baines Johnson. If the hill country provided its sons and daughters with an undaunted and unrelenting spirit, and if the culture of the region brought many different races and creeds together in a heady social milieu, the ancestral heritage of LBJ also contributed to his development as a leader. On the Johnson side, the men were rooted to the land, close to their families, and a part of the marrow of the people. The women of the clan brought brains and bearing. Conversely, the Baines men were all professional people. But their line was flawed, for they tended to be nervous and short-lived. Their wives and daughters had more stamina than they did. On both sides, many of the males had taught school, and all exhibited an uncommon amount of patriotism. Each side, too, was gifted in the art of storytelling and conversation.

There are individuals in the Johnson family tree whose accomplishments rank above those of the average person. Some, then, might be inclined to think that Lyndon obtained political prominence because he began with superior advantages. It ought to be pointed out, however, that his ancestors also experienced many of the same things that adversely affect ordinary men and women and often drag people down. Alcoholism, disillusionment, long widowhoods, single-parent homes, financial reversals, unemployment, dislocation, and illness resulted in broken dreams for Johnson's forebears. Sam and Rebekah were bequeathed a bittersweet heritage at best. The blood of the clan was not blue, and the individuals had to struggle even to survive. The most important quality that Lyndon inherited was hope. And until late in his life, he refused to despair personally or professionally.

Sam and Rebekah found it necessary to make many adjustments from 1908 to 1916, when children were born to the couple. Sam had to be absent from home quite often in order to tend to his legislative duties in Austin and to his business interests there and elsewhere. Rebekah, who became pregnant shortly after the marriage, experienced deep pangs of loneliness. Visiting was largely confined to nearby friends and relatives. Often Rebekah substituted books for companionship to help pass the long afternoons when it was too hot to work and the evenings that seemed never to end. In short fashion she realized that Sam was much different from her urbane and sophisticated father. He spoke with a coarse tongue, and his manners were sometimes embarrassing. To endure, she created a dream for her unborn son, and she shifted her focus from the present to the future.

Rebekah disappointed her husband in many ways as well. She tried to polish his manners and speech, and he resented her efforts to make him more like her father. Nevertheless, the two worked out their differences, and the arrival of children necessitated mutual lifelong bonds. The birth of Lyndon was the high point of the union. Rebekah later recalled: "We welcomed you—Daddy and I—with great joy. You have brought us great joy. We felt that in you we would realize dear dreams, cherished ambitions, and fond hopes. Our expectations were justified. You have been a noble, devoted son, a useful, capable citizen, and a true great-hearted man. I count you, darling, one of the truly great blessings of my life." [10]

Sam Johnson was not a man of letters. But his esteem for his first-born son was as great as the affection that Rebekah had for him. Father and son clashed often, yet others in the family had no doubts about the bond between them. Sam Houston Johnson, the second son, said that in spite of occasional "strains between daddy and Lyndon, there was a very decided sense of family loyalty between them, a solid standing together." [11]

The birth of a baby in the frontier West was thought to be a blessing. A man measured his wealth in land, in cattle, and in children. Many hands lightened the division of labor, and, in the case of a male, assured that the family name would continue. The fact that parents and grandparents on both sides of Lyndon's family were named junior and senior suggests that preservation of family line was important in the Johnson household. It was a joyous moment when the scream of a newborn child broke the stillness of the dawn on Thursday, August 27, 1908. Dr. John Blanton of Buda served as attending physician, and Grandmother Baines and Kate Keele, a paternal great-aunt, assisted. Rebekah remembered that Lyndon was a perfectly formed child who weighed seven pounds and was long and thin. Sam Ealy jumped on a horse and galloped down the road to tell his parents the happy news; so two generations were present to see past and present projected into the future.

That the boy was considered a special child is also evidenced by the fact that Lyndon did not receive a Christian name for months. Rebekah made long lists for submission to the father. Day after day, he rejected them as being "too sissy for a son of mine," or said, "I could never call my boy that, I knew a rascal by that name." Thus days slipped by into weeks and weeks became months and a quarter-year passed with the infant still called Baby. Then Sam's wife decided that her beautiful infant son must have a name. Rebekah went on strike from her household duties, refusing one morning in November to fix breakfast until a name had been selected. Sam offered the names of three lawyer friends, Clarence, Dayton, and Linden. The latter was acceptable to the mother as long as she could spell it Lyndon. Baines, the middle name, was added out of respect to Rebekah's father. The naming ordeal must have been related later to the boy, for the initials LBJ would one day emblazon nearly everything around him.

Little Lyndon meant different things to Sam and Rebekah. To the mother, he meant companionship and hope, a soft bundle of promise. She wrote: "The mother looked into her son's brown eyes, seeing in them not only the quick intelligence and fearless spirit that animated her husband's flashing eyes, but also the deep purposefulness and true nobility that had shone in her father's steady brown eyes." [12] Likewise, the father believed that something noteworthy had come into the dimensions of his daily activity. Sam and his father projected that their male heir would reach heights denied them. Grandfather wrote to his daughter: "I have a mighty fine grandson, smart as you find them. I expect him to be a United States senator before he is forty." [13] This prophecy was almost fulfilled.

Additional children came to the Johnson household with regularity. Rebekah Luruth and Josefa Hermine were also born on the family homestead between Hye and Stonewall in Gillespie County. Sam Houston and Lucia Hoffman arrived after the move to Johnson City in 1913. Lyndon felt it was his duty to oversee the activity of his brother and three sisters when Sam was out of town. Little Rebekah, Josefa, Sam Houston, and Lucia were assigned tasks which included chopping wood, feeding chickens, gathering eggs, as well as sundry other ranch and farm chores. On more than one occasion, his siblings resented the fact that their "supervisor" did little work himself, and they would threaten to tell on him when Papa came home. On the other hand, Sam Houston Johnson in his biography of his brother states: "He was always kind and protective toward me, and sometimes it caused him considerable discomfort and embarrassment."[14] Lyndon remained a surrogate father to his brother and sisters always. He found them jobs, opened doors for them in the business world, and loaned them money. The early assumption of family responsibility reinforced his parents' idea that he had been born to lead.

The birthplace of the future president was not pretentious, but it was much better than the average for country people. The house was constructed in 1886. It is located across from the family cemetery and just down the road from the Junction school. Sam Ealy Johnson, Sr., and a cousin, Clarence Martin, lived in the immediate vicinity. Relatives, the Pedernales River, dogs, horses, and wildlife made the acreage a pleasant place to start learning about the world. In a television interview, President Johnson explained:

> My first memory is on the banks of this [Pedernales] river. I remember running down and putting my feet in the water and watching the fish when I was four years old. I remember running away from home and coming to grandfather's house when he would give me an apple or some sticks of peppermint candy. My mother was always frightened, fearful that I would fall in that river. So I grew up on its banks and I raced horses up and down the slopes and I feel comfortable here. I'm at home here. It gives me serenity.[15]

The only scarcity Lyndon experienced was in the number of potential companions of his own age.

It was here, too, on the sandy banks of the Pedernales that Lyndon grew to know his parents and understand their dreams for him. Much has been written concerning the influence of Rebekah on Lyndon. These two had an unusual relationship. Their correspondence could sometimes be mistaken for the letters of husband and wife if one did not know they were mother and son. He discussed without embarrassment

his debt to Rebekah. Lyndon remembered his mother as a tall
frontier woman with strong features and an aristocratic bearing. Her hair had just enough red in it so that she could easily
be identified from a distance. "She was quiet and shy," said
her son. "But she was the strongest person I ever knew. When
she gets an idea in her head, she never gives up." [16] Her
strength, however, was not inherited. It had to be acquired. A
favorite family story concerns the time when the small boy
saw his mother in back of the house by the well sobbing while
she pumped a bucketful of water. Lyndon inquired into the
matter and discovered that Rebekah was afraid of staying
alone. "I'll take care of you," said the tot. And that he did
throughout his life. He put his mother and almost all of her
gender on a pedestal. Johnson became a knight errant and saw
himself as a protector of what in his day was thought to be the
gentler sex.

Sam Ealy Johnson, Jr., was a man's man, and far more
credit for molding his eldest son is due him than is ordinarily
given. Since he died at the beginning of Lyndon's congressional career in 1937, he never received proper recognition for
his role in raising a future president. A careful and detailed
search, however, indicates that the other members of the
family knew that Lyndon was, as the longest biography of
LBJ is called, *Sam Johnson's Boy*. Friends who knew both men
recognized similar traits. Wright Patman, who served in the
Texas and national legislature, said: "Sam was the cowboy
type, a little on the rough side, but he had good principles. He
used shortcuts in doing things, and he shouted slogans when
he talked. Sam was a very persuasive man; he would get right
up to you, nose to nose, and take a firm hold—just like his boy
Lyndon." [17] Both Sam and Lyndon were concerned with the
common man. Another acquaintance of Sam's commented
that he was "not a long-distance politician, he was a politician
of the area he lived in, and his primary concerns were with
those people in that area." [18]

Sam Johnson's boy stated on many occasions that he loved

First-Born

both parents. He told a journalist: "My daddy and my dear mother were equally affectionate, equally considerate with their children, and we responded in kind. When I was not prepared with my studies, daddy and mother both stayed up with me until they were satisfied that I had mastered the assigned subject. I looked at them with equal respect and cherished them with identical love." [19]

Early in his life, he credited his father, not his mother, with persuading him to attend college. And once he said: "My father was what we called in those days a 'well read' fellow. He could talk more intelligently than the average city dweller on current affairs in the world; and he had an appreciation for human values." [20] Perhaps the clearest statement came in a 1966 television interview. Johnson explained that "I wanted to copy my father always, emulate him, do the things he did." [21]

Also, Sam Johnson instilled in his son a desire to find his mark early in life. As a recent biographer has written, he was a man of physical, not intellectual, action. In this regard, the young LBJ was exposed to copybook maxims which had filtered by this time from New England to the sparsely settled Southwest. "Son," Sam would say, "get up now; every boy in town already has an hour's head start on you." [22] The boy frequently went to Austin with his father where he could observe the legislators as they conducted their business. He also enjoyed eavesdropping on conversations his parents had with politicians and other dignitaries when they visited the Johnson home. Then, too, he attended community picnics and barbecues with Sam. On one of these occasions, Lyndon said:

I received my first boyhood lessons in how folks in our beloved land choose their public servants. I went there [Johnson City] with my father; and my father taught me that a man should stand up before his fellow citizens and declare himself on every issue. My father told me that was the Texas tradition—and had been since my forebears stood up to be counted at Old

Washington on the Brazos and signed the Declaration of Independence. My father and my mother taught me to keep faith with the family tradition and that Texas tradition.[23]

Father and son frequently clashed, yet the tensions between them were personal, not philosophical.

Both Rebekah and Sam, it will be remembered, were former school teachers. It is natural, then, that they would involve themselves in the educating of their first-born son. Rebekah took the lead, reading to Lyndon in the afternoons and evenings when her husband had to be absent. Favorite selections included the Bible, history, biography, Mother Goose rhymes, and sentimental poems from the pens of Alfred Lord Tennyson and Henry Wadsworth Longfellow. She also used wooden building blocks with letters carved on them to teach Lyndon how to read at the age of two. When Sam was home, he would join Rebekah in listening to his son's recitations. The Johnson residence was a schoolhouse as well as a home.

Young Lyndon made his first contact with formal education at the age of four. He often wandered from his yard down along the banks of the Pedernales to the little Junction School, only a half-mile or so from the house, entering unnoticed and slipping into one of the double desks scaled to the size of the younger children. Rebekah, fearing her son might fall into the water on these adventurous expeditions, decided to enroll her eldest son in school, placing him under the expert tutelage of Miss Katie Deadrich. Miss Katie, however, soon discovered that her new charge had a special problem: called upon to read, "little Lyndon insisted that he was unable to do so unless Miss Deadrich held him on her lap, just as his mother did when he read."[24] The child progressed through a primer and reading book before a bout with whooping cough kept him home.

Those who were close to LBJ at home and at school singled him out as an extraordinary child. Miss Katie, who married Chester Loney and moved to Rough and Ready, California, later wrote that "Lyndon was a very smart boy. And I knew he would be a great man."[25] She was not the only teacher to award good marks. His report cards through the ninth grade would evidence a preponderance of A's. Another schoolmate, a relative, today provides tours through the boyhood home in Johnson City. She is convinced that those who knew him intimately believed that the lad from Stonewall was destined for the presidency of the United States. Hindsight helps prophecy, but there is much to indicate that the boy was an uncommon child.

During Lyndon Baines Johnson's boyhood, the American frontier was drawing to a close. An historian at the University of Wisconsin had achieved fame at the end of the nineteenth century by publishing an essay entitled "The Significance of the Frontier in American History." In this work Frederick Jackson Turner asserted that free land had shaped the American character, producing individualism, patriotism, and brotherhood. The Baineses and the Johnsons possessed these characteristics in abundance. They were pioneers endowed with self-reliance, love of neighbor, and, especially in Texas, a strong affection for homeland. The disappearance of the frontier, however, meant that an institution had to be developed to preserve this unique inheritance. Lyndon Johnson, like Turner, came to believe, as a result of his early experiences, that schools should be called upon to transmit the legacy of the land. The classroom would ensure the preservation of democracy. It would also aid mankind in the search for perfection. At long last, the strains of New England utopianism and western American democratic thought came together to form the rudiments of a great society in the mind of the first-born son of Samuel Ealy and Rebekah Baines Johnson.

CHAPTER TWO

Young Lyndon

"When I was a boy growing up, my mother frequently had all the children around the family table make pronouncements about what they wanted to be in life, what they wanted to grow up to be. It was very apparent to me, even at that early age, that mother wanted me to be a teacher or a preacher or a public servant. . . . Both of my parents had been teachers. My grandfather and my great-grandfather had been teachers. So I guess that early training led me into a teacher's college where I tried to prepare myself for the work that was ahead."
—Lyndon Baines Johnson, 1968

I N 1913, SAM and Rebekah moved to Johnson City, a small town thirteen miles to the east, toward Austin, in Blanco County. This settlement had been founded by James Polk Johnson, a nephew of Sam E. Johnson, Sr. Lyndon, Josefa, and little Rebekah accompanied their parents. Sam Houston and Lucia would be born within the next two years, making the family complete. In Washington the nation had just inaugurated its first professional educator as president, Thomas Woodrow Wilson. He would champion reforms in politics, conservation, labor law, pure food and drugs, and education. The phenomenon called "progressivism" reached its zenith during his two terms. Oscar Colquitt occupied the governor's chair in the Texas state capital. He would soon be replaced by Jim "Pa" Ferguson, the "farmers' friend." And

Ferguson's impeachment in 1917 would leave political thought in the Lone Star state a strange combination of agrarianism, populism, progressivism, conservatism, and liberalism.

Sam Johnson had hitched his wagon to that of Ferguson, and the governor's subsequent removal from office left the Gillespie and Blanco man destined to play only a minor role on the state's political scene. Rebekah remained a local personality as well for many years. She headed the school board, directed plays in the local Opera House, and gave private elocution and drama lessons. Meanwhile, the Johnson children entered the world of work and school.

In later life, Lyndon Johnson imagined himself as a kind of Abraham Lincoln, the son, as he once said of himself, of a tenant farmer, who learned his lessons by the flickering flame of a kerosene lamp. He recalled:

> The memories of childhood are always most vivid; and one of my memories is of our [evenings(?)] in a country home. After supper, my mother and one of my sisters would clean off the table, wipe the oilcloth cover with a damp rag, get the gravy and jelly off and set a big table, kerosene lamp in the middle of it. Then we kids would gather round with our books to get the next day's lessons. [1]

His early life, too, as remembered by friends and acquaintances, is put into the framework of the rags-to-riches stories so popular in the dawning of this century. Otto Lindig, a neighbor, reported he often saw Lyndon "following a double-shovel plow when he was eight" and "hauling cotton bales" at eleven. [2] At nine years of age he shined shoes "in the lone barbershop boasted by his hometown of Johnson City." [3] Others added that LBJ worked as a printer's devil for the *Record-Courier*, a newspaper owned briefly by the family.

Some believe that LBJ and his supporters exaggerated the analogy to Lincoln's boyhood. David Halberstam, the biting author of *The Best and the Brightest*, reported that Rebekah once chided her eldest son for his Lincolnesque statements.

Halberstam added: "He was, in reality, despite the poverty that was around him in those Depression days, a member of a part of the American aristocracy, albeit Texas hill country aristocracy."[4]

Mother and Father Johnson fashioned heroes for their son to emulate. In 1948, LBJ stated that "at my father's knee I was taught the wisdom of one of our great statesmen who said: 'The great cities rest upon our broad and fertile prairies.'"[5] (The quote is a famous line from William Jennings Bryan's "Cross of Gold" speech. Bryan was a champion of rural America at a time when cities were taking over political leadership in the United States.) Rebekah continued to read to Lyndon, concentrating upon biographies of political figures instead of popular fiction. She defended her choice of books by stating, "If part of this is not true, I'm not interested."[6] The two American presidents who captured Johnson's attention were Andrew Jackson and Woodrow Wilson. The boy thought that the former had not let his contemporaries tread on him and that the latter was at least a generation before his time. Lyndon read Wilson in school and sought to test the validity of his ideas against the pages of Texas history. Few can doubt the quality of his choice of heroes.

In more romantic moments, LBJ portrayed himself as "a cross between a Baptist preacher and a cowboy."[7] He shunned dancing lessons given by Mrs. Stella Glidden, the local postmistress, and violin lessons conducted by a gentleman named Brodie because such things were too effeminate. Instead, he envisioned himself as a Texas Ranger while riding horseback to and from school. Even his enthusiasm for classwork began to diminish, and it took great effort on the part of his parents to keep him in the harness. "Many times," confided Rebekah,

I would not catch up with the fact that Lyndon was not prepared on a lesson until breakfast time of a school day. Then I would get the book and place it on the table before his father and devote the whole breakfast period to a discussion of what my son should have learned the night before, not with Lyndon but with my husband.

Of course, Lyndon was too well trained to interrupt this table talk, and, forced to listen, he would learn. That way, and by following him to the gate nearly every morning and telling him tales of history and geography and algebra, I could see that he was prepared for the work of the day.[8]

Initially, such tactics worked to perfection, but later parental domination sowed the seeds of teenage rebellion in the youth.

From 1913 to 1917, Lyndon attended schools in Johnson City. He and his charming friend Kittie Clyde Ross were the most apt pupils in Florence Walker's first grade. The family returned to Stonewall when Johnson was nine. The fifth through seventh grades Lyndon completed at the Junction School. He took eighth grade classes two miles west of the farm in Stonewall. The next year, a horse was provided him to ride to the Albert school, near Luchenbach. Then Sam and Rebekah moved back to Johnson City so their eldest son could complete his last year at the high school there. Since the institution lacked a twelfth grade, the eleventh year became the final high school hurdle.

There were five students in the graduating class. Lyndon served as class president, played first base for the baseball team, threw the discus in track, and was a member of the debate team. He teamed up with Johnny Casparis in an attempt to win the Texas Interscholastic League debate, which focused on the topic "Should the United States withdraw troops from Nicaragua, where Wilson had sent them to prevent civil war?" They won the district contest in Blanco County but lost in the finals at San Marcos. Commencement day was May 4, 1924. Johnson's parents arrived early to decorate the stage with flowers and then sat back to see Superintendent Edward Bowman distribute diplomas. The Class Will prophesied that the six-foot-three, fifteen-year-old graduate would one day become the governor of Texas. The *Blanco County Record* took note of the occasion and said that Lyndon

Johnson "is the youngest member of the class and is believed to be the youngest graduate of the school." [9]

That summer Lyndon embarked upon a unique educational experience that lasted well over a year. Immediately after graduation from high school, he took a clerical job his father had found for him in Robstown, south of Houston. The pay was so low that he returned home (with eighteen dollars in his pocket), determined to seek richer pastures. He, Tom and Otto Crider, Payne Roundtree, and Otho Summy and his brother purchased a canvas-top Model T Ford. In July, the boys headed for California. Of this trip, the future president had mixed feelings. He once said: "I went to California to seek my fortune and almost starved to death before I got back to Texas." [10] Another time he recalled:

I'm not too old to remember my own boyhood [and] . . . . the first trip I ever made away from home, entirely on my own. I was fifteen years old at the time; some other Johnson City boys and I managed to save up enough money to buy a Model T Ford and we decided we'd go West. We slept along the road at night—burying what little money we had under the spot where we slept, and making the fattest boy in the gang sleep on the particular spot. When we got to the central valley in California, we thought it was the most beautiful spot in the world, with its fruit trees and its luxuriant gardens. I spent two happy years there—working at everything from picking fruit to running an elevator. [11]

Harold Lasswell, a pioneer in personality development, provides one of the most plausible explanations for this impulsive act. He says: "One thing of outstanding interest is the extent to which Johnson had to struggle to achieve independence from his mother." Rebekah, hypothesized Lasswell, was an ambitious, domineering lady who had married beneath herself. And it placed her eldest son in conflict because she pushed him very hard. "There is," Lasswell continues, "a tendency to accept domination and on the other hand a rebellious tendency to reassert one's independence and masculinity and sense of adequacy. . . ."[12] In this vein, then, Lyndon's leaving home was an attempt to remain independent by removing himself from outside influences. Sam Johnson sought to escape tensions in the home as well by seeking office in the legislature again, and then by drowning his sorrows with alcohol when ill health forced his partial retirement. His eldest son, too young for economic independence or alcoholic spirits, contemplated flight or fight, and fled.

It is also alleged that Johnson once told Wright Patman that he left home because "it meant one less mouth for my poor daddy to feed."[13] The truth of the matter is somewhere between these three positions; however, Lyndon Johnson had a habit of reconstructing his life to fit the situation at hand.

In the West, LBJ supported himself. The youth had some character flaws, but he was always willing to work—harder and longer than most of his associates. The boys were some ten years ahead of their Oklahoma cousins to the north in picking fruit in the Imperial Valley. They washed cars and dishes as well. But the longest stay for Johnson was in San Bernardino, where he ran an elevator in the four-story Platt building. This job had been obtained for him by a lawyer relative of Rebekah's.

Tired and despondent, after almost two years of hard work, Lyndon at seventeen thumbed his way back to Johnson City. There he began driving a bulldozer for a road construction firm at a dollar a day. He again lived with his parents, spending leisure time at the Casparis Café eating "Mexican T-bone" (chili), watching silent films at the Opera House, and dancing at a variety of halls including Hye, Stonewall, Twin Sisters, and German Fredericksburg.

Lyndon's search for independence continued. His restlessness grew into rebelliousness, and he frequently engaged in fist-fights between rounds of homemade brew. Both parents became disgusted with their strapping son. Sam told him that there were better ways of being noticed than engaging in town brawls. His mother's heart ached. One evening as she nursed his bruised and bleeding face, she threw herself on a bed and sobbed, "To think that my eldest born should turn out like this." [14] Nevertheless, Lyndon stubbornly refused to modify his behavior.

The California trip and the work on the road gangs at home, in addition to constant sermons from his mother and father, ultimately convinced the young man to attend college. Sam planted the first seed. He said: "It's fine to be satisfied with simple things. A man who is satisfied to be a laborer will never have much on his mind. Of course there won't be much in it, but those who are willing to devote all their lives to a road job really don't need much." [15] In February 1927, Lyndon capitulated. He told his mother, "I'm sick of working just with my hands and I'm ready to try working with my brain. Mother, if you and Daddy will get me in college, I'll go as soon as I can." [16] Former classmate Kittie Clyde Ross believed her friend had needed time and that when he made his decision it was a permanent one. She told David E. Conrad, co-author of a study on the young Lyndon:

> I really think that it was while he was on this road job that the impact of all his parents' teaching and admonitions took on new importance and Lyndon Johnson "became of age." It was then that he determined to make the most of the talents and abilities with which God so liberally endowed him. He had a goal and worked with all his might to attain that goal. [17]

Armed with the guarantee of a seventy-five-dollar loan from banker Percy T. Brigmon, of Blanco, Lyndon hitch-hiked to the Southwest Texas State Teachers College in San Marcos. Neither he nor the institution would ever be the same again.

LBJ officially enrolled in the college on March 21, 1927, the beginning of the spring quarter. The time prior to this he spent in the sub college, where he had to validate his high school credits. Johnson City, it will be remembered, did not have a twelfth grade, nor had the institution gone through the accreditation process. Johnson did not express disappointment at being denied immediate college entrance. David Votaw, who had broken the sad news to the fledgling student, remembered that he had taken the decision in stride. The youth "had planned a program for himself, and understood what needed to be done, and was perfectly willing to go into the subcollege to prove some of his credits," he said.[18] Rebekah, pleased at the determination of her son, moved to San Marcos temporarily to tutor Lyndon for his upward-bound examinations—especially in the area of mathematics. In less than six weeks, this obstacle had been overcome.

Southwest Texas State Teachers College in San Marcos, headed by President Cecil Evans, was a thriving institution in 1927. The campus contained ten major buildings, including Old Main, located high atop Chautauqua Hill and overlooking the headwaters of the San Marcos River, an area that had been converted into a playground called Riverside. An abundance of water ensured a campus sprinkled with green grass and flowering plants. It was the Texas Hill Country at its best. Girls outnumbered boys almost three to one, and all the students were instructed by a faculty of fifty-six, some of whom included the prestigious Ph.D. after their name. The degree programs, a Bachelor of Arts and a Bachelor of Science, encompassed a curriculum taught on the campus and in extension centers elsewhere. The institution is the sixth oldest in the Lone Star state.

LBJ acknowledged later his debt to Southwest Texas State in many ways. He returned to the campus almost as often as he visited the old homestead in Stonewall or his boyhood home in Johnson City. He once wrote to the dean of students: "It was there that you and the rest of the faculty took a raw country boy and tried to make a man out of me. To the extent I have succeeded in life, I can claim that you were successful."[19] John Dewey, now becoming known as an educational philosopher, put such thoughts a little differently. He was quoted in the campus newspaper of Southwest Texas State: "College is not preparation for life but is life itself."[20] Therefore, if Johnson could function well at STSTC, he could succeed in the world off-campus. Lyndon's letter to Dean A. H. Nolle was indeed high tribute. No doubt thousands of other youths who have attended relatively undistinguished schools feel the same way toward their alma mater, and perhaps with some justification. Baldwin, Dickinson, Kenyon, Williams, Union, Miami, Amherst, Whittier, and Southwest Texas, all relatively undistinguished institutions, have turned out national presidents.

Removed from the tension of his home, Lyndon threw himself into the task at hand. He later cast this experience, like that of his boyhood, in the Horatio Alger mold. After a lengthy interview with Johnson, a Texas newspaper reporter wrote:

> The young man who had scorned higher education now became a human sponge for the absorption of knowledge. Facts were his meat and bread. He recited his lessons aloud as he worked long after other students had left the school. He practiced oratory as he swept the halls which he kept clean. He made speeches to the walls as he wiped them down. He told tales of the ancients to the door mats which he shook free from dust.[21]

There is exaggeration here, but it is characteristic of the determination Johnson exhibited to succeed. Father and mother regularly received credit for his new-found commitment. In 1928, Lyndon wrote them: "Your letters always give me more strength, renewed courage and that bulldog tenacity so essential to the success of any man."[22] The proud mother retained her son's correspondence, reading and rereading the letters as often as possible.

Johnson completed his undergraduate work in two and one-half years, in spite of the fact that he took some courses by extension. He pursued a Bachelor of Science degree. It included approximately forty-five courses, in thirty-eight of which Johnson earned A's. LBJ majored in history, also electing to enroll in enough education courses to be granted a lifetime teaching certificate from the state of Texas when he graduated on August 30, 1930.

San Marcos, however, provided more than just an academic experience. Colleges, especially those that offered normal training, were still clinging in this era to the concept of *in loco parentis*. STSTC, then, became an extension of the home, a place to learn a vocation or profession, to acquire a moral code, and to mature socially. Lyndon and his classmates developed a style of life as well as gained an education.

The history and education major had a lasting impact on LBJ. Frederick Jackson Turner, then in his prime, was popularizing the idea that environment had shaped the American character. Another historian, Walter Prescott Webb, followed in Turner's footsteps, showing how local physical regions produced community cultural variations. Both Turner and later Webb, who taught at the University of Texas, succeeded in focusing the history at the national level on the American West. One historiographer has written that such scholars turned their colleagues toward the study of the "economic problems of the West, the influence of barbed wire on settlement, land speculation, railroad colonization of public lands, conservation, agrarian discontent, the sod-house frontier, Indian trade, transportation studies, the impact of frontier sectionalism, and the influence of the frontier on diplomacy."[23] Lyndon, as a result of this new scholarship, began to associate Texas with the West, not the South. And he looked at his section of the country as the place where goodness and virtue lived, while Easterners, by contrast, were cynical and greedy. Although it was not fully articulated, a distrust of Ivy League schools was felt on the campus of Southwest Texas State Teachers College during this period.

Unfortunately for the discipline of history, the Great Depression would usher in a school of historical scholarship that pointed out chinks in the democratic form of government, and the discipline began to lose its appeal. History was becoming more negative just as education was entering its Golden Age. STSTC brought in lecturers like Thomas Briggs and published reviews of books by Ellwood Patterson Cubberley, who believed that schooling and control of environment could transform impossible dreams into reality. An editorial entitled "The Call of Education," published in the *College Star*, proudly proclaimed:

> The value of a college education is greater in this age than any other.
> It will change your life completely. It will transform it from a humdrum, everyday existence to a vital, beautiful and interesting life of service. Education opens new opportunities for serving humanity; it develops latent powers and abilities; and it makes of a creature a man made in the likeness of his Creator.[24]

Many people have wondered why Johnson initially chose to teach instead of to politick. The answer lies in the brand of educational philosophy to which he was exposed at San Marcos.

Throughout most of his life, Lyndon Johnson thought of himself primarily as a pedagogue. In 1963, for example, he told an audience gathered to honor the teacher of the year in Washington that he still thought of himself as an educator "though my classroom career was momentarily interrupted about thirty-five years ago." He continued:

> I wouldn't ever want the teachers to believe that my teaching experience is limited to high school in Houston, because that, in our state, is usually regarded as where the big city boys live, and I started by teaching at a little town, San Marcos, in high school there. From there I went to Houston and made the great mistake of leaving the teaching profession and coming into Washington.[25]

Perhaps influenced by this idealistic view of education, LBJ also felt that control of the environment was necessary for building a happy, healthy society. In Congress, one of his first bills brought modern utilities to his hometown. A newspaper reporter who covered the dedication of the Pedernales Electric Power Project wrote that to the young man who only "a few short years ago studied his grammar school lessons by the flickering light of a kerosene lamp and dreamed of electric lights, Saturday was seeing his dream come true even beyond his fondest expectations."[26]

The two members of the faculty who contested for Johnson's career choice were H. M. Greene, professor of government, and Cecil Evans, an educator and president of the college. Professor Greene was a rugged individualist and a nonconformist who took delight in putting deans and other administrators in their places. He lived in a Thoreau-type cabin in the Devil's Backbone area, west of San Marcos. He taught by the Socratic method and coached the college debate team. Greene urged Johnson to choose a career in politics, pointing him toward the United States Senate. And, later in life, he credited Johnson with being "the best student in government and politics I ever had the pleasure of teaching."[27]

That Greene had a great impact on Johnson is without question. But the influence was a long-term one. Lyndon had become an organization man and a team worker by the time he entered the collegiate program. The cynicism of Greene must have been invigorating, yet it was something LBJ simply could not adopt. His student editorials in the *College Star* were geared toward honor, duty, and country. Furthermore, there is little evidence that Johnson continued a close relationship with Greene after going on to a career in politics. On the other hand, Evans and LBJ worked well together while the two were on campus, and they saw much of each other in subsequent years. LBJ could always call on President Evans to provide a radio endorsement or a speech introduction, or to offer sage political advice in a moment of desperation.

Cecil Evans had been the general agent for the Conference for Education in Texas prior to assuming the reins of Southwest Texas State Teachers College. He held a Bachelor of Arts degree from Oxford College in Alabama and a master's degree from the University of Texas. His family was involved in Texas politics, and a brother, Hiram Wesley Evans, achieved no small degree of notoriety for his association with the Ku Klux Klan. Evans put STSTC on his feet, and he labored long hours to obtain funds from the legislature for new buildings and programs. The students appreciated this effort and respected Evans as a man and leader. He received many tributes from the young men and women entrusted to his care. In 1930, the year Lyndon graduated, the student body dedicated its yearbook to the president. The inscription said: "To an understanding leader in clean, sportsmanlike living—To a character beautiful in genuine simplicity and friendship—To a sympathetic friend of cultural and social influence—And to a man, President Cecil E. Evans, we lovingly dedicate this."[28]

Rebekah Johnson and Cecil E. Evans had similar ideas about the importance of education. Therefore, it is not strange that young Lyndon and his mentor formed a genuine friendship. Rebekah had talked to Evans about her son attending Southwest Texas State when LBJ finally made his decision to enroll in college. Too, since Sam Johnson had served in public office in Texas, there is little doubt that he and Evans frequently found time to chat about educational and personal affairs. The president found work for the Johnson City student and rented him a room over his garage. When there was no other employment, Lyndon and his roommate painted the garage to pay their rent. One anecdote suggests that LBJ painted the building five times in one year.

Johnson and Evans worked hand in hand at STSTC. Shortly after he matriculated, Lyndon earned his tuition by serving on the maintenance staff. He filled a vacancy in the president's office within a short period. His initial duties included hand-carrying messages to the faculty and staff from

Evans. Some people got the idea, one which Johnson certainly did not discourage, that the instructors had to go through him to see the chief administrative officer of the institution. This position lifted Lyndon's prestige on the campus. Some alleged, for instance, that students who were friends of his received the easiest and highest paying jobs on the work crew. But more important, the "administrative" position taught him many organizational lessons and helped him to develop professional skills such as letter writing, supervising employees, and understanding the relationship between politics and education. Johnson didn't forget the experience, and later his administration sponsored many internship programs for budding civil servants.

The organizational life of the campus also pointed LBJ toward a career in education. In 1962, when STSTC awarded an honorary LL.D. to him, a Dallas newspaper reporter listed the number of extracurricular activities in which he had been involved. He discovered that Johnson had been a reporter, editorial writer, and editor-in-chief of the *College Star*, a member of the student council and the Harris-Blair Literary Society, and secretary of the Schoolmaster Club. The association with the newspaper deserves close attention, for Johnson was identified with the *Star* longer than any other campus group. Perhaps he enjoyed it the most as well. He once told the White House press that he relished being the Lippmann, Evans and Novak, and Drew Pearson of his school. Nor could he resist a short lecture. "When I was a newspaperman I never had any trouble getting along with the president. I believed," he added, "every word he said. Perhaps I should have taken a leaf from his book by inviting Washington newspapermen to sleep in my garage, as he did."[29]

College and high school newspapers were in their heyday in the 1920s. Educational institutions often exchanged their copy with other schools so that links between different regions could be established. Then, too, the papers were sent to alumni, which, in the case of STSTC, meant mostly teachers.

The stories, reports of speeches, and book reviews, therefore, helped to keep people in the field abreast of new developments in their area. The first year Lyndon was on the campus, the *Pedagog*, the institution's yearbook, summarized the general mission of the *Star* in the following manner:

> In its efforts to mirror the activities on the hill, the *College Star* has done its best. It has attempted, as a mouth piece of the student body, to voice the student opinion at all times, but in so doing it has not conflicted with the aims of the administration. It has been the medium through which the student today has been kept posted as to the activities of the college as a whole. In the capacity of news bearer, the *Star* has printed all the news pertaining to student activities.[30]

Johnson joined the staff in the summer of 1927. Manton Ellis, editor-in-chief, thanked Johnson for editorials "whose outbursts gained wide comment."[31]

Johnson later became editor of the school newspaper, serving from 1927 to 1929. His chief contribution was as an editorial writer, and the themes he developed reflect the characteristics of his personality. Vernon Lynch, who collected these editorials in 1965, provides some convenient categories. He wrote: "Special days and holidays particularly received the young editor's attention. At other times, he lectured his school fellows on personal and civic virtues, naming his own heroes as models. A recurrent theme was the value of education and the worth of teachers to society."[32]

The titles of some of his editorials give us a clue about LBJ's early themes:

UPLIFT
"Higher Ideals," August 10, 1927.
"Vision," February 1, 1928.

SEASONAL
"Constitution Day," September 24, 1927.

"Armistice Day," November 16, 1927.
"Thanksgiving Day," November 23, 1927.
"The Twenty-First of April," April 25, 1928.

PERSONAL DEVELOPMENT
"He Who Conquers," October 5, 1927.
"Play the Game," October 12, 1927.
"Duty," October 26, 1927.
"Personality," November 9, 1927.
"The Cynic," December 7, 1927.
"The Apostle of Thrift," January 18, 1928.
"Sincerity," May 16, 1928.
"Getting Ahead," July 31, 1928.

EDUCATIONAL
"Guilty of a Wasted School Year," September 28, 1927.
"The Call to Rally," November 30, 1927.
"The Greatest of Vocations," April 18, 1928.
"The Advantage of College Training," May 2, 1928.[33]

In these Johnson evidenced that he had inherited from all limbs of his family tree, for one finds traces of the preacher, the teacher, the politician, and even, at times, the poet.

Lyndon learned the rudiments of good essay writing while he was on the staff of the *Star*. He usually began his editorials by quoting a famous figure—William Gladstone, Charles Lindbergh, Woodrow Wilson, Theodore Roosevelt, Benjamin Franklin, Abraham Lincoln, Isaac Watts, Joseph Bailey, or Robert E. Lee—to prove or disprove a particular point. He seldom left his readers in doubt about the point he wanted to make. And if the students didn't appreciate him—he was not in the athletic "in" group—he at least had grown fond of them. In a final editorial, "Farewell," he said of this experience: "To the *Star* we bid farewell. It has been a pleasing privilege to serve our college and its students and faculty. It has been a deep gratification to employ in a measure in the pages of the

Star the ideals and hopes that animate college journalism. It has been a happy task. Now it is completed; so farewell, good luck and may fortune's blessing attend."[34] This goodbye was not permanent. But later, the *Star* had to vie with other activities for Johnson's attention.

Of particular interest here are Johnson's editorials on education. The influence of Cecil Evans is clearly apparent. First, Lyndon evidenced great loyalty to his school, the faculty who taught him, and the state that made his training possible. For LBJ the worst sin that a subordinate could commit was to not give first allegiance to the policy or program at hand. Second, the columns in the *Star* repeatedly stressed service to mankind, a concept that must have pleased his public servant father and civic-minded mother. There is also a strong emphasis on providing an education for poor and underprivileged rural youth. To his dying day, Johnson believed that schooling could unlock doors for those on the lower end of the socio-economic ladder. And last, the editorials ascribed teachers with near supernatural powers for good. Of the pedagogue, he concluded: "He leads the student to love learning for its own sake, as well as to appreciate it for the powers and advancements it brings. As the Pied Piper with his flute charmed the children to a wonderland beyond, so the ideal teacher leads his students into a magic land of beauty whose treasures await their grasp."[35]

The editorship of the *Star* led to Johnson's election as president of the campus Press Club in 1930, the year of his graduation. This group had been formed in 1925 "for the purpose of fostering and stimulating a higher type of college journalism."[36] During his senior year, he also served as secretary for the Schoolmaster's Club, an organization "sponsored by the college for the social and educational benefit of its men students and faculty members."[37] This organization, in a day when teachers were judged in the community by the same standards one expected of clergy, provided an outlet where men could get together for fun and relaxation. The high point of 1930 was a watermelon feast held at Wimberley.

Lyndon became a class officer, a member of the student council, and a debater for the Harris-Blair Club. The latter agency brought him into contact with Professor Greene outside the classroom, while he teamed with Elmer Graham and participated in several debates. Graham called Johnson a specialist in finding the weaknesses in arguments of others, one who hammered away relentlessly to score crucial debating points.

The college also offered an active social life. Johnson attended the Christian, rather than the Baptist, church, a move which no doubt irritated his mother. One of his best-known accomplishments on the campus was to create a secret group known as the Alpha and Omega Club, sometimes called the White Stars. Alpha and Omega succeeded in dominating some of the campus elections and in making college life more open. This venture seems to have convinced LBJ of the inestimable value of personal persuasion. Perhaps he had the White Stars in mind when he wrote an editorial entitled "Personality." In it he stated that personality "is power. It has force and strength, charm, and attraction. The man with a striking personality can accomplish greater deeds in life than a man of equal abilities but less personality."[38]

At San Marcos, too, Lyndon became more aware of the presence of the other sex. He dated many girls, but one, Carol Davis, particularly captured his attention. The two often walked down Chautauqua Hill in the evenings to the waters around Riverside and the fish hatchery. But, to a man in a hurry, there was no time for serious romance. Money also may have been a problem, because late in the summer of 1928, Johnson, who had already earned a two-year teaching certificate, took a job at Cotulla, Texas, a small rural community located about halfway between San Antonio and Laredo. He was hired to teach the fifth through the seventh grades at the Welhausen School in the Mexican section of this border town.

In addition, when he reported for work, the superintendent convinced him to serve as principal at a salary of $125 per month. Johnson enrolled in two extension courses per quarter in an STSTC center at Cotulla so that he would lose no time in finishing his schooling.

The Welhausen School obtained a real bargain in Lyndon Johnson. He spent a part of his first paycheck on "athletic equipment for the students who otherwise had none of the essentials for play and recreation except space."[39] He arranged competitions in athletics and debate with neighboring schools, and one local citizen complained that he was thinking of selling his automobile, because the principal had him continually driving pupils to away contests and games. The faculty lounge was patrolled, and teachers were told that this room was not a place to smoke, drink coffee, or loaf. A lunchroom was organized to ensure hot, palatable food. Mexican children were punished for speaking Spanish, for the principal believed that assimilation was necessary to enter society at large successfully.

More consequentially, however, the young teacher became aware of impoverished minority students. Cotulla today is much like it was during the fourth decade of this century. Houses are built on stilts to prevent termite infestation. The streets are dirt, with deep ruts that become muddy traps when the rains come. The community is dotted with small bars, and inside and outside these establishments one sees people whose eyes exhibit despair and lack of hope. With the exception of a theater, the schools provide the only entertainment for the locality: athletics, music, and debate are the major recreational outlets for parents as well as children.

The Cotulla school board appreciated the efforts of their new principal and offered to continue his contract for another year. Johnson, however, declined this invitation, for he wanted to return to San Marcos to complete his college degree. By combining his junior and senior years, it would be possible for him to graduate in the spring. Sam Johnson approved of his son's decision. He was re-entering politics and believed it might be possible for him to secure a patronage position for his son. In June, then, the young teacher bade his students goodbye and left for San Marcos to become a student once again himself.

Lyndon Johnson left Cotulla, but Cotulla never left him. The plight of this community later served as the model for modernizing rural America. "In those days neither America nor her schools shared any abundance. We had only five teachers. We had no lunch facilities. No school buses. Very little money for educating the young people of this community," Johnson recalled.[40] Then he listed legislation his administration had backed in education and health, showing the impact on Cotulla. "Education," he explained another time, "will not cure all of the problems of society, but without it no cure for any problem is possible."[41]

Except for a few courses he took later in Washington, D.C., Lyndon Baines Johnson ended his formal educational training in 1930. It is just as well that he did not pursue advanced degrees, for the restless youth had never learned to enjoy learning for its own sake. He seldom read books, though he became most proficient in reviewing large stacks of reports and suggestions relating to his professional life. LBJ's future wife, a journalist by training, filled in his literary gaps and frequently forced her activist husband to consider literature at the dinner table, as her mother-in-law had done earlier. On the other hand, LBJ left the campus of the Southwest Texas State Teachers College with skills that would serve him well. California, San Marcos, and Cotulla had made him a "jobs-and-contract" democrat with a faith in the goodness of people and government. He also had gained confidence and self-reliance. Friend and foe alike believed that someone unusual had resided in their midst. And so did LBJ. The traditions of the family, and his own experiences, now combined to make public service his goal for the future.

CHAPTER THREE

Learning to Be a Bureaucrat

"I am concerned about the whole man. I am concerned about what the people using their government as an instrument and a tool can do toward building the whole man, which will mean a better society and a better world."

—Lyndon Baines Johnson, 1946

A MERICAN INSTITUTIONS experienced rapid transformation in the generation between the end of World War I and the beginning of World War II. The home, the church, the educational system, and the government at every level were all revamped during these twenty years. Unemployed and underemployed parents resolutely vowed that they would labor to provide for their children more opportunities and more material possessions than they had enjoyed. The social gospel of Charles M. Sheldon and the Salvation Army, among others, decreed that the church should pay attention to the here and now, rather than simply promising a better life in the hereafter for the righteous. The New Education of Charles William Eliot and the Wisconsin Idea of Bob La Follette combined to alter the character of the university, while philosophers like John Dewey and muckrakers like Joseph Mayer Rice infused new vigor into the common schools. The referendum, the initiative, the recall, and the city manager system were developed by reform-minded politicos to rescue a troubled democracy. Nationally, the seniority rule and the direct election of senators were adopted in an attempt to make the House and Senate more responsive to the welfare of the general public. Urbanization and the second industrial revolution were the unifying threads of these diverse changes. The American of the future would live in the city and work in a factory. And isolationism drew its last breath when President Franklin Roosevelt requested a declaration of war in 1941.

It was an exciting era for Lyndon Baines Johnson to learn to be a bureaucrat. He studied under social architects whose activity and philosophy are virtually unparalleled in the modern past. LBJ, in tune with his age, moved from San Marcos to Houston after spending one month teaching in the tiny town of Pearsall, located just north of Cotulla. He persuaded his superintendent to hire his sister Rebekah in his place, and then he headed toward the cities, where he would spend the rest of his life. Henceforth, Houston, Austin, and Washington, D.C., would be home, except for the solitude of the ranch near Stonewall. But the latter was more of a reminder of the past than a portent of the future. In 1964, Johnson said: "I have a little house where I was born, the son of a tenant farmer, a picture of which is hanging up in my bedroom, because every night when I go to bed and every morning when I wake up, I call it the 'opportunity house.' No one," he continued, "could look at that house and the way it looks, and not say 'there is still opportunity in America.'"[1]

In the fall of 1930, LBJ moved to Houston to teach at Sam Houston High School. His younger brother Sam accompanied him to attend the University of Houston. This high school position had been secured partially through the good offices of Uncle George Johnson, a gregarious bachelor relative who headed the history department. "The Senator," as the students called him, specialized in the Age of Jackson in addition to being well informed on politics in Texas. In the latter area, he often held forth on the oratorical ability of Joseph Weldon

Bailey, who represented the Lone Star state in the national Congress from 1891 to 1913. Lyndon and Uncle George became fast friends. Besides history and politics, they shared a mutual interest in debate and in the general welfare of their students.

W. J. Moyes, the principal of Sam Houston High, spoke highly of his new teacher. He believed that Lyndon Johnson was loyal, devoted, and efficient—a welcome addition to the faculty. Lyndon appreciated the teaching job in the dark depression days, and he pledged all of his energies to successful completion of his duties. "As a teacher in one-room schools and finally in the Houston system," he would say later, "I did not always agree with the policies of the school board, but I never did seek to attack the board, split it wide open and instill a spirit of distrust in the people who were dependent upon that board for its administration." [2]

LBJ taught speech and coached the debate team. Gene Latimer, a student thought to be typical of his peers, praised the new teacher. "At first," he said, "I didn't think he was as good as the speech teacher we had. But it didn't take long to change my mind." [3] Latimer went on to become an outstanding debater. He and his colleagues won the city meet for the first time in four years and lost the state title by the barest of margins—by only one vote. The vigor that Johnson exhibited indicated a future characteristic: long hours, hard work, and a continual pushing of subordinates to achieve a goal became an integral part of his professional psyche. Principal Moyes was pleased with the team's success. In 1931, he remarked: "Credit for the work of these boys . . . is due to the splendid work in all lines of public speaking done by L. B. Johnson, who is making a great record in his first year as a teacher in a Houston school." [4]

As the 1930–1931 academic year closed, a banquet was held at Sam Houston High School to commemorate the many high points of the term just completed. Two politicians, former Governor Pat Neff of Waco and State Senator Welly K.

Hopkins, were invited to speak. Neff had been a longtime friend of Sam Johnson, and Lyndon had managed Hopkins's campaign for the Texas Senate. Neff could not attend, but a close friend delivered comments for him. He and Hopkins singled out the accomplishments of the youthful Lyndon Johnson. Moreover, the student newspaper published a full page headed "Who's Who in Sam Houston," and LBJ's photograph appeared in this report. Underneath, an explanatory caption read: "Pleasing in personality, indefatigable in his labors, zealous in all his undertakings. Although one of our newest faculty members, he has carved for himself a place in Sam Houston as one of the outstanding teachers."[5] LBJ made the transition from country to city with a resounding splash.

Next September, when the young pedagogue returned to campus, events transpired that would permanently change his career plans. About one month after school started, Lyndon received a call from Richard Kleberg, the son of one of the owners of the King ranch. Kleberg had recently been voted to Congress in a special election to fill an unexpired term. He asked Johnson, apparently on the advice of Welly Hopkins, to come to the ranch to discuss an appointment as his private secretary in Washington. The two conferred, and on November 30, 1931, the *San Antonio Express* reported that an offer had been tendered and accepted. Sam Houston High School extended a leave of absence, and Lyndon recommended one of his STSTC classmates for his teaching position in Houston prior to catching a train for Washington. In his early twenties, the former teacher was short on experience but long on enthusiasm. Kleberg, as had Cecil Evans at San Marcos, often wondered exactly who was working for whom.

Kleberg and Johnson reached Washington in December 1931 and worked together until 1935. Thus began for Johnson a tenure in government and politics that would span almost four decades and finally land him in the Oval Office for five years. The young bureaucrat took a room in the Dodge Hotel, which he later discovered housed many of the congressional aides. There he roomed with Malcolm Bardwell, whom he had first met in San Antonio when Kleberg was running for Congress. Bardwell said of his colleague:

> He was just a likeable type of fellow. He seemed to make himself agreeable with you, and he would listen to you. He wouldn't carry on all the conversation. He would at that time sort of draw you out as to what was going on and what was going on in your territory, and acted like he wanted to be of personal service to you, so it made every one of us feel good. [6]

Listening skills had been difficult for Johnson to learn. At last, however, he realized the importance of his father's advice to the effect that when you are talking you are not learning.

In Washington, as in San Marcos, Lyndon Johnson absorbed information rapidly and touched bases with as many colleagues as humanly possible. One acquaintance reported that when he and co-workers went to the All States Restaurant for lunch, Johnson would run to the head of the line to be served first so that he would be free to talk while others were eating. He also developed friendships with the other Texas delegations, including those of Senators Tom Connally and Morris Sheppard. The senators, however, followed established protocol and remained somewhat aloof from Kleberg and Johnson. LBJ paid daily visits to Wright Patman and Sam Rayburn, both friends of Sam Johnson. Initially, John Nance Garner extended a friendly hand, but Johnson's relations with him became strained because Rayburn and Garner both became candidates for the speakership of the House of Representatives.

In 1934, Lyndon enrolled in Georgetown University, where he studied law in the evenings. But because of a change of jobs, he never completed his degree. His role as secretary to "Master Dick" Kleberg served as a substitute for graduate school and provided the opportunity to develop further the rudimentary administrative skills he had learned at STSTC.

He became so efficient at his job that his boss increasingly permitted him to conduct business while he, Kleberg, played polo at the park and golf at Burning Tree Country Club. Johnson answered much of the office correspondence, and he personally visited individuals and groups who sought government pensions. In this, he was much like his father who delighted in serving the man on the street. The long hours he spent on these matters surprised his friends. Bob Jackson, aide to another Congressman from the Lone Star state, commented: "You couldn't imagine the enormous degree of energy that boy had. It was unheard of for aides . . . to work past noon on Saturdays, much less Sundays. We just couldn't understand what motivated Lyndon at times."[7] Estelle Harbin, another assistant to Kleberg, added that she and Johnson worked so late that inexpensive restaurants were closed by the time the office door was locked each evening.

Johnson's deft organizational ability exhibited itself in many ways during the Kleberg years: on one occasion, "Cactus Jack" Garner's attempt to control the appointment of postmasters in Texas was thwarted by advance information Johnson received through interoffice contacts. But LBJ's major accomplishment relates to his election as speaker of the "little congress." This group, composed of congressional aides, paralleled the national House of Representatives. It provided a forum for debating issues concerning the operation of congressional offices. Normally, the head position of the little congress was reserved for a senior aide. Johnson, however, persuaded many people to join who heretofore had not belonged, thus securing an unusually large delegation to appear in one of the hearing rooms on the night scheduled to select a new leader. Lyndon easily acquired a substantial majority by promising to hold different types of meetings. "The fifty or so hardcore members," said Bob Jackson, "sat in their chairs dumbfounded— they didn't know what had happened."[8] Johnson's maneuvering here bears a close similarity to his formation of the White Stars at Southwest Texas State.

One other incident during his period as a congressional aide needs retelling because it never left Johnson's mind as long as he served in public office. The young bureaucrat was one of those hundred thousand people who stood on the steps of the Capitol on March 6, 1933, to hear Franklin Delano Roosevelt's inaugural address. From that moment, Lyndon became a supporter of the administration identified as the New Deal. Remembering that speech, Johnson explained, "Today some say that the New Deal was an experiment. Some say it was a 'failure.' Some say that it became 'outmoded' and 'obsolete.' But," he added, "I say that the philosophy of government which helps people to help themselves against depression, against unemployment, against old age will never be outmoded or obsolete in civilized society."[9] The pockets of rural poverty and the ghettos of Houston and San Antonio needed governmental assistance to enter the twentieth century. That cold, gray day in 1933 became the touchstone by which all legislation could be judged. Johnson believed that he as well as the American people had a "rendezvous with destiny."

Representative Kleberg came to believe that he had made a good choice in hiring the ex-schoolteacher as his aide, and he paid him well for his long hours and total loyalty. The salary enabled Lyndon to marry Claudia Alta "Lady Bird" Taylor, a shy but charming girl from Karnack, Texas, who lived with her father. Lyndon and Lady Bird met in the Austin office of C. V. Terrell, who had replaced Pat Neff as chairman of the Texas Railroad Commission. They were introduced by Eugenia Boehringer when she arranged a blind date for her friend Lyndon with a girl named Dorothy McElroy. Johnson's eye, however, was caught by a second petite lass, and he immediately invited her to breakfast at the Driskill Hotel. During the next two months Johnson made endless telephone calls and offered proposals of marriage. Lady Bird soon succumbed, and the couple married on November 17, 1934, at St. Mark's Episcopal Church in San Antonio. The newlyweds enjoyed a brief honeymoon in Mexico prior to moving into an apartment in Washington at the Kennedy Warren apartments on Connecticut Avenue.

Lady Bird resembled Rebekah Baines Johnson in many ways. Both had suffered loneliness and had experienced family tragedy, and both had sought refuge in books. The newest member of the Johnson clan read as much as Rebekah. "Of all the talents I wish I had," she said, "the one I admire most is the ability to make words march and sing and cannonade. . . . When I think back over my own life, books seem always to have been with me, throwing open windows to the wondrous world outside." [10] The two women were also alike in unselfishly helping Lyndon to obtain his goals. Though a graduate of the University of Texas, Lady Bird did not seek a career. Instead, she cooked meals for a busy family and a variety of political cronies and often pitched in at the office to meet deadlines. In spite of occasional disappointments, she never regretted her decision to marry Johnson. She told a Democratic Women's dinner in 1964 that Lyndon was "an exciting man to live with; an exhausting man to keep up with; a man who has worn well in the twenty-five years we've been together." [11]

Rebekah and Lyndon had corresponded frequently while Lyndon was in the service of Richard Kleberg in Washington. The letters exchanged between them date from the first week after leaving Texas. "I'm still a 'baby' in your only letter to me since my departure a week ago yesterday," the son wrote. He also was a bit miffed that Rebekah had hinted that she would write *just* in response to his notes, an obvious attempt to keep her sweet boy, as she called Lyndon, close to her apron strings. "No, Mother dear," he retorted back, "I've never played that way with you all of these ten or twelve years I've been writing you and I refuse to start now." [12] The close attachment of mother and son could have spelled trouble for the new marriage. But both Rebekah and Lady Bird were too clever to become caught in a contest over Lyndon's affections. Lady Bird visited with her mother-in-law prior and subsequent to the ceremony in San Antonio. And if Rebekah was miffed at not being invited to the services, she never once made mention of the fact.

On Tuesday, November 30, 1934, just after Lyndon and Lady Bird had moved into their apartment, Rebekah sent a moving letter to the couple, here quoted in full.

Thinking of you, loving you, dreaming of a radiant future for you, I someway find it difficult to express my feelings. Often I have felt the utter futility of words; never more than now when I wish my boy and his bride the highest and truest happiness together. That I love you and that my fondest hopes are centered in you, I do not need to assure you, my own dear children.

My dear Bird, I earnestly hope that you will love me as I do you. Lyndon has always held a very special place in my heart. Will you not share that place with him, dear child? It would make me very happy to have you for my very own, to have you turn to me with love and confidence, to let me mother you as I do my precious boy. My heart is full of earnest wishes for your happiness. From a mother's standpoint however I can scarcely say more than this. I hope, and hope you know is composed of desire and expectation, that Lyndon will prove to be as tender, as true, as loyal, as loving, and as faithful a husband as he has been a son. May life's richest blessings be yours, dear little girl.

My darling boy, I rejoice in your happiness, the happiness you so richly deserve, the fruition of the hopes of early manhood, the foundation of a completely rounded life. I have always decreed the best in life for you. Now that you have the love and companionship of the one and only girl, I am sure you will go far. You are fortunate in finding and winning the girl you love, and I am sure your love for each other will be an incentive to you to do all the great things of which you are capable. Sweet son, I am loving you and counting on you as never before.

Now, my beloved children, I shall be longing to see you

soon. Write me. Enjoy your honeymoon in that ideal setting,
then hurry home to see us.
My dearest love to you both, Momma.[13]

Rebekah had never before used the word *Momma* in closing.
Perhaps the fact that Lady Bird's mother had died young
provided the opening for a long and close relationship between
the two women.

Marriage and a growing uneasiness within Kleberg's office
indicated that it was time for LBJ to think about changing
positions. Some observers feel that Congressman Kleberg
became annoyed at Lyndon for assuming too much responsibility in the day-to-day decision-making functions and that
hard feelings developed. There is, undoubtedly, some truth to
this conjecture. But the real reason for Johnson's leaving stems
more likely from Master Dick's lukewarm reception of the
New Deal. Johnson put a premium on loyalty, and when he
could not fully support his superior's actions, he had no choice
except to resign. Then, too, as Roosevelt created agency after
agency during the presidential-congressional honeymoon,
thousands of front-line positions needed to be filled. Lyndon,
remembering his commitment to youth made at San Marcos,
Cotulla, Pearsall, and Houston, wanted to be involved with
young people again. And so he passed his job with Kleberg to
his brother Sam Houston, found employment for his sister at
the Library of Congress, and then left for Austin to become
the first director of the Texas National Youth Administration.

In October 1933, President Roosevelt convened an educational conference in Washington to discuss the problem of
unemployed youth. Some prior assistance for young people
had been provided under the auspices of the Civilian Conservation Corps, but this legislation had little or no bearing on the
four hundred thousand students who had dropped out
since 1931. The education brain trust, or task force, as Johnson
would later name his advisory committees, recommended the
formation of a Federal Emergency Relief Administration to

provide funds so that 10 percent of a school's students could be put to work on a part-time basis. This quota was soon increased to 12 percent, and some one hundred thousand students took advantage of the provisions of the act. However, the battle was not yet won: the Bureau of Statistics estimated in 1935 that 3.9 million young people aged sixteen to twenty-five were in need of jobs or schooling. Simultaneously, a document released by the Works Progress Administration equated adult unemployment with undereducation.

Franklin Roosevelt issued Executive Order Number 7068 on June 26, 1935, creating the National Youth Administration. This organization, called the NYA by the New Deal alphabetizers, was to be administered by the Works Progress Administration. The nation, according to Roosevelt, needed to "do something for the nation's unemployed youth because we can ill afford to lose the skills and energy of these young men and women." [14] Two groups, a National Advisory Committee and an Executive Committee, were formed to offer counsel. Each state NYA director and five regional centers were also to have citizen overseers, with membership coming from the ranks of labor, business, agriculture, education, and youth. In general, the program provided funds for keeping students in school, for part-time employment of the children of relief families, for the encouragement of job training, and for the development or extension of constructive leisure activities. Aubrey Williams, the head of the executive committee, devised three broad NYA divisions: the Student Aid Program, the Works Projects Program, and the Guidance and Placement Program.

The precise manner in which Lyndon Johnson obtained appointment as the head of the NYA in Texas at twenty-six years of age is somewhat uncertain. Many stories have circulated, and interpretation depends upon the teller's relation to Johnson: friend or foe. It is clear, nevertheless, that Johnson's commitment to the principles of the New Deal, his congressional contacts, and his friendship with prominent Texans who now held high positions in the new democratic regime were of much value. In August 1935, Johnson attended a meeting of state directors and then flew to Austin, where he established headquarters on the sixth floor of the Littlefield Building. He lived in the home of Robert Montgomery, an ardent New Deal supporter who taught economics at the University of Texas. His tenure as NYA Director in Texas provided a final bureaucratic training ground for a man who had already decided that he would make the national Congress a home away from home.

As an administrator, Lyn, as his friends and associates called him, proved indefatigable. He arrived at the office early in the morning, left late in the evening, and then held impromptu conferences at his home until the wee hours of the morning. Like Theodore Roosevelt, he frequently visited his employees incognito at project sites. But long hours and dedication were not enough. Johnson had learned in Washington the necessity of a completely loyal staff who pledged allegiance to one person. He made no decisions as a public servant more cautiously than those regarding choice of personnel: the right man or woman had to be matched with the right job. Johnson sought advice from all quarters, held discussions with Lady Bird, and passed some sleepless nights while he sorted and digested data. This selection process changed little in future years.

Staff selections for the Texas National Youth Administration, then, were chosen with great care. The individuals who received appointments were often graduates of public (not private) universities, and they were usually from Texas. Jesse Kellam, who had attended Southwestern Texas State, agreed to serve as deputy director, in spite of the fact that he held a responsible position in the Texas State Department of Education. Sherman Birdwell, a boyhood friend, consented to become the state finance director. And Willard Deason, a fellow White Star at San Marcos, was named director of district operations. The memberships of the various advisory committees and boards were made up just as carefully. Four regional divisions were established in Dallas, Lubbock, Houston, and Austin, and eight smaller units were situated in Marshall, Fort Worth, Waco, San Antonio, Laredo, Amarillo, San Angelo, and El Paso. With most major appointments made and organizational machinery completed, the director set about to make the Lone Star state an NYA model for the nation.

Much of Johnson's success in Texas can be attributed to the good working relationship he created with Aubrey Williams and Richard Brown in Washington, his use of local and state organizations, and his adroit publicity skills. Williams, a southerner, felt that his own man in Austin was too young to shape policy, so he encouraged Lyndon to touch base frequently with people such as Alvin Wirtz and Maury Maverick. Johnson peppered his superiors with correspondence. For example, he hoped that Williams could convince FDR to come to Texas, where a nationwide radio hookup would be made available to the President to speak to the youth of the nation. LBJ cultivated Richard Brown slowly but surely. He urged him to visit so that Johnson could get "to know my chief, and the man, Dick Brown, a little better." LBJ sent photographic displays, exhibit materials, and letters from schoolchildren to his superiors as well as personal testimonials. Then he used flattery. "We have been going day and night to get the job done and it would be gratifying if you would come down and look us over. We need some suggestions from you and we know that the benefit of your experience with other states will be most helpful to us," he wrote.[15] FDR did not come, but his wife Eleanor included Texas on her itinerary, and she provided a glowing account of her visit to newspapers and her husband.

Early in his administrative career, Johnson learned to know the value of broad public support for programs that he was associated with. In Texas, he wrote college presidents, spoke as often as he could in person and on the radio, and he involved the PTA, the Rotarians, the Kiwanis, and other organizations in his activities. State officials in every quarter were sought and singled out for what has since become known as the Johnson treatment. Newspapers became a special object of concern, and soon editorials and column comments came regularly from the *Austin Statesman*, the *Waco News Tribune*, and the *San Antonio Express*. Richard Brown, like many others, was amazed at Johnson's ability to generate press coverage. He wrote: "In hardly any other state has there been such a complete cooperation of the press as you seem to have had. I congratulate you and hope that your good fortune may continue." [16]

These plaudits, however, led to the formation of some unsavory personal qualities that persisted long into the future. Lyndon continued to cast himself as a boy Lincoln who had risen from utter poverty by hard work and determination. Some of the photographs of this period portray a man with an arrogant manner who had little time to praise or support subordinates. Too, Johnson ruthlessly eliminated people from the payroll in order to present an image of thrift. The author of *Sam Johnson's Boy* combed state newspapers of the period and concluded that Johnson could not tell a credible story and that his exaggerations were often cornpone. He quoted the following from an interview to show Lyndon's less favorable side.

"Sure," says Dir. Johnson, propping his feet on the desk and grinning broadly. "I guess I know a little bit about youth's hard lot in life. You don't mind if I relax, do you?"

I didn't. In fact, a man talks better when he does relax. Then he told me how he started out.

"Received my early education in a country school in the Hill Country. After schoolin', I got a job as a day laborer on the highways. I chopped weeds, earned a dollar here and a dollar there, always with an idea in my mind to finish a college education."

It was this same desire which put Lyndon Johnson into college. He worked and studied at San Marcos. He learned how it felt to come home at night dog tired, turn on the lights, and try to whip a tired body into shape to absorb some mental training. [17]

The remainder of the essay is too tedious to quote. But this image must have caused Rebekah and Sam to shake their heads in disbelief on more than one occasion.

The initial thrust of the National Youth Administration in Texas was to keep young men and women in school. In September 1935, over one hundred educators gathered at the University of Texas to outline plans for aiding college students. Johnson estimated that one hundred twenty-three thousand Texans between the ages of sixteen and twenty-five were on relief and required assistance. The director, determined to reach as many people as possible, limited elementary and high school students to five dollars per month instead of the allowed six and suggested that college and graduate students receive only fifteen instead of the allowed twenty dollars. High school students generally performed work on the campus, but on occasion, they worked in the local community. College students did the same, but on a more specialized level. William Knippa, a San Marcos student who wrote a thesis on the early political life of Johnson, discovered that history majors catalogued documents in the State Library, chemical engineering candidates researched the hardening characteristics and carbonization of steel, biology students performed as laboratory assistants, and, at Baylor University, sociology majors counseled Waco public school dropouts. The latter achieved an unheard-of record by reinstating almost seventeen hundred people to their classes.

The biggest problem Johnson encountered in the Student Aid Project was lack of money. He told some of his troubles to Richard Brown in a long letter dated Christmas Eve of 1936. Approximately half of the student applicants could not be

given help. During that year, funds were granted to 102 graduate students and about ten thousand high school students. In
an effort to increase funding, Johnson attempted to supply
Washington with figures and survey results to show the program in the best possible light. Experienced administrators,
however, could see through the management of data. "I
think," wrote Brown, "on the whole that the investigation
could have been a lot more intensive and covered a good many
more items than you included. I feel also that some of the
questions are fairly leading questions or else the authorities
have worded their answers along too general lines." [18]

Johnson's one significant innovation in the area of student
aid was to suggest relocation of Civilian Conservation Camps
near college campuses so that people could take university
classes while they worked. He told Aubrey Williams, "We
have a big state, consequently a big job; and since our time is
short, if we are going to put the program over, we must start
moving." [19] A long report was attached which suggested the
creation of camps in the College Station, Austin, and
Kingsville locales. When no response came immediately, he
wrote again, this time asking that the situation be discussed
with President Roosevelt. This idea eventually gained approval, and it was put into action in Texas as well as in several
other states.

Outside of insufficient funds, the major difficulty with
school aid concerned the fact that Texas had Jim Crow laws on
statute books. In consequence, Johnson appointed a Negro
Advisory Committee to advise him on programs for black male
and female youths. Early leaders on the board were W. L.
Davis, principal of Harper Junior High (Houston); Marsh
Branch, president of Tillotson College (Austin); L. Virgil
Williams, principal of Booker T. Washington High School
(Dallas); Mrs. J. O. Conner, home economist (Prairie View);
and Joseph Rhoads, president of Bishop College (Marshall).
The separate board was justified in a letter to Brown, where
Johnson said: "The racial question during the past one hun-

dred years in Texas, and particularly since Texas entered the Union, and again after the Civil War, has resolved itself to a system of customs which cannot be upset over night."[20] In addition to securing school aid for blacks, LBJ sprinkled fifteen freshman college centers throughout the state. These agencies offered "college work of the first-year level that is taught by teachers certified for work relief to students whose families are subject to work relief."[21] National inspectors gave the project good marks, and the program became a model operation.

The next point of concern for the National Youth Administration in Texas received designation as Works-Progress. This program was designed to provide jobs for unemployed youth. Funds did not become available, however, for Works-Progress until January 1936, so, in an effort to get the program moving without delay, Johnson thought it necessary to find some large department or division in the state to serve as a sponsor. His own experience building roads reminded him that the Texas Highway Department might need additional employees. He courted this agency, and many youths were put to work at road building and maintenance. A suggestion by a highway engineer named Gib Gilchrist brought a significant innovation—one that eventually became standard in many states. Gilchrist conceived the idea of constructing "pocket parks," or "roadside parks," as they are now called, and some one hundred fifty of these were built throughout the Lone Star state. Another Johnson project which captured national publicity was the restoration of the *Villita* Street Spanish village, an adobe and caliche settlement on South Presa Street in San Antonio that dated back to 1835. The Carnegie Foundation joined with Mayor Maury Maverick to plan the development, and young Texans brought *La Villita* to completion at a cost of approximately $100,000.

Phases three and four related to the formation of instructional resident centers and vocational guidance and job placement. The former provided training for out-of-school youths while the latter attempted to locate employment for them. Close to these two activities were the women's camps, and the heartwarming story of their operation in Texas deserves much more space than can be provided here. This program took single women, usually Negro or Mexican-American, and gave them two months of training in a rural setting by certified public school teachers. In the first four weeks the girls were given dental and medical checks. A physical and psychological case history was kept on each individual and most people were found to have bad teeth, swollen gums, open skin sores, inflamed tonsils, and other health problems, some very severe. Almost all were malnourished, and many suffered from depression and anxiety because of their financial plight.

Initially, the women were taught the basic fundamentals of healthy daily living. Good food, fresh air, and rest changed attitudes and gave bodies a more robust and zestful appearance. As the students ate, they were instructed in diet, nutrition, and modern methods of preparing foods to retain vitamin content. Hiking and swimming built up strength, while singing and games provided a feeling of warmth and companionship. Both posture and countenance improved. Then, too, instruction in sewing assisted the girls in making dresses and underclothing. Students were also encouraged to improve grammar and conversational skills. All of these activities were designed to restore confidence, instill hope, and assist the pupils so that they could handle job interviews successfully after termination of the program.

The second four weeks brought a more formal, but still practical, curriculum. History and civics in outdoor classrooms became short courses on governmental affairs, and the need "for better living conditions and for adequate health and safety protection in employment was a topic of never-ending interest."[22] English classes concentrated on pronunciation and spelling to help those who wanted to seek jobs as secretaries. Sessions in arithmetic included playing dominos and cards and enabled classes to review enough mathematics so that graduates could become clerks in department stores. Other elementary and high school subjects were handled in a similar manner. One teacher in a San Antonio camp concluded: "I know of no other two months in which the investment of time has shown as much visible profit, and it is my opinion that these girls will make good citizens if they can be immediately put into positions of usefulness by the committee appointed by the National Youth Administration to follow up the two months of camp activities."[23]

Most individual case histories document substantial improvement. Only a few girls left camp prior to the festivities that signified graduation, and those who stayed gained weight and improved in health. Many girls were able to use the work skills they had acquired. This was the aspect of the National Youth Administration that had something of a humanizing effect on Lyndon Johnson. These camps burned such an image in the mind of the young bureaucrat that he could never forget the program. "Those were the great days," Johnson told a newspaper reporter. "Those kids came into the units as we established them, railing at fortune and circumstances, and cowed by the economic conditions that had left them without a job and without the means to live on the self-supporting independent basis that should be every American boy's and girl's birthright. And their frowns were soon changed to smiles."[24] These students, undoubtedly, reminded him of himself during the time he had left home to seek economic improvement in California.

Jesse Kellam, who served as deputy director and later as director of the Texas NYA provides a good summary of the whole program in a letter to William Knippa in 1967. He wrote:

An evaluation of the National Youth Administration tempts one to mention the Little Chapel in the Woods at Denton, *La Villita* in San Antonio, a workshop here, a training program there, numerous roadside parks throughout the State and the

Student Aid program. Three decades later the vantage point translates these tangible things into what then were the intangibles—and now are the educators, business and professional men and women, who, had it not been for the National Youth Administration, would have become "drop-outs."

The real contribution made by the National Youth Administration involved people—not things—and the program is still paying dividends. [25]

Sherman Birdwell added: "For years I've been amazed at the number of secretaries and dieticians and even heads of big factories who come up to me and say they got their start in the youth program." [26]

It all ended as quickly as it started. In February, 1937, Representative James P. Buchanan, whose district included Johnson's home county, died of a heart attack. Days later, Lyndon sent his resignation to Aubrey Williams. He mailed a separate note to Richard Brown, who had provided him with sterling support. "In leaving the National Youth Administration I feel a deep sense of regret, for in doing so I have removed myself from active association with some of the finest men with whom I have ever worked." [27] The job had entailed a unique combination of teaching, administering, and politicking. So ended Lyndon Baines Johnson's career as an appointed official. He had decided to seek elective office. Now he faced a new challenge. It was best stated by Senator Hubert Humphrey years later. "I know," he said to Johnson, "you've proved you're tough and smart—a goddam great Texan. I'm waiting now for the day you also prove you're a goddam great American." [28]

LBJ did not neglect the National Youth Administration after he left the directorship. He continued, in elective office, to support the organization when the opportunity permitted. In 1940, Franklin Roosevelt asked Congress to increase NYA funding from $75 million to $123 million. Johnson spoke in support of the program as follows: "It is my conviction, Mr. Speaker, that no agency of the Federal government has done more constructive work both for the present and for the future of America than the National Youth Administration." Then he reviewed the history of the organization, explained how it had helped youths attend college, and how it relieved pressure on the job market. He added, in conclusion: "Evidences of it lie across every state of the Union and our possessions. It is all a monument to the youth who built it and which trained and learned under competent leaders and instructors while it was working."[29] Forever afterward, Johnson associated improvement of instruction, student aid, health programs, and job training with the good life. The purpose of government, he felt, was to assist other people and to provide them with an opportunity house.

CHAPTER FOUR

Roosevelt's
Lieutenant

"In America the schools not only foster freedom, but show the way in which freedom can be conserved. They teach that to live in liberty is to live in order, that the only perfect freedom is found in perfect law, that the true lover of liberty not only desires to be free himself, but he desires to 'see all, everywhere free.' Freedom of thought, freedom of speech, freedom of hearing, freedom of press, freedom of learning and freedom of reading, result from the teaching of freedom and make America truly a land of liberty."
—Lyndon Baines Johnson, 1932

ON THE EVENING of August 24, 1938, Lyndon Baines Johnson, a newly elected congressman, shared his innermost thoughts with the summer school graduates of the Southwest Texas State Teachers College who had gathered to hear a fellow alumnus speak at commencement exercises. The title of the address, "The South Will Rise," suggests that the honored guest was beginning to feel the pressure of representing a region, not just a section, of the United States. Johnson spoke with more feeling than eloquence about the "land where our fathers came a century ago and established in the wilderness a new land, a new civilization, and a new culture." Those who lost the Civil War suffered greatly, and Texas had received little help in combating persistent problems such as depleted soil, polluted water, low per-capita income, poor housing, inadequate educational facilities, substandard health care, starvation wages, shortages of credit for business, and exploited natural resources. "Most insidious of all," concluded the speaker, "there has been built up in the South a spirit of agriculture against industry."[1]

Then came a search for solutions: How was the South to enter the mainstream of American society? He posed a series of rhetorical questions to show the merits of the New Deal, which had become controversial since Franklin Roosevelt's attempt in 1937 to pack the Supreme Court with appointees who he hoped would rule upcoming reform legislation constitutional. "If you had the choice," Johnson asked, "would you do something or would you do nothing?" More specifically, he asked:

> Should we lend money to insurance companies and banks to save them and the money of their thousands of investors? Should we lend funds to railroads to keep them solvent, to move our traffic without interruption? Should we take money from tax collections and insure bank deposits, so that we may take our money out of banks as we put it in? Should our farmers receive benefit checks? Should they be paid to revive, restore, and rest their soil? Should tenant farmers and share-croppers be lent money at low rates of interest over long periods of time so they can till land of their own? Should farm mortgages be refinanced to keep our southern farm land in private hands and prevent its concentration in the hands of absentee mortgage holders? Should every boy and girl denied the right of an education because of economic upheavals be helped to train for a place in this highly specialized world? Should we take jobless boys and put them into civilian conservation camps? Or place them on National Youth part-time projects, where they can gain constructive work and experience? . . . Shall we give the hopelessly forlorn hordes of unemployed WPA work until such time as normal business can again absorb them? Shall we borrow money at two or three percent and lend it out for public works at four and five percent, to build such permanent improvements as your labora-

tory school and auditorium, your student union and your girls' dormitory?[2]

The remaining text details statistic after statistic, all supporting the need for governmental assistance to solve pressing human conditions.

If the New Deal constituted an answer to immediate social difficulties, Congressman Johnson believed education was the means to prevent disaster in the future. Schools and colleges ought to train an elite for leadership positions. But, in addition, he believed that degrees meant better paying jobs, which would result in higher personal income and the collection of more taxes for the general welfare. He put the problem in personal terms, using STSTC as an example: "This school took us in when we had no money," he said, "gave us four years of work and found us jobs."[3] The address closed with a statement to the effect that the classroom is a gateway to the world that lies beyond.

Standing before his audience, LBJ must have reflected briefly on the process that had brought him to the podium in front of the student body. The death of James P. Buchanan had given him a start. Informed observers had known that the late incumbent's wife intended to announce for the vacancy. Johnson felt that she would be a sentimental favorite. Thus he and others who were interested would have to get their names before the public in quick fashion. Then, too, an issue of great significance would have to be found to separate him from the crowd of aspirants. Two personal complications needed attention as well: Sam Johnson had just experienced a serious heart attack, and the family had no financial reserve to support his retirement. Moreover, a congressional campaign called for more funds than Lyndon and Lady Bird had saved in their short marriage.

Quick consultations with Senator Alvin Wirtz and Lady Bird indicated that Johnson should enter the race. The latter called her father and asked that $10,000 of her inheritance from her mother be deposited in the bank the next morning. It was there when the bank opened the next day. Wirtz provided the campaign issue. His political protégé was to run in support of the New Deal and in defense of President Roosevelt's decision to expand the membership of the Supreme Court. If Johnson entertained any doubts about running, the change in Sam Johnson's face erased them. "My father became a young man again, as he saw me announce my candidacy from the porch of the house in Johnson City," recalled Lyndon. "He looked out into all those faces he knew so well and then he looked at me and I saw tears in his eyes as he told the crowd how terribly proud he was of me and how much hope he had for his country if only his son could be there in the nation's capital with Roosevelt and Rayburn and all those good Democrats."[4]

The first political campaign of Lyndon Johnson's career was an exciting one, and he worked day and night to win it. In 1937, the Tenth District was composed of ten counties: Blanco, Burnet, Hays, Travis, Williamson, Burleson, Bastrop, Washington, Lee, and Caldwell. Its dues supported a culture with which the Johnson clan was familiar. Next to Austin, the largest city had a population of only eight thousand. The region had racial mixtures of Germans, Poles, Wends, Swedes, Bohemians, blacks, and Latin Americans. Franklin Roosevelt, in his 1936 bid for re-election against Alf Landon, had carried the Tenth District by a comfortable nine-to-one margin.

Nine candidates announced for the vacant congressional seat. Only one was not affiliated with the Democratic party: Stanley S. Smith ran on the Republican ticket. The eight Democrats included Merton Harris, Lyndon Johnson, Sam Stone, Ayres K. Ross, C. N. Avery, Houghton Brownlee, Polk Shelton, and Edwin Waller. The candidacy of the last man drew chuckles from many quarters because, as Bob Ripley in his syndicated "Believe It or Not" column reported,

Waller had run for office thirty-four times without success.

Johnson launched his campaign at San Marcos in the auditorium of the Southwest Texas State Teachers College on March 5. There were some seven thousand people in the audience, including Rebekah and the ailing Sam. Judge Will Burnett introduced the candidate. Lyndon came directly to the point in his comments. He said:

> I believe the hungry should be fed; I believe that jobs should be furnished the unemployed; I believe that the home of the farmer and the city dweller should be saved from the greedy grasp of mortgage foreclosures. I believe agriculture should be put on parity with industry; I believe that the people of this country are behind the president in his effort to bring all this about. If the people of this district are for bettering the lot of the common man; if the people of this district want to run their government rather than have a dollar man run it for them; if the people of the district want to support Roosevelt on his most vital issue; then, I want to be your congressman. But if the people of this district don't want to support Roosevelt, I'll be content to let some corporation lawyer represent you.[5]

Johnson, nicknamed the "Blanco Blitz," unequivocally identified himself as a Rooseveltian.

Johnson made few, if any, mistakes in the initial campaign. In the next four weeks, the candidate distributed handbills, made some two hundred speeches, pressed the flesh, and frequently brought his program to the people over the radio. He stressed his prior experience in Washington, his youth, and his enthusiasm for getting the job done. Big Jim Farley came to Texas to dedicate some post offices, and he encouraged the voters to vote for Roosevelt's champion. Johnson's unwavering support for the court-packing scheme drew some national attention. "I don't have to hang back like a steer on the way to the dipping vat," LBJ told his listeners. "I'm for the president. When he calls on me for help I'll be where I can give him a quick lift, not out in the woodshed practicing a way to duck."[6]

The strategy proved successful. He almost doubled the vote of his nearest rival; Merton Harris received 5,111 votes and Johnson 8,280. (Edwin Waller did surprisingly well, garnering a record with 18 votes.)

Johnson himself was not at the polls on election day. Shortly before, he entered Seton infirmary in Austin for an emergency appendectomy.

Sam and Rebekah Johnson were enthralled with the election results. The latter wrote to Lyndon without delay. "My darling boy," she began,

> beyond "Congratulations Congressman," what can I say to my dear son in this hour of triumphant success? In this as in all of the many letters I have written you there is the same theme: I love you; I believe in you; I expect great things of you. Your election compensates for the heartache and disappointment I experienced as a child when my dear father lost the race you have just won. How happy it would have made my precious noble father to know that the firstborn of his firstborn would achieve the position he desired.[7]

Sam, too, must have felt vindication for the Johnson clan, since his grandfather—in violation of his Christadelphian precepts—had run for Congress and lost. Moreover, Sam must have silently applauded Lyndon's courage in not becoming openly associated with the oil interests in Texas. Like his father, Johnson identified more with individuals than corporations. He also eschewed being shoved into any particular wing of the Democratic party.

Johnson was to serve six successive terms in Congress as a representative of the Tenth District. When he was released from the Seton Infirmary, he joined Franklin Roosevelt, who was vacationing in the Gulf of Mexico on a fishing cruise. Texas Governor Jimmy Allred introduced the two men in Galveston on May 12. This meeting also produced an invitation from FDR to ride with him through Texas on his Presidential train. The fact that Johnson had been a strong New

Deal supporter put him in good stead with Roosevelt from the very first. The two men constituted a strange pair, one from the most aristocratic section of New York and the other from the backwoods Texas hill country. The train journey northward "began a friendship that endured for the remaining eight years of Roosevelt's life."[8]

In May 1937, Lyndon Johnson formally joined the U.S. House of Representatives, an institution that he would learn to love and respect. The oath of office had been administered by William B. Bankhead. Johnson had flown from Austin to Washington with Maury Maverick, who stated that his friend had won his recent election "on the issue of supporting President Roosevelt's policies, including the president's court reorganization program."[9]

One of Johnson's first acts was to place a memorial in the *Congressional Record* to commemorate the six senators and fifteen representatives who had died during the preceding twelve months. They were all "great and good men," he wrote. Then he singled out his predecessor, Buchanan. "It is beautiful to remember that he passed away as he wished, in the saddle riding hard."[10] Of himself, Johnson hoped that God would make him worthy to follow in the footsteps of the deceased legislators.

Lyndon Johnson's close identification with President Roosevelt proved of inestimable value to his career. He obtained a committee assignment on naval affairs, an agency that greatly interested the president. And this led to other defense activities, including the establishment of a naval reserve officers training program at the University of Texas, a naval reserve unit at Dallas, and the expansion of shipyards in Houston and elsewhere. He also served as a New Deal lieutenant for Roosevelt, and in this capacity he attempted to secure other benefits for the state of Texas: he voted in favor of government farm credits, championed lower freight rates for the Southwest, participated in the construction of slum-clearance projects, and supported existing programs such as the

72   THE COMPASSIONATE SAMARITAN

Civilian Conservation Corps and the National Youth Administration. In 1939, Roosevelt offered Johnson an appointment
as federal administrator for the Rural Electrification Administration. Johnson refused this position, however, because of
his strong desire to remain in elective office.

The House of Representatives consists of many time-
honored traditions. Since the powers of the speaker were
reduced during the progressive era, seniority had become
more and more important in determining duty assignments.
Freshman legislators, like children, were expected to be seen
and not heard. Therefore, Johnson was content to work
behind the scenes, associating with and assisting men like
"Mr. Sam" Rayburn, who would become Speaker of the
House in 1940, and Carl Vinson, the powerful chairman of the
Naval Affairs Committee. This soft approach was not without
risks. Some of LBJ's colleagues were amused at what often
seemed his rubber-stamping of any legislation that had
Roosevelt's approval. At home, critics dubbed the man from
Johnson City a toady. T. A. Price of the *Dallas News* ended a
lengthy 1941 interview of Johnson with the question: "Are
you a yes man?" The interviewee immediately responded: "I
am a yes man for anything that will aid in the defense of this
great republic. I am a yes man to the commander-in-chief as
every good soldier should be in time of emergency." [11]

Omar Burleson, a Texan who had struck up a friendship
with Johnson during his National Youth Administration
period, felt that it was necessary for LBJ to be a team player.
He believed that frequent contact with Sam Rayburn was a
prerequisite for passage of legislation and for holding the
Texas Democratic delegation together. This was the last era
"when we had what might be comparatively very great
harmony in the Democratic party. And I would give Mr.
Johnson credit for having kept welded a cohesiveness in the
factions in Texas." [12] Johnson had another reason for operating
as a member of the team, however. He did not aspire to power
in the House; his eyes were on the Senate and perhaps upon
the presidency as well.

Personally, Johnson had two major objectives as representative of the Tenth District of Texas. For one, he continued to support improvement of the educational system. In 1939, at the St. Anthony Hotel, where STSTC alumni had gathered, he stated that never in the history of civilization had a teacher had greater obligations. He thought that instruction that did not help a person to live a happier and fuller life could only be described as a failure, and that the application of learning to life was just beginning to be understood. He continued: "One of the great shortcomings of our modern educational system is its tendency to lean toward converting all of the material which comes to its hands into doctors, lawyers, newspapermen, engineers, professors, financiers, bond salesmen, archaeologists, anthropologists, economists, and genealogists." Conversely, what the average person wanted to know was: "How can I find myself a place—a little niche—in this community so I can be a part of it and live a normal, happy, comfortable and useful life in it, contributing something to the general welfare as I enjoy and insure my own welfare?" [13] In the future some would view such statements as being anti-intellectual. And, in part, they were. LBJ had grown somewhat distrustful of Roosevelt's professorial brain-trust, the members of which knew how to create new ideas but did not know how to institutionalize them into legislation. Johnson chose to look at the world as it was instead of looking through rose-colored glasses.

Good health and equating health to education also became a frequent theme of the legislator. His clearest statement in this regard came in a speech he delivered on the floor of the House toward the end of World War II. Statistics revealed that Texas had a higher selective service rejection rate than many other states. Of every hundred Texans drafted, seventeen were rejected for syphilis, fourteen for illiteracy, nine for heart ailments, nine for muscular-skeletal defects, eight for poor eyesight, seven for mental illnesses, six for hernic problems, five for nervous afflictions, three for tuberculosis, and three for substandard hearing. The solution was to educate for health as well as increased learning. This speech closed with familiar words. Said Johnson, "I am concerned about the whole man. I am concerned about what the people, using their government as an instrument and tool, can do toward building the whole man, which will mean a better society and a better world." [14]

While Representative Johnson frequently spoke on the subject of education, he did not initiate major bills to extend federal aid to schools and colleges during his years in the House. Except for the Northwest Ordinance of 1787 and the Land-Grant College Act of 1862 (and its various extensions), Congress had separated the state from education as well as from the church. A story from Lyndon's school days in San Marcos illustrates this point. LBJ remembered that he had failed an examination regarding what the Constitution permitted in regard to aid to education:

> I remember on the final examination I got an F. The question was: What does the Constitution say about education?
>
> I wrote about six or eight pages. When I got my theme back telling what the Constitution said about education, the professor gave me an F and wrote on it, "nothing."
>
> So if any of you think that the Constitution charters you to do a lot in the field of education, you will have to read between the lines instead of the lines. [15]

Personally, the legislator was willing to read between the lines, but the crisis of the Great Depression and the war clouds in Europe left little time for braving new frontiers. The National Youth Administration, however, had opened the door of federal aid to education a little wider, and the moment neared when old barriers would come crashing down.

From 1937 to 1941, Lyndon Johnson's life began to grow more complex, and he experienced some great personal and professional disappointments between triumphs. The long hours of exhausting labor often left him tired, resulting in medical treatment for a variety of illnesses. After his appendectomy, he wrote Rebekah that he strengthened himself by "eating country eggs, drinking sweet milk and sleeping."[16] Then he had trouble with his throat and tonsils, and later he underwent extensive tests for kidney stones. He did not have them, but he continued to drink mineral water as a preventative measure. His worst illness yet came in January 1941. On the twentieth, he told his mother that he had been out of commission for three weeks and that he was sitting at his desk for the first time of the new year. He still did not feel well, but he returned to work on that morning so that he could stand in the clear air and sunshine at noon to see his aging commander-in-chief once again be inaugurated. He worried, too, about Roosevelt's health that day and was happy to report, "It was a tremendous event and the spirit of confidence and assurance in the man who has led us through eight years gave more thrill than anyone else. I suppose you heard him repeat his oath of office on the radio, so I don't need to tell you how forceful it was."[17]

Lyndon's family, too, proved a source of strength as well as of personal heartache. His father's ill health awakened in him the feeling that no one was invulnerable. Rebekah, as a consequence of Sam's illness, had to continue to rely on her eldest for assistance. She wrote in September 1937 that "Daddy had a restless evening Wed. but slept after midnight. . . . When you come home bring any books you may have dealing with politics. I have an arduous task keeping him entertained."[18] Sam died shortly thereafter and did not live to see his son occupy a congressional office. Lyndon, then, had to assume full responsibility for Rebekah's financial needs.

Sam Houston caused concern, too. He had refused to campaign for his brother in the congressional race. Not long after, he started on a stormy personal life, which included drinking bouts, unhappy marriages, an inability to retain jobs, and other problems. In an undated letter, Rebekah pleaded with her eldest to continue looking after his siblings: "The younger ones try you, darling, but you are loving and strong and patient and are a great and potent influence for good in their lives. See how you did with Joseph and Billy. Mother appreciates it all *and is* so happy to see you do the things she wants to do but is unable to do herself. Am so proud and happy to have you to help me in shaping their lives." [19]

Rebekah kept Lyndon in mind day and night. She wrote on one occasion, "I dreamed of you last night. I ran in at Lucia's and there you sat, a splendid surprise, but I woke before you kissed me." [20] Birthdays were special, and both attempted to see each other at this time each year. Lyndon's thirtieth brought a special response. "Conserve your strength," Rebekah warned. "There is so much to do that you are eager to be doing, but you must not travel too swiftly. Restraint now may add years to your life." [21] Once when LBJ threatened no more help for his brother and sisters, she said: "I go right on turning to you. You have always been my confidant and friend—son, and I turn to you as the flowers to the sun." In the same message she told him, "Not having the children about me to love and to do for is the greatest cross old age brings me. Try to love each other and bear with each other for our own sakes. You are a noble son." [22] And, in his better moments, he was.

Meanwhile, the year 1941 was a watershed in the life of Lyndon Johnson, as it was for most Americans. Those eventful twelve months contained more than one bittersweet occasion. With national elections coming again, it was obvious to many people that both Roosevelt and the New Deal were in trouble, and newspaper headlines suggested that the rise of Adolf Hitler might imperil the security of the United States. Rebekah, always sensitive to Lyndon's future course of action, wrote: "These are indeed troubled times. I am eager to hear your opinion of present conditions. If we can stay out of the war it will be wonderful." [23]

The family was pleased, however, to hear that President Roosevelt had big plans for his young protégé. Rebekah wrote of the thrill she had when Walter Winchell mentioned Lyndon as the president's choice for heading the Rural Electrification Administration.

She would have been even more pleased, however, to know of Drew Pearson and Robert S. Allen's 1941 syndicated column in which much of the credit for preventing a Grand Old Party congressional landslide was given to her son. "Three weeks before November 5 [1940] you could have cut the gloom around Democratic congressional headquarters with a knife," a columnist said.[24] The Republican party only needed forty-eight votes to capture control of the House of Representatives. Democrats and Republicans were running close contests in one hundred districts. Floor leader John McCormack and Sam Rayburn visited FDR because Pat Drewry's campaign committee had collapsed, in their words, like the deacon's one-horse shay. The trio decided to put Johnson in charge. After a three-hour breakfast with Roosevelt, LBJ opened an office in a downtown business building and went to work. When the results were in, the Republicans had lost six seats instead of becoming the majority party in the House. The landslide victory convinced many in Washington that Johnson should think of running for the Senate.

On April 22, 1941, LBJ discussed with President Roosevelt the possibility of running for the Senate to replace Morris Sheppard, who had died only days before. FDR urged the thirty-two-year-old politician to announce his candidacy from the steps of the White House. Johnson did. The speech was brief. He said:

> I am a candidate for the United States Senate. Texas must fill a seat now vacant—left vacant by one who fought the good fight for democracy. This fight must go on under the banner of Roosevelt and unity. Senator Sheppard, who will be written in history as one who died working to save and serve, supported President Roosevelt always. In failing health he fought on. His loss is great; perhaps no one can fill his place.

If Texas voters believe me worthy, I offer my ten years experience with national problems and pledge that my long and consistent record of support of our President will be continued no matter what trials may face it.[25]

Until a special election could be held, Governor W. Lee O'Daniel appointed Andrew Jackson Houston, the eighty-six-year-old son of Sam Houston, to represent the Lone Star state.

President Roosevelt probably did not do Lyndon Johnson a service by convincing him to run for the Senate so early in his political career. Most observers thought that Representative Martin Dies, chairman of the House Committee on Un-American Activities, would be the major opposition. Dies had many enemies in Washington because of his frequent clashes with the Department of Labor and the Department of Justice, but he had a campaign issue that would appeal to patriotic Texans. He believed that Communists had placed some of their members in prominent government positions. Moreover, he was a rough-and-tumble campaigner who had access to large contributions from monied interests. Texans now had to choose between a man loyal to a popular president or a man who believed the nation itself was in jeopardy because of a radical world movement. Like Johnson's first congressional race, his campaign for the Senate seat would be of interest to the nation at large.

A single issue campaign, however, did not materialize because Governor W. Lee "Pappy" O'Daniel entered the race. In addition, Gerald Mann, a leading Texas lawyer, announced his candidacy. With three well-known opponents and several obscure names in the race, Johnson had to broaden his base. First, he continued to support Franklin Roosevelt without qualification, to the extent of bringing Preparedness into the public spotlight. Second, he decided to make extensive use of educational institutions—often making them divisional head-quarters. This was predicated partly on the fact that his strength at the polls lay with young people and partly because

Martin Dies had questioned the loyalty of students and faculty at the University of Texas. Last, Johnson's strategists believed it necessary to stump the state and make as many speeches as possible. The goal was two hundred public appearances. About $30,000 was budgeted, including approximately $7,000 for purchase of radio air time. Subsequent rumors, however, suggested that as much as a half-million dollars was expended.

President Roosevelt offered indirect as well as direct support for the youthful candidate. Too, Harry Hopkins had helped Johnson weigh the pros and cons of running prior to a formal announcement of Lyndon's candidacy. A. J. Wirtz, undersecretary of the Interior, Grover Hill, assistant secretary of Agriculture, and Harold H. Young, an associate of Vice-President Henry Wallace, all became involved in his campaign. In addition, FDR sent personal letters and telegrams for publication in newspapers, suggesting that the two men worked together in close concert. The most important of the president's messages, obviously an attempt to swing some of the older voters to the Johnson camp, arrived in June. The president wrote:

> I have your letter favoring further help for our senior citizens over sixty years of age. As you remember, you and I discussed this problem before the Chicago convention of the Democratic party last year. Our ideas were incorporated in the party platform, which called for the early realization of a minimum pension for all who have reached the age of retirement and are not gainfully employed. I agreed with you that the implementation of this pledge is the best solution of this problem. I hope you will come in and talk with me about it when you return.[26]

Texas colleges and high schools were used to contact both students and parents. At the Stephen Austin Hotel, for instance, Johnson spoke to campus representatives of "Lyndon Johnson for Senate" clubs. He told the delegates that in "times like these when our young men and women are being called upon to give training and energy to the defense of their country, there is nothing more fitting than that they have an active hand in the selection of government leaders."[27] He also had his office in Washington mail letters to high school graduates. These nonpartisan messages congratulated high school seniors on completing their studies and then added:

> If you or your parents feel that I might be of any assistance to you in making your plans, or once made, carrying them out, I would be mighty happy to have you write me about it. . . . Please consider me a friend who is eager to know you better, to prove my friendship for you by service in your behalf, and to have you know how proud I am of your past record and how much I wish you every success in the future.[28]

The high school students, of course, could not vote; but their middle-aged parents could.

Johnson delivered many speeches on college campuses. In early May, he spoke to an overflow crowd of three thousand in the auditorium at Southwest Texas State Teachers College. Cecil Evans provided an introduction, and LBJ emphasized preparedness, castigating isolationists for causing suspicion and sowing discord against Roosevelt. He also promised to see that Fifth Columnists, foreign agents, Communists, and Fascists were brought to justice. And he pleaded for support of a Great Britain that was "mighty wobbly." America, he added, was not immune from the war: Hitler would invade this country the day after conquering England and Europe. He then told those assembled that he hated war, but that if the time comes "when my vote must be cast to send your boy to the trenches, that day Lyndon Johnson will leave his Senate seat to go with him."[29]

Johnson used the *Congressional Record* as an instrument to defend Texas educational institutions from the charges of Martin Dies. Inhabitants of the Lone Star state, according to Johnson, were loyal Americans, and they knew better than most the necessity of defending liberty. "Even though there may be some trying months to come," he explained, "perhaps sorrow and sacrifice and tears, my hope and belief is that the same undying courage, the same love of freedom, the same unconquerable spirit which raised the flag of independence over Texas one day will raise it over a democratic world."[30] A week before, he had gone into more details on Texas traditions in a speech before a joint session of the legislature on San Jacinto Day. "The riflemen at San Jacinto didn't have much. They possessed scanty and inadequate supplies. They were few in numbers. They won because they used what they had of men and supplies a full one thousand percent. And that's what we have got to do."[31]

The Senate campaign ended on the steps of his boyhood home in Johnson City. Rebekah and Lady Bird stood beside the candidate. The initial vote count gave a jubilant Johnson a 5,000 lead over O'Daniel. Mann ran third and Dies a poor fourth. It appeared that the prophecy of Grandfather Sam had come true. The Johnson clan had a U.S. Senator who was under forty years of age. Unfortunately for Lyndon, however, delayed returns and recounts gave O'Daniel an edge of 1,311 ballots. The months that followed, the loser told a biographer, were "the most miserable in my life. I felt terribly rejected, and I began to think about leaving politics and going home to make money. In the end, I just couldn't bear to leave Washington, where at least I still had my seat in the House."[32]

The election results were not contested, in spite of the closeness of the count, and on July 14, 1941, the state election board certified O'Daniel as the victor. Silently, however, Johnson must have vowed that he would pay closer attention to key precincts in the future. He again threw himself into his work but continued to use "a world on fire" as a theme, the tone he had set in a talk given at Fort Worth:

We're going to reach out across the Atlantic and the Pacific and put our first line of defense thousands of miles from our American shores. We're going to drop the dictator's bombers over the water. We're not going to try to shoot them down on the ruined streets of New York and San Francisco and Fort

Worth and Dallas. We're going to fight Hitler, if we have to fight him, far away from the Rio Grande or the jungles of Panama or Brazil.[33]

In early July, a smiling, pacing, nervous loser boarded a plane at Love Field for Washington. His chief, he told well-wishers, had ordered him back to the nation's capital. Rebekah wrote two letters to her son the week he departed. The first commiserated with Lyndon. "You have been in my mind and heart all day. I keep thinking with great pride of your splendid statesmanlike campaign and the calm courage with which you met the final outcome. . . . You are very young and there will be other opportunities to go to the Senate."[34] Further, she suggested that friends be put to work in the counties where the vote was small. Johnson probably concurred in this matter, for he told Harry Hopkins that one of the reasons for his loss was that he did not have a statewide organization when he announced. But Rebekah struck a sore spot next. She advised Lyndon to have his tonsils removed and to take some lessons in public speaking. "You grow everyday in statesmanship and oratory but you are still better before a direct audience than over the radio."[35] Lessons would have helped. Johnson had patterned his public speaking after Huey Long, but he did not have Long's ability for rapid-fire speechifying, and as a result he was unable to stir the people with a machine-gun tongue like that of the Louisiana demagogue.

Not long after Johnson's return to Washington, he had to face another crucial decision. On the morning of December 7, 1941, Japanese aircraft inflicted severe damage on the American naval fleet stationed at Pearl Harbor on the island of Oahu. Johnson cast his vote in favor of retaliation and then, true to his promise given at San Marcos, he enlisted for active duty with the U.S. Navy. He received the rank of lieutenant commander and was ordered to report to the Twelfth Naval District headquarters at San Francisco. Lady Bird pitched in to help with his congressional duties. Before Lyndon left, he wrote his mother that he could not correspond so often any-more, as he was spending his days "at the Navy Department and trying to take care of my congressional office at night."[36] It is likely that Johnson never had a second thought about his enlistment. In the Texas tradition of the family, he had to now take his stand on the Brazos.

From California, Lieutenant Commander Johnson proceeded to the South Pacific. This was his first glimpse of the Far East, and the wide gap between rich and poor was permanently impressed into his memory. But at present the war effort had to be dealt with. LBJ spent eight months in New Zealand and Australia with Douglas MacArthur, who was then engaged in a holding action while awaiting much-needed supplies from the United States. Johnson served as a liaison with Washington in regard to the supply situation, and he assisted in untangling a potentially hot racial maelstrom: the Aussies did not want U.S. black troops in their country. Conversely, the Japanese were hoping for a knockout blow that would enable them to occupy Australia. Japan now had partial control of New Guinea and had only to push the Allies out of Port Moresby before accomplishing its goal. Johnson worked feverishly while in the South Pacific as a liaison officer, losing twenty-five pounds as a result of his rigorous schedule.

The time LBJ spent under MacArthur's command did pro-duce some tangible results. A gap between American and Australian commanders narrowed significantly, particularly in the acceptance by the Aussies of black soldiers from the United States. Then, too, General George C. Kenny replaced General George H. Brett, and this transfer, which had been recommended by Johnson, helped to smooth relations between MacArthur and the air force. Logistic logjams were also unclogged, making it possible for the historic Battle of Midway to commence on June 4, 1942. Lieutenant Colonel Samuel E. Anderson explained the importance of Johnson's mission in these words:

A problem read in a report is entirely different when the
problem is one demanding attention and solution. Those people
had critical problems of getting the gasoline they needed so
badly just to keep the planes in the air. They had to scream and
beg and even borrow (from the Australians) the bombs and
ammunitions needed to fight the war. Feeding the men was a
constant aggravating problem. They didn't even have the
clothes they needed for everyday war! Reading about a shortage
of shoes when you're in Washington and walking barefoot on a
hot desert may be the same problem, but it's a long way
different in its individual meaning. The people in the SWPA
were at the real end of the line at that time, and it was rough
going for them.[37]

In addition to helping solve supply problems, Lieutenant
Commander Johnson was eager to engage in actual combat
operations. On or about June 8, 1942, he volunteered, against
orders and against advice, to observe aerial combat operations
in and around New Guinea. The plane in which Johnson
flew, the Heckling Hare, piloted by Alter Green, lost a gen-
erator prior to reaching Lae, the bombing destination. It had
to drop out of formation as it had become the target of eight
Japanese Zeroes. Saburo Sakai, an enemy pilot, said after the
war that he had fired most of the shots at the B-2 in which
Johnson was a passenger. If so, LBJ was most fortunate, because this ace ended the war with sixty-two credited kills.
When the Hare returned, General MacArthur awarded the
Silver Star to Johnson for gallantry in action as well as for his
hard work on the supply situation.

Congressman Johnson enjoyed his wartime venture at the
time, and he remembered the experience later. The South
Pacific films he took were shown on many social occasions. He
almost always ended a showing with the comment that the
Australians were good people—men and women that you
could go to the well with.

Lady Bird, though busy in Washington, kept Rebekah
informed of Lyndon's whereabouts when she knew about

them. She reported on the bombing raid in detail. One letter she wrote immediately after the attack on the Hare revealed that a recent Associated Press release had stated that Johnson did not know he had been placed on the ballot for re-election in the Tenth District. "That means," she confided, "he did not get a couple of cablegrams John [Connally] and I sent him around and after the filing date. . . . So you see the situation is really quite in the dark." [38] Rebekah lost no time in contacting her son when he returned to Washington in the summer of 1942. A letter addressed to her son began: "How wonderful to have you back in Congress! I am so happy to have you home again." [39]

The Silver Star made up for much of the disappointment Johnson experienced in losing the Senate seat. And the war record he compiled would be helpful in the future—should he consider running for that body again. His days on active duty also produced a personal identification with the military establishment, a relationship he thought was reciprocated. Moreover, his trip to the Asian borders seldom left his consciousness. When time permitted, he mused about developing closer ties between the East and the West.

But meanwhile, there was a war to be won on the home front as well as on the battlefields in Europe. Senator Gerald Nye from North Dakota had held an inquiry into the causes of World War I in 1934–1935. His commission had concluded that American munitions makers in particular and businessmen in general had drawn the United States into the first great global war of the twentieth century by extending excessive credit to foreign countries that wanted to buy armaments from the U.S. Eventually, according to the Nye Commission, America had had to declare war on Germany: if England had been defeated she would have been unable to repay her loans, and many American businessmen might have had to declare bankruptcy.

Lyndon Johnson and many other American politicians decided not to let businessmen run unchecked during World

War II. He thought he had learned a valuable history lesson from the Nye Commission. It was enough that the citizenry was sending its sons and daughters to fight, he felt; their elected representatives ought to see to it that the people's economic security was not threatened as well. In a summer graduation exercise speech delivered in San Marcos, Johnson let his constituency know how he stood on the latter question. He said: "Selfish groups are fighting over the question of what patents will be used, where the plants will be built, what character of basic raw materials will be utilized and behind it all, who will get control of industry and get the profits after the war?"[40]

Johnson identified an issue in this speech that later would take on great importance. A colleague from the state of Missouri, Harry S Truman, would soon head a committee to investigate military and civilian waste and inefficiency. Partly because of the publicity he received, Truman would receive the vice-presidential nod from Roosevelt in 1944 and succeed his superior in 1945. Had Johnson won the Senate seat he wanted in the 1941 election, and had he continued to speak against waste and inefficiency, he might have been selected by FDR to serve as vice-president instead of Truman. This situation might have made the man from Texas the youngest president in the nation's history.

CHAPTER FIVE

Grassroots and Heel Leather

"I am a free man, an American, a United States Senator, and a Democrat, in that order."
—Lyndon Baines Johnson, 1963

N ATIONS ARE NOT unlike men: they are tested by trial as well as by time. The United States experienced a threat from within during the Great Depression and then a crisis from without during World War II. That famous debate between the Committee to Defend the Allies and the America First Committee quickly became irrelevant when the Japanese attacked native soil. The bombing of Pearl Harbor in short fashion convinced citizens that aggression must be met with determination, though few believed that the latest conflict would end war forever. The holocaust did, however, produce sweeping changes on the domestic scene, especially altering the family unit. Men worked longer hours than in the past and brought home inflated paychecks. Wives and mothers donned blue collars and punched time clocks in defense and defense-related industries. Children, less supervised than before, saved pennies to purchase war bonds, chanted obscene songs about Adolf Hitler, and traded photographs of war weaponry as they had baseball cards in the past.

Perhaps those affected most by the war were the youths of

high school and college age. Many males found themselves suddenly transported from their hometowns to armed forces induction stations and something called boot camp. Young women volunteered for active duty in the service auxiliaries and received training on the campuses of colleges and universities so that able-bodied men could be sent to the trenches. The latter were taught by professors who reserved a part of their working day for research, seeking substitutes for rubber or analyzing microbes and plants from distant lands. Saturday movie matinees and Sunday sermons both portrayed the Germans and the Japanese as fanged monsters. Young adults sought alcoholic highs to escape thinking of what the morrow might bring. Most important of all, this generation saw the end of free security. The military industrial complex, of which Dwight Eisenhower would warn in the future, was in the process of creation, and Americans needed a grassroots leader with thick heel leather to represent their interests in a rapidly changing world.

Lyndon and Lady Bird Johnson resembled their fellow Americans in many ways. They became parents, for example, just before the baby boom reached its zenith. The first child, Lynda Bird, arrived red faced and screaming in 1944, and the second, Lucy Baines, appeared three years later. The girls saw little of their ambitious father, and Lyndon would mature as a parent only when his daughters reached their sub-teens. The impending presence of children in the Johnson household dictated that more thought had to be given to the future, and the parents began to ponder the necessity of generating more personal income. Loose change and dollars they invested in savings bonds. Then, on January 25, 1943, the Federal Communications Commission approved the sale of radio station KTBC in Austin, Texas, to the family. Lady Bird used the remaining funds from her mother's estate to launch the venture. The FCC later increased the power of the system and permitted unlimited broadcasting. Affiliation with the Columbia Broadcasting Network catapulted the operation into the big time. By 1962, Johnson claimed that the business had made him a millionaire.

It has been charged that Lyndon Johnson used his political influence to purchase the station at the right price and that he looked after the facility so that it was free from competition. One writer, J. Evetts Haley, devoted an entire chapter of his book *A Texan Looks at Lyndon* to the subject. He repeated in print many accusations that had only been whispered before. Haley wrote that some people in the Austin area felt that Johnson was unethical in money matters and that Lady Bird was fanatical in her effort to turn a profit for the family. His portrait of both individuals is unflattering indeed. Such an interpretation is unnecessarily cruel. More to the mark is that Lyndon and Lady Bird were children of the Great Depression. He worked long hours as a politician and she as an investor to provide financial security for themselves and for their children. If, at times, their zealousness went beyond the bounds of propriety, neither person should be excused. The Johnsons, however, both in their desire for security and their efforts to maintain it, were not much different from many other Americans who came of age in a time of economic chaos.

Simultaneously, Congressman Johnson increased in confidence as a person and grew in stature as a politician, though there was not much time to spend on his first love, education. He made the transition, as longtime friend William White has noted, from "Dr. New Deal" to "Dr. Win the War" without difficulty. But a second rite of passage proved harder. LBJ continued to serve on Sam Rayburn's "Board of Education," a group of congressmen who met each day in an isolated room to drink bourbon and discuss present and future legislation. He was one of the first members of this group, however, to understand that the days of rescue and reconstruction were over. America had to find its place in the world and to convert its institutions back to peacetime. This comprehension produced a reassessment of his current political position, initiating a turn to the moderate left. Furthermore, Johnson came to regard the antiquated machinery of the House of Representatives as a detriment to progress. It was geared more to collective than individual action, the latter being more compatible with the upper house. Only in the Senate, among the options immediately available to him, did he feel he could deal effectively with the social and economic vicissitudes born out of the internal and external upheaval of the thirties and forties.

As World War II came to a conclusion, two events associated with the leadership of the Democratic party opened the way for the emergence of new personalities. The first event was the death of Franklin Delano Roosevelt at Warm Springs, Georgia, in 1945. News of FDR's demise shocked Johnson. He told one confidant that "he was like a daddy to me always; he always talked to me just that way."[1] Likewise, Speaker Sam Rayburn's loss of power to Joseph Martin in 1946 caused Johnson much personal consternation. Rayburn and Roosevelt had held the Democratic party together; the demise of one man and the descent of another left room for somebody born in the twentieth century to gain prominence. "The greatest need," Johnson thought, "underlying all others, was for national unity. The country must be drawn closer together so that, with a new spirit, it could confront the massive enigmas of its new world leadership."[2] Thus LBJ strove to become a more visible politician.

Johnson served on only three blue-ribbon committees during his last years in the House of Representatives. He continued to enjoy his duties as a member of the Armed Forces Committee, rising to the point where he might have been made chairman in 1948 if the Democrats had won the election that year. He participated, too, in the Select Committee on Postwar Military Policy. But the real high point came in 1947, when Speaker Martin elevated him to the Joint Senate and House Committee on Atomic Energy. These assignments, in part, evidenced Johnson's growing interest in foreign affairs. He cast his vote for the Truman Doctrine because he felt that the only thing a bully understood was force. He reminded his

colleagues that "the America Firsters . . . exploited the hesitancy of many of our citizens to prepare for adequate national
defense. The tactics of these ostriches and their fellow travelers encouraged, indeed if they did not induce, Hitler to ignore
us and the Japs to attack us."[3] He approved of the Marshall
Plan as well. He told a Texas reporter that he would support
and vote for the Marshall Plan for two reasons. "One is because it is a humanitarian plan. The other is from the standpoint of selfishness because I don't want to spend three hundred
billion dollars on another war."[4]

Johnson's increasing political breadth is best marked by
analyzing the speeches and documents he placed in the *Congressional Record* from 1942 to 1948. He spoke more often than
before and on a broader variety of subjects. In regard to
foreign affairs, LBJ supported aid to allies and items that
would strengthen America's defenses. For example, he voted
for Senate Bill 2202 in 1948, stating that "by sending food, by
sending financial aid, by sending faith abroad, we contest with
the evil in a battle for peace."[5] Measures for defense often
reminded him of the time he spent in the South Pacific. He
strongly supported air power. "Let us free ourselves of the
hidebound faith in the invincibility of a larger land army, and
give the air force the equipment, planes, and personnel it
needs to fulfill its fundamental role in our national defense."[6]
The lessons of World War II in regard to preparedness stayed
foremost in his thoughts as well. He told his colleagues that
should larger military appropriations not be obtained, the
United States risked paying in blood and dollars with interest,
as England had paid when attacked by Hitler.

Benefits for veterans and their families occupied much of
the time that the Tenth District congressman from Texas
spent speaking before his House colleagues. "The soldier
turned civilian," he explained, "finds the streets are not paved
with gold. His path, in fact, is strewn with stones."[7] Johnson
sought to amend the Surplus Property Act of 1944 so that
ex-GI's could obtain a priority in purchasing materials that

they had used to win the war. Johnson always supported educational benefits for veterans. And he approved of efforts to see that widowed women and the sons and daughters of men killed on the battleground received a college education. The example that he wanted to see widely emulated was the attempt of the Ex-Servicemen's League associated with the University of Texas to raise a million dollars for scholarships to help educate such people. He told those assembled in chambers on February 14, 1946, that "I consider this scholarship program to be an inspired concept of what a war memorial should be—an unusually vital and appropriate commemoration of the names and spirit of the men who made the supreme sacrifice . . . in order that we might continue to live as freemen and to improve, through education, our individual and national standards for democracy and all things that are really worthwhile."[8]

Johnson also continued to believe that government should intervene in the lives of the citizenry to raise the nation's social and economic levels. Rural America was his favorite cause. He drew on this theme in a discussion on electrical power: "If there was an enterprise wholly American in concept and character, it is the program of extending the blessings of electricity to all the people who live in the rural areas of our land."[9] He added that urgency was necessary. The farmer had to be kept independent, he warned, or the country would have "ghost villages, towns, and cities scattered throughout the States and Nation—the result of man's folly of doing too little and too late."[10] The farmer was also important in preserving freedom. Our world, he thought, was divided between godless communism and Christian democracy. Bulgaria, Yugoslavia, Rumania, Albania, and Czechoslovakia had fallen into the Soviet Bloc. The Communist parties in Italy and France were growing at an alarming rate. And some felt that Latin America and China had been lost already. The United States, therefore, had to prevent the expansion of what some called "stomach communism." "Democracy's only hope," Johnson felt, "is to provide more than promises, more than empty words, more than stiff-necked diplomacy. Democracy must roll up its sleeves and get to work—answering the cries of the hungry with food, replacing desolation with construction, replying to hopelessness with a new and active faith." [11]

The American home front drew attention, too. Johnson urged Congress from 1942 to 1948 to appropriate large amounts of money for the social well-being and health of the people. Improvements, for instance, were needed in housing (with a special break for veterans) and medical research, the latter involving investigation into the parasites and disease-producing organisms brought home by those who had served overseas during World War II. In addition, Johnson wanted steel and oil production to be increased. He pushed programs in this area because of their relation to defense, and also because it was a matter of concern in Texas. But more important, inflation was causing concern. Here LBJ developed a concept called "Operation Breadbasket." He called for the formation of a bipartisan committee "to dig into the causes of inflation and come up with solutions." [12]

Given the enormity of the task of converting the country to peacetime, Representative Johnson persistently spoke out on the subject of public service. He voted for pay increases for postal workers, who, he said, brought messages of happiness from one home to another. "This small pay increase," he said, "is a step in the direction of lending dignity to public service." [13] In July, 1947, he made public service to the nation the topic of an entire speech.

> Some parents feel that they prefer their children to go into the fields of medicine, law, agriculture, or engineering when they reach the age to determine their life's work. A certain amount of suspicion and distrust has been created because of the failure of a few public servants to live up to the confidence reposed in them. "Politics" and "politicians" carry a stigma and a taint to some that parents would like to see their children spared. [14]

Further remarks on this subject came in an address he mailed
to the Johnson City high school. The speech, which he had
intended to read in person, was entitled "The Atomic Age
Needs Heart and Soul."

In the text of the speech, Johnson evokes the memory of his
own high school graduation speaker, who had painted a rosy
picture for his generation. The Great Depression and World
War II, however, had clouded the happiness of many
Americans. Next, he launched into a treatise on the importance of the individual and the need for civilization to follow
the Golden Rule. The world ought to be made a better place,
he wrote, and this was to be the challenge of those now just
entering adulthood. "I do not mean better for me as an individual. Nor better for the rich man nor the poor man; for Jew
or gentile; for black or white or red or yellow; for Catholic or
Protestant; but a better place for all the people." [15] How could
this be accomplished? He said:

> Yours is the challenge to nurse back to health and well-being a
> sick and diseased and confused world. For we cannot hope,
> merely because we are American, that we will remain a fertile,
> green oasis in the midst of a deadly desert. Either our oasis
> must grow and expand to cover the desert, or its deadly poison
> gases and death-laden winds in time will erase that last spot of
> fertility.
>
> So I am convinced that we, as individuals and as a Nation,
> must furnish the leadership and the moral courage that will
> serve as an inspiration to the rest of the world. . . .
>
> When we practice the Golden Rule in our daily conduct
> with our neighbors, it is understandable to them. They have
> the same language, religions, and faiths and customs. If we are
> to become world leaders we must act so that what we do will
> be understandable and intelligible to peoples who speak in
> tongues strange to us, with customs different than ours, and
> even with faiths we may find repugnant to our thinking. [16]

These words on the brotherhood of all mankind and the need

of Americans to practice the Golden Rule he would repeat many times in the future.

Lyndon Johnson's speeches during his last years in the House of Representatives echoed sentiments widely shared by the citizenry of the United States. Those twin perils of depression and war had bred optimism and confidence in the goodness and greatness of America. The nation's inhabitants believed that a decent home, a living wage, and good health were rights, not privileges. And government should aid in securing these things. Henry Garland Bennet, a Midwest educator soon to be appointed to head the Technical Cooperation Administration created under Point 4 of Truman's inaugural address, summed up this viewpoint when he said: "I should like to see one generation . . . reared and educated from cradle to maturity with the benefit of all that we know about medicine, health and hygiene, formal education and psychology. . . . Truly, I believe here lies the pathway to Utopia." [17] Moreover, now that the United States had helped to achieve international peace, an effort must be made to extend these concepts abroad. The Marshall Plan and the Truman Doctrine were only a beginning. Africa, Asia, and Latin America needed a window to the twentieth century. Their cries, plus a fear of communism, became for Lyndon Johnson a missionary call, leading him to seek for a second time a seat in the United States Senate.

In the spring of 1948, Johnson decided to make his intentions public. But this time, unlike seven years ago, the Senate contest would not be a special race; that is, he could not run for two offices simultaneously. The actual decision itself was agonizing for Johnson because his re-election to the House seemed a sure bet. He had beaten Buck Taylor, who published *The Middlebuster*, by a comfortable margin in 1944. Two years later, Charles King, a University of Texas student, and Judge Hardy Hollers had fallen just as easily. On the other hand, the thought of being turned out of office frightened him. Johnson later told a biographer: "At first, I just could not bear the thought of losing everything."[18] But in June he told the "good people of Texas" that he had decided to place his name on the ballot. "In 1941," he added, "I lost this great office by 1,311 votes. Three voters changed in each county would have meant my election. . . . Lots of people said they'd support me next time."[19] Undoubtedly, too, the prophecy of his grandfather—that Johnson would be a United States Senator by the time he was forty—lingered in the back of his mind. Whatever the motivation, LBJ found himself at a most crucial point in his life.

Altogether, ten candidates paid a filing fee for the Senate post and contested with each other in the Democratic primary. Of these, two men—George Peddy, a Houston Lawyer, and Coke Stevenson, governor of Texas—were regarded as the toughest opposition. Martin Dies also entered, but he soon withdrew. The polls put Stevenson ahead. He had 46.6 percent while Johnson had 36.8 percent and Peddy only 12 percent. LBJ selected for his slogan "Peace, Preparedness, Progress." The tone for the campaign came from a kickoff rally held in Houston at Wooldrige Park. "We're the kind of people," the candidate remarked, "who started life in a . . . little town. You'll find those people in filling stations and hardware stores. Teaching in country schools. Riding a tractor across the black lands—or following a plow furrow as I did in my boyhood."[20] The simple country boy had returned.

The campaign of 1948 was ill-fated from the beginning. Shortly after the race got underway, Johnson developed acute pains in the abdomen. These were later diagnosed as kidney stones. Surgery, he hypothesized, would force him to miss campaigning completely, so he quickly boarded a plane and flew to the Mayo Clinic in Rochester, Minnesota, for treatment. The staff there was able to dissolve the hardened substance through medication, though the problem returned periodically and reduced the Texan's strength. The loss of time created some severe difficulties in speaking schedules. Some method had to be uncovered to narrow the gap delineated by the polls published in the newspapers. An answer came on June 16. Johnson announced that some World War II veterans had leased a helicopter so that he could visit more towns and cities each day than by automobile or train. The "Johnson City Windmill" first stopped at Marshall, then went on to twelve other communities before nightfall. Johnson made personal contact with about six thousand people by this means. His staff was elated, and Lyndon vowed he would average twelve thousand people per day until the lease expired on the aircraft.

During the summer, two major issues surfaced. One centered upon support or nonsupport for the Taft-Hartley Bill, a measure recently adopted by Congress to curb the power of labor unions, which had been gaining strength since the early days of the New Deal. Johnson voted for Taft-Hartley, though he had been labor's friend during the Great Depression. Coke Stevenson attempted to sidestep the issue, and this drew some bitter barbs from LBJ. In return, the governor publicly chided Johnson for his unabashed activity in the area of federal aid to education. The specific question related to a bill by Senator Robert Taft to subsidize the salaries of public school teachers. Johnson addressed himself to this issue on June 22. He said: "My crafty, do-nothing opponent has tried to make an issue of federal control of the schools either by deliberately distorting the facts, or by being too lazy or careless to learn what the facts are." Then he continued: "The federal aid bill that I endorsed was written by Senator Taft, who is probably the most conservative man in Congress. All anyone has to do to learn the simple truth, is to read the bill. It simply says that the federal government should give the states five dollars per pupil per year so that teachers' salaries could be raised. There would be no federal strings whatever on the money."[21]

By July, federal aid to education became the paramount issue of the campaign. The attack by Stevenson in this area did much to cost him the election: Johnson hammered away on

the benefits of such programs, and he organized the schools
and colleges in the state on his behalf. The propellers of the
"Johnson City Windmill" spun faster and faster, with advance
announcements of its stopping points coming the day before
on the radio. Most of these broadcasts made it seem as if the
Lone Ranger was coming into town. A typical program began:
"From out of the rugged Hill Country a new day's dawning in
Texas politics. A new day born by the Johnson City
Windmill, the whirly helicopter that is carrying Lyndon
Johnson over the state." [22]

The speeches in July centered upon home and family and
the right of parents to provide the good life for their children,
including education. The clearest statement in this regard
came on the second day of the month. With growing confidence, Johnson ascended the steps to center stage in Abilene
and said:

> Some one has said that a politician looks to the next election;
> while a statesman looks to the next generation. By that defini-
> tion, every mother is a statesman; for every mother gives her
> life to her children. The most thoughtless girl becomes the
> most thoughtful and unselfish mother. She forgets her own
> well-being and rebuilds her life around her children. She
> guards them; she will strive to feed them; she will fight to
> protect them. [Everybody(?)] owes his continued existence on
> earth to that deep protective mother-love.
>
> The child's training starts at home; it continues in church
> and school. Then the child goes out in the world where laws
> were made by men. Jealous of the future for their children,
> women demanded and won the right to vote, so that they
> might have a voice in forming that future. And they shaped it.
> Look to the history of our social reforms . . . the humanitarian
> laws of yesterday which we take to the improvements in our
> education system . . . and the emphasis upon international
> affairs . . . because women long ago realized that what is
> happening elsewhere in the world is happening to us. [23]

Ten days later Johnson gave more vocal support to the Taft

education measure and identified the villains opposed to federal aid. In so doing, he evidenced that he knew the nature of the Texas populace. The discovery of oil in this state had created some sharp social divisions. Dirt farmers and ranchers, for example, struggled to make ends meet. They did not resent those who bettered themselves by hard work and skill. But this element developed enmity for those who joined the nation's super-rich simply because black gold had been discovered on their property. Moreover, a small percentage of these oilmen generously gave funds to archconservatives who opposed federal aid to the masses, thus doubling the resentment. Johnson knew that such feelings existed, and he gained votes by making wealthy oil men the culprits when it seemed expedient. He was particularly angry at this time at the opposition to education, retorting: "The Taft Education Bill specifically says that there shall not be any Federal control. I don't know what their real objection was, but I *do* know that the big money boys down in Houston are having a mighty hard time living on two hundred fifty thousand dollars a year out of their million-dollar income."[24] Few people questioned the validity of the accusation.

The same day, he pointed out to his listeners that Texas land-grant colleges and veterans were now receiving federal aid without disastrous controls resulting. He used a biblical injunction to show that he was on the side of the Right. "Some principles endure," he explained, "because they are based on eternal truth. Go back with me to your Sunday School days and recall this verse from the gospel according to St. Matthew: 'No man can serve two masters; for he will hate one and love the other or else he will hold to the one and despise the other. He cannot serve God and Mammon.'"[25]

From July 15 to 23, LBJ continued to champion federal aid to education and enlisted leading educators throughout the state to support his position. On one evening, the following individuals provided testimonials: W. J. Moyes, principal, Mirabeau B. LaMar High School, Houston: Charles M.

Robers, past president of the Texas State Teachers Association, Amarillo; E. B. Comstock, assistant superintendent, Dallas; Mary Wildenthal, principal, Cotulla; R. H. Shelton, Stephen F. Austin College, Nacogdoches; and B. Dickson, superintendent, San Angelo. On July 23, President Cecil Evans of San Marcos walked onto the firing line. His words left no doubt of what he thought about his former student at Southwest Texas State Teachers College:

> I know, love, and honor Lyndon Johnson as I would a son. Lyndon has my endorsement as to character, honesty, integrity, and all-around ability. His election to the United States Senate will promote our common cause of education, conserve the best interests of Texas and the nation, and give Texas an outstanding young statesman for service in the Senate. I commend him wholeheartedly to every friend of education in Texas—and that means every Texan.[26]

On Saturday evening, July 24, the Texas Election Bureau broadcast the results of the election. George Peddy received 20 percent of the vote, coming in third with a count of 237,195. Johnson captured 34 percent of the ballots; 405,617 fellow Texans had checked his name in the election booth. Both men, however, trailed Stevenson, who obtained 40 percent of the vote, or 477,077 actual tallies. No one received the necessary 50 percent to capture the nomination. Thus, a runoff was scheduled approximately thirty days later. Johnson, then, had to formulate a new strategy without delay. Stevenson decided to go to Washington for conferences with people in high offices, a move which gave him maximum news coverage. Johnson hired a new speech writer, Horace Busby, and he went after the Peddy vote. The second phase of the campaign was scheduled to start in Center, Peddy's home county. Johnson threw even more issues into the hopper. During the next month, his speeches touched upon legislative experience at the national level, know-how, a fair deal for farmers, fifty-dollar-a-month pensions for retired people, methods for enticing industry to Texas, internationalism, and the menace of communism. Moreover, Johnson stated that he and Colonel Peddy essentially agreed on most matters of importance.

Federal aid to education continued as a major theme, however. LBJ reminded his listeners that his Grandfather Baines had served as the second president of Baylor University, and he spoke of his own experience at San Marcos, in country schoolrooms, and as director of the Texas National Youth Administration. One five-minute radio speech was devoted entirely to this subject. The text reads as follows:

This is Lyndon Johnson speaking. I am a candidate for United States Senator. I want to discuss with you how we can pay our teachers a salary as big as their jobs, without burdening the little home owners of Texas.

The way is by federal aid to education. *Without* federal control. That principle has worked for fifty years at A. and M. College which is largely supported by federal funds. Federal aid has been used to teach vocational education in most Texas high schools and in many colleges. A half-million veterans got federal aid for their education. Those who oppose federal aid to education must oppose all of those things. He also must be against federal aid to support farm prices; to make REA loans; to build farm-to-market roads and highways; to pay old age pensions. Big money has painted a black picture of federal aid to education. The propaganda has been carefully calculated, and no expense has been spared in spreading it across our land. That kind of money was never spent because somebody feared federal control.

The same folks who are screaming federal control today, screamed state control a few years ago when Jim Ferguson proposed state aid to the little red schoolhouse. Jim put it across and called it the egalitarian principle. That very same principle is used in federal aid. The state did not dominate the local schools. And the kind of federal aid I propose will not change the local control of schools top, side or bottom.

The most conservative man in the United States today is Senator Taft of Ohio. Senator Taft is the author of the Federal

Aid bill. It is almost unbelievable that we could have anybody in the race for the United States Senate more backward than Senator Taft.

We want schools to teach Americanism: that by industry and hard work, any boy or girl can rise to fame. It's the teachers' job to plant this American dream in the hearts of our children. Yet that dream hasn't come true for the teachers themselves.

Like you, Lyndon Johnson wants to make that dream come true. As your United States Senator, I will vote for the bill which will make possible a pay increase of four hundred dollars a year for every Texas teacher. If you believe in that goal, contact your local Johnson committee. . . .[27]

Later, in the Senate, Johnson developed close ties with Robert Taft and regretted some of his harsh words toward him. He respected Taft's personal courage and integrity, though he often had misgivings about his narrow political beliefs. The senator from Ohio had become worried during World War II about the shameful neglect of public education. Money for schooling and housing had to be found to repair the damage that had been done. He knew that the Constitution did not authorize the national government to regulate schools—this clearly was a function of the state. On the other hand, the Congress, through its power to spend money, could move into this area if necessary. Taft's only concern was that the government not interfere with the local school process. In 1948, he made this clear. He explained: "Nothing contained in this act shall be construed to authorize any department, agency, officer, or employee of the United States to exercise any direction, supervision, or control over, or to prescribe any requirements with respect to any school, or any State educational institution or agency. . . ."[28] Johnson and Taft both agreed, in spite of other political differences, on aid to education. When Taft died in 1953, Johnson wrote: "I have never known a man with whom I could work more smoothly. He was a great statesman and an honorable Christian gentleman;

and during the time we worked together . . . he became one of the best friends I have ever had." [29]

As the Senate race neared a conclusion, Johnson, panicked by the polls, struck as hard against organized labor as he supported federal aid to the schools. Carl Estes, an East Texas newspaperman, now spoke on LBJ's behalf. His approach was to tie labor to the much feared and so-called "communist conspiracy" in Texas. Should the people elect "Calculating Coke," Estes said, every CIO-PAC-AFL labor boss in the country will step up organizing in the Lone Star state. "I also," he added, "lay down the proposition, ladies and gentlemen, that the true working man in Texas, once he is in possession of all the facts, will not on August twenty-eighth be against Lyndon Johnson and the American way of life, and for the theories of Harry Bridges, John L. Lewis, Henry Wallace, and Vito Marcantonio—or any of the rest of the ragtag and bobtail of those whose political coats, plainly speaking, range from pale pink to blood red." [30] Simultaneously, Richard M. Nixon of California, another congressman running for the Senate, printed on pink paper the biographical details of his opponent, Helen Gahagan Douglas. It was a day to bait Communists.

When the votes from the 1948 Democratic primary in Texas were counted, it become clear that Johnson's hesitancy in running had some basis in fact. The election results were too close for comfort. Court battles on two levels had to be fought for many weeks and did not stop until a black-robed justice of the Supreme Court had determined whose name ought to appear on the ballot of the November general election. The initial results were announced on Saturday, August 28. The Texas Election Board reported that Stevenson led, 470,681 to 468,787. By Sunday afternoon, Stevenson's margin had dwindled to 315 votes, and by midnight LBJ had captured the lead, with 10,000 votes yet to be counted. The situation reversed itself again on Monday. The governor now had 119 votes more than Johnson. But some 400 ballots had not been tabulated yet. Stevenson's margin rose to 362 on September 2, and what were thought to be final results on September 3 gave him a 114-vote margin.

The counting, however, was not over. Officials in Jim Wells County reviewed the balloting and reported 967 for Lyndon Johnson and 61 for Coke Stevenson. Earlier, they had reported 765 for Johnson and 60 for Stevenson. Jim Wells and the neighboring counties were under the jurisdiction of a political boss named George Parr, who over the years had acquired the title of "Duke of Duval." Subsequent rumors place him as the kingmaker for this election. This vote change precipitated a court battle. On the local scene, Alvin Wirtz, J. Allred, John Cofer, Ed Clark, and John Connally worked out a defense for Johnson's case. On the national level, the law firm of Thurman Arnold, Abe Fortas, and Paul Porter succeeded in convincing Justice Hugo Black to put Lyndon Johnson's name on the November ballot, where Johnson then defeated Jack Porter, a Houston oil man, by a 350,000 vote margin. The Johnson family at last had a United States senator. But he was a senator called "Landslide Lyndon" by some wags.

The close vote count and the details of the scoring process itself caused Johnson embarrassment in the future. His strong antilabor position and his phobia of Communists caused some to label him as a modern John Calhoun. But the most significant aspect of the election was his development into a consensus politician. In the future, Johnson would deal with both liberals and conservatives on an equal basis. Moreover, he had learned a lesson about issues. He would henceforth support those which had popular appeal. And paramount among those was to be federal aid to education. Americans might disagree as to how funding should come about, but most believed in good schools. Johnson, then, once more became an avowed school man.

Altogether, Lyndon Johnson had served eleven years in the United States House of Representatives. His service as an individual cannot be called distinguished, but he did become a part of an effective team that changed the character of American government, swinging it substantially to the left of center. The New Deal established once and for all that Washington had a direct responsibility to the populace in providing leadership and legislation aimed toward improving health, education, and welfare. Johnson belonged to the younger bureaucracy that did not simply devise but implemented visionary programs. He had profited much from listening to others and from learning how decisions on important matters were made. This information would remain in his mind until he himself occupied a seat of real power.

Just as the New Deal altered the philosophy of government in America, World War II indicated that the people of the United States were now citizens of the world, meaning, among other things, the end of free security. Friendly neighbors to the north and south and the wide expanse of the Atlantic and Pacific oceans to the east and west no longer ensured immunization from the ills of Asia or Europe. Johnson's move from the House office building to the Senate office building was a virtual journey across the world, for the upper chamber had direction over foreign affairs. Lyndon Johnson now occupied a position where he was in the national and international spotlight. He quickly assembled a staff—the youngest and most poorly paid in Washington—to meet the challenges ahead. Most of these names are now familiar: Mary Rather, personal secretary; Leslie Carpenter, publicity; Sam Houston Johnson, all-around troubleshooter; John Connally, administrative assistant; Walter Jenkins and Warren Woodward, second in command; and Horace Busby, speech writer.

The new members of the Senate class of 1948 were a star-studded group. Estes Kefauver, Hubert Humphrey, Paul Douglas, Clinton Anderson, Robert Kerr, and Russell Long headed those freshmen who took the oath of office along with Harry Truman. All of these men, including Johnson, obtained choice committee assignments, and they were ready to move from New Deal to Fair Deal.

President Truman set the tone for the next four years in his inaugural address. He made four major points on January 19, 1949: he reaffirmed support of the United Nations, pledged to put his full weight behind the European Recovery Program, promised to help strengthen freedom-loving nations against the dangers of aggression and to develop a bold new program for aiding underdeveloped nations to enter the twentieth century. "Democracy alone can supply the vitalizing force," he concluded, "to stir the people of the world into triumphant action, not only against their human oppressors, but also against their ancient enemies—hunger, misery, and despair."[31]

CHAPTER SIX

A Master
of Congress

"Give to the world the best you have, and the best will come back to you."
—Johnson City high school senior class motto, 1924

THE SENATE OF THE United States received Lyndon Johnson into membership about the time he and the twentieth century reached the midpoint of their lives. In another sense, though, the Senate was just coming of age. Until the direct election of solons in 1913 (under the provisions of the Seventeenth Amendment) the Senate had had no great political consequence. A convincing case could be made that this body had been the weakest link in the system of checks and balances. Tradition and the Constitution relegated it to advising and consenting on presidential appointments, initiating only nonrevenue bills, voting on other measures, and approving or rejecting international agreements in which the American people had a stake. At the turn of the century, David Graham Phillips, in his biting series of essays entitled "The Treason of the Senate," labeled the organization a rich man's club, hinting that members often purchased their seats. What public attention senators did obtain usually came from personal charisma or extraordinary skill in debate. But the expansion of the national bureaucracy during the New Deal and the increased importance of foreign affairs after World War II provided the foundation for an enlarged mission. Ironically, at the time the Senate assumed these added duties, the established hierarchy had passed its prime. Men such as Carl Hayden, Theodore Greene, Richard Russell, and Robert Taft were already at or beyond normal retirement age. Thus it was time for the mantle of leadership to be draped over other shoulders.

At forty-one, LBJ was ready for increased responsibilities. He had developed some individual color, and his speaking skills had improved. Moreover, the nation needed a "master of Congress," because the last four years of the Truman Administration at home and abroad were difficult by almost any standards. The Cold War had polarized the globe, and many domestic American institutions were antiquated well past the limits of safety. The Fair Deal of President Truman called for significant advancements in housing, social security, health care, tax reduction, and education. However, John Tabor, chairman of the House Appropriations Committee, insisted that frills be eliminated from the budget. His stand and Truman's strong pronouncements on civil rights in 1948 split the Democratic party, creating ideological as well as geographic differences.

Events associated with the Iron Curtain countries produced the problems that occupied most of the new senator's time throughout his first six years in office. The policy of Containment, the perfection of the atom bomb by the Soviets, the fall of China, the formation of mutual security pacts such as the North Atlantic Treaty Organization, the scramble for resources in underdeveloped countries, and the Korean conflict—all necessitated that domestic issues be put on the back burner. Quite naturally, then, Johnson's speechmaking focused on the international horizon. One significant domestic problem did surface just after he took the congressional oath, an issue that had to be dealt with before the Senate could get down to the routine of handling ordinary or extraordinary business. The division in the Democratic party over civil rights had to be addressed.

In 1948, the Democratic party's platform contained a strong civil rights plank. In line with Truman's February 2 message on civil rights, it advocated the creation of a Fair Employment Practices Commission and called for passage of federal legislation to prevent lynchings and to end discriminatory poll taxes. HST's surprise election victory in November gave heart to those who wanted Congress to adopt a twentieth-century civil rights bill. But each time this subject had come up in the recent past, filibusters, real or threatened, had thwarted discussion of the matter. Soon after the Senate convened in 1949, civil rights supporters asked for the amendment of Rule 22. This procedure, popularly known as the Anti-Filibuster Rule (or Cloture Rule), had to be changed if a civil rights bill were to be introduced. The battle lines were soon drawn. Northern liberals wanted to limit debate and southern conservatives wanted unlimited discussion on the floor to postpone a vote.

The cloture question put Lyndon Johnson in a precarious position. His foremost objective in the Senate was to make the transition from a regional to a national politician. But now, after only two months in the upper house, he would have to cast a ballot which would put him in either the liberal or conservative camp unless he could devise a strategy to lift him above the fracas. It was not even possible for Johnson to duck the issue and remain silent: to do so would have affected his relationship with Richard Russell of Georgia, who vehemently opposed anti-filibuster legislation, and LBJ had chosen Russell for his sponsor in the Senate as Rayburn had been in the House. He needed to keep Russell's goodwill. Since he could not avoid taking a stand, Johnson chose Rule 22 as the topic for his maiden speech. His comments were delivered in the month of March. His announced topic was cloture, but the address is more revelatory of how he viewed the Senate and how he would use that body to make his name a familiar one in American households in the future.

In his speech on cloture, LBJ spent much time comparing the Senate to the House. He pointed out that the large number of congressmen prohibited more than a few minutes each for speechmaking, and this in turn prevented members from securing national newspaper headlines of the type that swayed public opinion. Likewise, the two-year term in the House made representatives vulnerable to the election process. This meant that an inordinate effort had to be allocated to the homefront to secure re-election. Also, Johnson theorized, two years was not enough time to intimidate a strong president. The smaller number of senators and the six-year term of office left "to the Senate the role of a national forum, where the underlying philosophy of legislation—as well as the surface details—can be laid bare for the public to contemplate,"[1] Johnson explained. Those who heard LBJ so far could anticipate what was coming next. He opposed limiting debate or voting cloture on the grounds that oratory was a central Senate function. Debate could inform the public as well as force a president to do his homework.

His exact wording is worth repeating. The freshman senator stated:

> It is my conviction that the right of unlimited debate here in the Senate is an essential safeguard in our American system of representative government; first, as a safeguard for the public's right to full information on all legislative decisions; second, as a safeguard against the deliberate or accidental destruction of the distinctions between the legislative and other branches of government; third, as a safeguard for members here—both majority and minority—against rash, impetuous action, or action predicated on incomplete or inaccurate information.[2]

Johnson wisely chose to champion free speech instead of directly opposing cloture. On the opposite side of the coin, he somehow had to dispose of the civil rights issue in a manner that would not offend liberals. This, too, he handled deftly.

The speaker disclaimed that he had any personal prejudice toward any minority peoples. "My faith," he said, "in my fellow man is too great to permit me to waste away my lifetime with hatred of any group."[3] Then he went on to state that he thought it unfair to associate the filibuster with only the American South. Dixie, for example, had voted to curb floor time during World War I by supporting the Underwood Resolution, which limited remarks to an hour-and-a-half when the nation was at war. Discrimination was an age-old and universal problem that ought to be redressed by schools, LBJ said, not by legislation. "I do not concede to federal law an obligation which I think rightfully belongs to education, and which education alone can discharge," were the speaker's actual words.[4] The suggested solution probably did not surprise those in the audience, for Johnson's utopian faith in the power of pedagogues was well known by this time.

Johnson carefully selected examples to illustrate salient points, making sure that the precedents he cited came from men who had lived and worked in the South. LBJ thought of himself as a westerner, yet he had to have the support of states below the Mason-Dixon line if he was to play a leadership role in the Senate. Thus, he quoted Senators Thomas Reed of Missouri on cloture, Joseph Robinson of Arkansas on the necessity of free speech, Lister Hill of Alabama on the importance of the Senate as a national forum, and J. William Fulbright of Arkansas on the imperial presidency. Shorter references were made to Walter George of Georgia, Tom Connally of Texas, and former greats John Calhoun and Henry Clay. Only one northerner—Daniel Webster—received Johnson's attention. The last three men were included because they all had a history of making lengthy speeches in the Senate.

As Johnson warmed to his task, he was not content to offer data just from America to illustrate his position. He jumped across the ocean to England and France and then moved backward in time to the days of the Roman empire:

I am no historian, but as I have studied the history of governments gone before us, I have been impressed by the fact that
the freedom of unlimited debate in legislative chambers has
been given up many times by members themselves who were
irritated by a minority. But, so far as I have found, once that
freedom has been yielded, it has never been returned. If we
now give up this freedom in the Senate, I, for one, do not
expect to live to see it return. For that reason, I cannot and will
not join hands with those who seek to throw this freedom out
the window now.[5]

Two final points brought the speech to a close. He directed
strong words toward journalists who cast southerners as the
culprits impeding civil rights reform because they insisted on
limiting floor debate:

I should like to point out here to the writers with their wrath-
ful pens, to the commentators with their caustic voices, to the
cartoonists with their derisive skills, and all those who join the
throng to keep alive the cries against unlimited debate, that we
here in the Senate . . . cherish our freedom of expression as
they cherish theirs. But for the grace of God . . . we might
today be debating the limitation of their freedom to speak out
or that of the press, rather than our own.[6]

Last, Johnson reminded Americans that the Soviets often
repressed personal liberties. If only one freedom could be
exported behind the Iron Curtain, "I would send to those
nations the right of unlimited debate in their legislative chambers. It would go merely as a seed, but the harvest would be
bountiful; for by planting in their system this bit of freedom
we would see all freedoms grow, as they have never grown
before on the soils of eastern Europe."[7]

The attempt to limit debate in the Senate did not pass;
Johnson's speech, however, had little to do with the outcome.
President Truman had made some intemperate comments in
public that hurt his own cause. He had also failed to choose able

defenders to support his effort to amend Rule 22: Carl Hayden, a Democrat, and Robert Taft, a Republican, were not natural and popular leaders. Somebody remarked that Hayden had not spoken on the Senate floor since the twenties, while Taft's extreme conservatism alienated him from the mainstream. The leaders against cloture, Richard Russell and Arthur Vandenburg, easily defeated the bill. Truman lost prestige. The Fair Deal surrendered ground that could not be easily regained. Blacks had to wait another decade for a civil rights bill. Perhaps only Lyndon Johnson profited. He had fought on the winning side, had supported the noble cause of free speech, had retained respect in the South, and had secured favorable personal publicity.

Johnson delivered only one or two other major speeches in the Senate in 1949. (On August 23, he spoke in favor of increasing appropriations for public power programs.) He instead reserved most of his energy in 1949 for national defense matters. He championed in particular additional expenditures for experimentation and research. He feared that the lack of a hot war might lead to an American complacency, leading in turn to an obsolete weapons arsenal. Many diverse subjects received his attention, but the supersonic jet got the lion's share of his time. In one presentation, he warned his colleagues: "The era of the subsonic military aircraft . . . is at an end. If ever the fate of the world is again decided by aerial conflict, the aircraft involved will fly at supersonic speeds."[8] Scientifically, America was a mere babe in the supersonic wilds, but more money, LBJ argued, could hasten the arrival of the jet age.

Johnson returned to the field of education in late 1949 and early 1950. During the 1949 Thanksgiving school recess, he addressed the delegates of the Texas State Teachers Association. He had not talked to this group for eighteen years, and perhaps this long absence provided the incentive for offering some particularly pertinent remarks.

Two issues preoccupied him on this day: salary increases for teachers and the dangers of overspecialization. He began by sympathizing with those who were lobbying for pay raises. "I suppose," he said, "that I stand before you tonight as living evidence of what happens to teachers when they are underpaid: one way or another, they get into politics."[9] But demands for higher pay held some dangers. Traditionally, parents had kept tabs on the comings and goings of pedagogues. Social habits, church attendance, and family life were scrutinized. Yet if teachers were paid more, then some significant changes might be expected: larger salaries, Johnson believed, would invite communities to take a more careful look at what went on inside the school itself. He said: "In doing this . . . you have virtually invited the public to cross the threshold of the classroom for the first time and judge you as a teacher rather than as a model of virtue and commendable private life outside the classroom."[10] Here the speaker turned out to be a good prophet. As school budgets expanded, beginning in the late 1950s, the public did demand more involvement in the educational process and requested more accountability from those who directed learning. Curriculum and teaching strategies as well as goals and objectives were to change at a rapid pace. More administrators were hired to supervise, and many teachers experienced pressures that had not been felt in the past.

Overspecialization was a different matter. European existentialism, born in the bombed-out rubbish of the Western free world, had now crossed the Atlantic. This philosophy emphasized the present at the expense of the past; old values diminished in importance as pupils were taught to see the world as it actually was rather than how they wanted it to be. History and philosophy moved aside to make room for practical subjects, especially vocational education. Johnson believed that, because of these ideas, students were not being instilled with a faith in the American way of life. He did not blame educators for this situation: they had "merely responded to the ill-advised cries of our time for the kind of security that makes the present secure—and assumes that tomorrow will be secure, also." [11] But he viewed this trend with alarm. Again, he correctly predicted the future: Johnson, a liberal arts major himself, recognized that less functional subjects would be squeezed out of the curriculum. "What we need, I think, is the teaching of a sort of 'workable morality' in our schoolroom. When I say 'workable morality,' I am speaking of the morality of usefulness and unselfishness which our society—in its mad rush for personal gain—often fails to encourage or produce." [12]

Finally, Johnson stated that science and technology were increasing in importance. They were necessary in the atomic and jet age; but they were only a means to an end, not an end in themselves. More than anything else, he believed, science should help people not to fear the unknown and not to worry about what lies over the horizon. Johnson thought that the citizenry should be optimistic instead of pessimistic, but he recognized that the age of confidence had not quite arrived: "We seem to be afraid to start climbing the stairway to the stars until we are sure that the handrail is in place." [13] Johnson had an abundant faith in the educational system to preserve the best of the past and to shape an American who had no qualms about living in the decades ahead.

This theme received further attention in an Atlantic City speech Johnson gave early in 1950 to the annual convention of the American Association of School Administrators. LBJ identified defense as the major topic of the day, asking, "What is the best defense our country can have?" The best defense, he answered, was to ensure that the citizenry were taught the principles of liberty and freedom in the classroom. America had an advantage over certain other nations, he said, because it had "a long history of free public education, which has given us the world's greatest reservoir of enlightened manpower. We have the further advantage of freedom, which permits the full use of the minds and learning of our citizens." [14]

Two recent events motivated this phase: China had joined the ranks of communist nations, and the Soviet Union had

perfected an atom bomb a full seven years earlier than predicted by the American scientific and intelligence communities. No single invention, therefore, could ensure security for
anyone. "Modern politics," continued the speaker, "and
modern science have made it impossible for any nation to be
certain that its defenses are adequate." [15]

How right he was! On June 28, 1950, Johnson wrote a note
to Harry Truman, who had recently ordered the armed forces
of the United States to join the United Nations in aiding
South Korea's fight against aggression from the north. "Your
action," he told the president, "gives a new and noble meaning
to freedom, gives purpose to our national resolve and determination, and affirms convincingly America's capability for
freedom." [16] The mission of the United States was to preserve
liberty here and to help it thrive elsewhere as well. Sixteen
days later, Johnson shared this same message with other members of the Senate. The speaker reiterated his "too little, too
late" caution of World War II and called upon patriotic
countrymen to approve the expenditures needed to win the
war: American boys "who had fallen into the hands of this
enemy are dying a slaughterhouse death—dying from bullets
fired into their faces." [17] Johnson wanted to mobilize the entire
nation quickly. The Korean conflict produced a halt in educational planning, and it created a national and international
situation which would occupy the mind and actions of
Lyndon Johnson until the middle of the decade.

Though Johnson advocated increased defense budgets, he
wanted good value for all money spent. He did not like to see
dollars wasted. In July he accepted appointment to the Preparedness Investigating Subcommittee of the Senate Armed
Forces Committee, more popularly called the "Truman committee of the Korean conflict." Estes Kefauver, Virgil
Chapman, Lester Hunt, Styles Bridges, Leverett Saltonstall,
and Wayne Morse worked under his chairmanship. Johnson
promised the public that his group would not "hunt headlines
or exploit the sensational or play politics. Above all, we must

not try to establish this subcommittee as a Monday morning quarterback club, second-guessing battlefront strategy."[18] Nevertheless, the subcommittee offered a unique opportunity to an ambitious man. And at least one Washington journalist, Doris Fleeson, concluded: "It is already being said that Lyndon Johnson wants to be president."[19]

The Korean conflict reinforced the idea among Americans that their country had reached the end of free security. Henceforth, in times of both war and peace, the nation would have to maintain a modern and superior fighting force. Defense, in its broadest sense, became the personal mission of LBJ. And budget items, small and large, were examined with his eagle eye. He protested when surplus equipment was sold to civilians at reduced cost when it should have been rushed to Korea instead. Then, too, he watched the list of stockpiled minerals to see if any items were getting dangerously low. He devised the phrase "siesta psychology" to warn the bureaucracy as well as to keep the public alert to all these possibilities.

The initial report of the Preparedness Investigating Subcommittee became public approximately six months after the Korean conflict began. Johnson informed fellow senators first, in an address entitled "Necessity for National Preparedness." LBJ portrayed Korea as a war for the survival of the United States. He also expressed the fear that the battle might linger on as long as twenty years. He leveled criticisms at the executive branch, the Department of State, and the Joint Chiefs of Staff for not ordering mobilization immediately. Far too much of the decision-making, it seemed to him, had been done on the spur of the moment, and what planning was done used World War II as a basis rather than current conditions. The tactics of the last great world encounter, according to Johnson, were outmoded and inapplicable to the present situation. "Obviously," he concluded, "we need new approaches, new plans, and new goals."[20] Johnson realized better than most that old myths had to give way to new realities. The world had changed and so had warfare.

The report of the Senate Preparedness Committee touched upon the state of the domestic economy. Inflation had taken and would continue to take a heavy bite from the paycheck of the American worker. The wholesale price index, for example, now stood at an all-time high. In the previous thirty days, it had reached 171.7, representing an increase of 12.3 percent over the past six months. The cost of some war materials had greatly exceeded this rate. During the previous one-half year, the price of burlap had risen 75.6 percent, copper 32.6 percent, lead 61.9 percent, tin 85.3 percent, wool 67.6 percent, and crude rubber 209.5 percent. What did this mean insofar as defense tax dollars were concerned? The committee gave these specific illustrations:

The tax dollars which would have bought 100 miles of field wire before Korea would buy only 85 miles in September and only 78 miles in November. The tax money that would buy 10,000 barrels of fuel oil before Korea would buy only 6,500 barrels in September and only 4,700 barrels in November. The money that would have bought 1,000 truck tires in April, before Korea, would buy only 830 in September and just 720 in November. The money that would have bought 10,000 pairs of Khaki trousers before Korea would buy only 8,500 pairs in September and only 7,600 in November. The money that would have bought 10,000 pairs of wool socks before Korea would buy only 9,000 pairs in September and only 8,500 in October.[21]

The committee recommended that future budgets be carefully examined by the Congress. "I think," Johnson said, "we must dispense with the idea that because one segment of government increases in size, all segments must increase."[22] Growth in the bureaucracy, Johnson explained, must be justified in each and every case.

The *Washington Star* used the concluding lines of the address for one of its banners the next day. "Is this the hour of our Nation's twilight, the last fading hour of light before an endless night shall envelop us and all the Western World?"[23] The story itself added some hitherto unknown details to Johnson's speech. Full mobilization had not been declared because George Marshall feared that a national alert would create additional problems for the United States. If, Marshall reasoned, the Communists eased up on the Korean front, then America would be left with a large standing army and converted defense plants that could not produce peacetime goods. Such an action was politically and economically unwise on several counts. Moreover, the Department of State was committed to following a policy called containment. George Kennon explained this concept in an article published anonymously in 1948 by *Foreign Affairs*. Kennon suggested that America not attempt to liberate people inside the communist bloc, but instead simply contain them within present boundaries. The goal in Korea, therefore, was to push the enemy over the thirty-eighth parallel and there to stop.

Altogether, the Preparedness Investigating Committee issued forty-six unanimous reports. These recommendations—or at least those implemented—saved many billions of dollars. Johnson's contribution to this group made him one of the leaders of the Senate. Newspapermen as well as politicians sympathized with the idea that wars were fought to be won, and won as fast and decisively as possible. An article in *Nation's Business* by Henry S. Pringle, a Pulitzer prize-winning biographer, supported the point of view recently espoused by Johnson in the Senate. At home in Texas, the *Fort Worth Star-Telegram* and the *Tyler Courier-Times* reprinted some of Pringle's essay. And local editors took pride that one of their own was making positive headlines throughout the country. Personnel associated with the *Courier-Times* believed that the junior senator had made the transition from politician to deep-thinking statesman. Too, the report increased LBJ's standing in the Senate. Wayne Morse, from Oregon, offered the following:

> I want to say in passing that the Senate is aware of the great work which is being done by the Subcommittee on Prepared-

ness of the Committee on Armed Services. However, I think it is quite proper that I should comment on the floor of the Senate today on the courage, fearlessness, absolute fairness, and impartiality of the chairman. . . . The committee under his leadership has been carrying out the promise we made at the outset of our work that we should be entirely impartial and fearless, and that we would let the chips fall where they may.[24]

Morse's words drew warm applause, and in the same month, the Senate increased the responsibilities of Lyndon Johnson.

The Democrats met on January 4, 1951, to hold new leadership elections. Arizona's Ernest McFarland garnered enough votes to become majority leader. The same group also designated Johnson as whip. The duties of the latter position were not onerous. Primarily, they involved collecting information on how fellow senators would vote on upcoming legislation.

McFarland had never been an outstanding leader, and now his advanced age rendered him less effectual than usual. This provided LBJ an opportunity to assume some of the power that rightfully belonged to McFarland. Elevation to the post of whip and the chance to help the majority leader inflated Johnson's ego. He told a future biographer: "Well, right here in the Senate I have to do all of Boob McFarland's work because he can't do any of it. And then every afternoon I go over to Sam Rayburn's place. He tells me all about the problems he's facing in the House, and I tell him how to handle his."[25]

While duties as whip were not particularly taxing, they did help Johnson to better understand the inner workings of the Senate. The big issue of 1951 was the defense budget, and Johnson soon found himself embroiled in a debate over Senate Bill 1. He wholeheartedly supported a section establishing universal military training for all college-aged males. This act advocated raising a standing army of 3.5 million and would ensure that the nation had a sizeable ready reserve that could be placed on active duty on short notice. The Armed Forces Committee had recommended approval of Senate Bill 1 because the population of countries behind the Iron Curtain had quadrupled in the last five years, whereas the number of free men and women in the Western World had only doubled. Johnson hoped to increase the military without raising havoc with American college and university enrollments. He explained:

> We do not accept the idea that all colleges should be turned into military training camps. It would be most unwise to place institutions of higher learning under the thumb of the military. There could be no more uncertain step toward a militaristic state than that. We want to safeguard academic freedom. We do not want to reduce our learned professors to drill-master status. [26]

Not all of Johnson's colleagues liked Senate Bill 1 as written. John Bricker of Ohio and Edwin Johnson of Colorado introduced an amendment on February 28. Both men feared that the proposed National Security Training Corps would interrupt normal college matriculation. Likewise, they believed that the proposed seventy-five thousand deferrals were not enough to meet the needs of the learned professions. The junior senator from Texas rejected this view. "I think," he said, "I am safe in saying that more study has been given to the subject of universal military training and to the program set out in this legislation during the past five years than has been given any other aspect of national defense." [27] And he was right: it had.

The Postwar Policy Committee of the House of Representatives, the Compton Commission, and the Armed Forces Committee had urged passage of the bill. The final version was influenced more by the House than by the Senate. Johnson, however, won enough essential points to convince his colleagues that he was a man who would continue to rise in the ranks of this august body.

The second session of the Eighty-second Congress was really an extension of the previous session. With more old business than new, Johnson's passions were aroused only once. He had to contend with the thorny question of oil rights in the Texas tidelands. Both the state and the federal governments claimed jurisdiction. The problem was not resolved until later, but the situation did force monied interests in the Lone Star state to deal with LBJ. His hard work on behalf of Texas businessmen resulted in a more solid political base at home and diminished his reputation as a political maverick in Texas. In the future, LBJ would not have to worry unduly about his re-election to the Senate.

A more difficult situation from 1950 to 1952 for Lyndon Johnson was how much he should support Harry Truman. The Fair Deal was close enough to the New Deal so that LBJ did not have serious ideological reservations about the man in the White House. On the other hand, Truman's public opinion ratings were dropping at an alarming rate, largely because of the Korean war. Also, labor leaders were still upset with the Taft-Hartley Bill. Wildcat and organized strikes were becoming more common. Critics were questioning the loyalty of many public officials in high offices, especially in the State Department. And finally, several government employees had accepted questionable gifts from lobbyists. It was therefore risky to associate too closely with the president, who did little to help himself. His sharp tongue resulted in adverse publicity at a time when he needed every bit of support he could get. Truman and Johnson would become fast friends, but only after the feisty Missourian retired.

Neither did the presidential election of 1952 appreciably help Johnson determine where he should stand politically. Adlai Stevenson, who had recently won the gubernatorial election in Illinois by the largest plurality in the history of the state, was too liberal for most Texans. And Johnson and others resented his hesitancy in seeking and accepting the Democratic nomination. Conversely, the standard-bearer for the Republicans, Dwight David Eisenhower, was one of the most popular figures of his time. He was a World War II hero, and his promises to go to Korea in order to effect an armistice had wide appeal. Americans were getting tired of wars, especially one in which the government sought only to contain rather than to crush the communist opponent. In the end, it was Ike's promise to visit the war zone that brought victory to him and the Republican party. His margin at the polls might have been even higher if it had not been for the dubious conduct of his vice-presidential nominee, Richard M. Nixon, who was rumored to have had an illegal campaign slush fund. Eisenhower kept Nixon on the ticket, but he could have gotten more votes for the Republicans if he had replaced him.

The 1952 election brought disaster for the Democratic party. The Republicans captured the majority in the Senate and the House as well as bagging the presidency. For Johnson personally, however, it was a stroke of luck. Arizona's Barry Goldwater, a Republican, had defeated Democrat Ernest McFarland in that state's senatorial election. This meant that when Democrats met on January 3, 1953, they had to choose a new person to head their party in the Senate. The most logical choice to serve as minority leader was Richard Russell of Georgia, but he did not want to lead a party not in power. Johnson, who had ascertained Russell's feelings prior to the organizational meeting in January, obtained Russell's support for his own bid. He used the Georgian's endorsement to capture the votes necessary for victory before many of his colleagues realized that a race was in progress. On January 3, LBJ became the youngest minority leader in the history of the Senate.

Simultaneously, the Republicans experienced difficulty in selecting the right man to serve as the Senate's majority leader. Nebraskan Kenneth Wherry got the first nod. His program faltered with the death of Robert Taft in the summer. William Knowland of California replaced Wherry in 1954. He was a capable man, but his liberal beliefs separated him from the mainstream of Republican thought. President Eisenhower did not often invite him to the Oval Office, and when he did no substantive consultations took place. This again put Lyndon Johnson in an advantageous circumstance: in effect, it left him in a position where the leader for the minority had more influence than the leader for the majority. Eisenhower and Johnson held a mutual respect for each other and soon developed a harmonious personal and legislative relationship.

The new Senate minority leader had much in his favor. His youth, vitality, and vision served him well. On February 14, 1953, he spoke in Washington and surprised many when he said, "The role of the minority party is to hammer out a program that will solve the problems of America—not just to obstruct the work of the majority party."[28] Here was something refreshing, a politician who at least on the surface put his nation ahead of his party. His constituency at home and his colleagues in the Senate applauded Johnson's elevation to minority leader. In March, for example, the Texas congressional delegation presented a citation at a testimonial dinner: "We . . . proudly salute you as one who has attained the heights of Senate leadership through brilliant and patriotic service. . . . You have brought honor to our state, our nation, and our people."[29]

Senators echoed similar sentiments. Both liberals and conservatives supported Johnson's efforts to be civil to legislators regardless of their views. Also, the split in the Democratic party caused by the 1948 convention diminished. Here again, Johnson's fairness stood out. At the end of the summer, senators from South Carolina, Louisiana, and Wyoming singled Johnson out as a man with good common sense and praised him for fighting communism without raising hysteria. Gore of West Virginia added one more plaudit: Johnson had "an appealing sense of humor and also genuine personal kindness."[30]

It was a generous Johnson who summed up the year's work in the summer of 1953. He thanked many of his colleagues by name, including Earle Clements of Kentucky, his whip. He cited Morse, Knowland, and Richard Nixon as members of

the opposition who had been cooperative. He also congratulated personal staff, such as "Skeeter" Johnson (no relation)
and Bobby Baker. Then LBJ asked how one should judge the
failure or success of a session—was it by bills passed? by hours
in session? by implementation of the president's program?
No! he responded. The real yardstick, he said, was "What has
Congress done to promote the security of America and the
prosperity of its citizens?"[31]

Such statements added to Johnson's stature in the country
and in Congress. Perhaps the most grateful person, however,
was Dwight David Eisenhower. Ike was not a professional
politician, and long years of military service under crisis conditions had sapped his endurance and patience. His most
perplexing leadership problem stemmed from the fact that the
Republican party had few moderates. Bob Taft and Bill
Knowland held extreme positions, and Ike regarded Joe
McCarthy as a dangerous fanatic. In fact, Lyndon Johnson, a
fellow Texan, was closer to Ike's political philosophy than
most in his own party. Their mutual respect enabled them to
conduct the country's business in a difficult age.

Johnson continued to serve as minority leader when the
Senate reconvened in 1954. But other things occupied his
mind as well. Six years had passed since he had left the House
of Representatives, meaning that he had to stand for re-election again in Texas. Elections always frightened Johnson. The
last one had been a cliff-hanger, and now rumors from Austin
indicated that the popular two-term governor of Texas, Allan
Shivers, would provide primary opposition. On the other
hand, there were some new assets since 1948. Johnson was
now the senior man from Texas, as Price Daniels had replaced
Tom Connally in the Senate. Moreover, the position as minority leader had made Johnson a national personality. Then,
unexpectedly, Shivers announced that he would seek an unprecedented third term as governor. This elevated Johnson's
spirits and confidence. The race would be made with gusto.

Still, he would have opposition in the June Democratic primary. Dudley Dougherty, from Beeville, decided to make the race. He had served in the Texas legislature, and his extensive oil and ranch holdings meant that he would spend considerable sums of money. An angry and vengeful Coke Stevenson quickly offered to serve as Dougherty's campaign manager. Six years had not erased the pain of Stevenson's 1948 defeat. His strategy was to have his candidate present himself to the public as a conservative, in spite of the fact that he had given huge sums to Adlai Stevenson two years before. Dougherty campaigned hard, spending much time riding on the back of a vintage fire truck through rural Texas. Dougherty attacked Johnson personally by asking embarrassing questions regarding Johnson's attainment of millionaire status. He also questioned America's participation in the United Nations, took a firm stance against revision of Taft-Hartley, and labeled his opponent soft on communism.

Johnson relied heavily on the advice of Sam Rayburn in the 1954 election. He ignored personal comments and retaliated only to the charge that he was politically pink. This approach must have worked, because when the Texas Election Bureau announced the final vote, Johnson had defeated Dougherty by a margin of 875,000 to 350,000. The good news reached the minority leader while he was on the floor, and business stopped for ten minutes so that Republicans and Democrats alike could extend their best wishes. Johnson did not need to worry about the November elections at home. Winning the Democratic primary in Texas, as in many states below the Mason-Dixon line, was tantamount to victory. He used free time in the fall to help other Democrats in their senatorial campaigns. In November, the House of Representatives returned to the Democratic fold. Sam Rayburn, who had lost the speakership in 1952 because of Eisenhower's groundswell that year, once more held the speaker's gavel. The situation in the Senate was less clear. But when Wayne Morse, an Independent, agreed to side with Democrats, the party of Jefferson and Jackson regained control. On January 5, 1955, the

Democratic caucus voted Johnson majority leader of the Senate. This moment was a proud one for Texas, as native sons now headed both segments of Congress.

Ambition, however, demands human sacrifice. And in Johnson's case, the recent campaigning and his dawn-to-dusk working schedule had left him in a weakened condition. The day after his election to the post of majority leader, he was forced to leave the Senate for two months because of ill health. Physicians at the Mayo Clinic diagnosed his current problem as kidney stones. LBJ felt that he could not spare the time necessary for an operation, but he did promise to rest and change his life-style. It was a resolution that he no doubt fully intended to keep at the time. Johnson had just purchased property on the Pedernales River, just across the stream from where he was born. Perhaps, he hoped, he could in the future spend more time there making the ranch a model of its kind. Unfortunately for Johnson, the nation had a divided leadership, and patriotic Americans had to help make the system function. The month of March found Johnson back at his duty station in the Senate, working as if he still possessed his youth.

CHAPTER SEVEN

Our Battlefield Is the Classroom

"Our battlefield is the classroom. Our real struggle is our struggle to educate our youth."
—Lyndon Baines Johnson, 1959

T HE YEAR 1954 heralded great changes in American education. Perhaps the single most important catalyst in bringing schools to the attention of the public was *Brown v. The Topeka* (Kansas) *Board of Education.* This ruling outlawed segregation in educational institutions, stating that dual systems harmed the social and psychological development of blacks. The *Brown* decision spawned a revolution, and soon activists attacked *de facto* as well as *de jure* segregation. Other educational questions, too, were debated during this momentous year. McCarthyism remained alive. His fellow travelers continued to examine teacher loyalty, curriculum worth, and library holdings. Many critics angrily wondered why some young men had not yet returned from China to America after the end of the Korean conflict. More and more citizens demanded that teachers sign loyalty oaths or lose their positions. Then, too, the rapid technological advances of the Soviet Union frightened much of the citizenry. A worried public wanted to know why children could not read, write, spell, and cipher better than they did. The nation needed mathematicians and physicists to keep pace with a mushrooming Cold War.

These developments led to the formation of difficult questions. Should force be used to integrate schools, such as Central High in Little Rock, Arkansas? Ought the federal government bear some responsibility for the destruction of a high school in Clinton, Tennessee, that had been bombed in the middle of the night by a mysterious stranger shortly after the Warren Court banned school segregation? Did America have a moral obligation to ensure equal educational opportunities for minority and disadvantaged youth? And even more encompassing, should the federal government offer aid to education in order to strengthen a school system that had not been able to keep pace with international developments since before World War I? A world spotlight focused on this country, and its beam shone on America at a time when a champion of education neared the zenith of his popularity. By the summer of 1955, Lyndon Baines Johnson had mastered the job of Senate majority leader, and he was ready to help schools and colleges modernize to meet challenges at home and abroad. A few even hailed him as man of the hour.

Stewart Alsop, syndicated columnist, believed that Johnson had the bones and blood of the Senate in him, and he urged Americans to observe him closely. "There is something peculiarly satisfying about watching a genuine professional at work," he wrote, "whether on the field of a baseball diamond or on the floor of the U.S. Senate. Anyone who wants to see in action the best professional floor leader of our time need only visit the Senate gallery at a tense legislative moment and keep his eye on the tall, lanky, slow-moving form of the majority leader as he ambles about the floor below."[1] The Texan had twenty-five years of public service behind him, and he handled with more light than heat legislation dealing with topics as diverse as the Paris Accords, reciprocal trade, agricultural appropriations, and Colorado River reclamation projects.

Other prestigious journalists responded in kind. Albert Clark, in a column written for the *Wall Street Journal*, thought that Johnson ran the smoothest show in years and called the forty-six-year-old "one of the most adroit politicians to occupy the post in recent years."[2] Arthur Krock, Walter Lippmann, and Frank Kent were equally impressed. Local newspapers did not neglect Johnson either. A writer for the *Waco News-Tribune* marveled at the fact that the Democrats only had a majority of one, yet they solved problems intelligently and quickly. Louise Evans, an Amarillo reporter, published a series on famous Texans in her newspaper and put Lyndon near the top of the list. She stressed his tutelage under Roosevelt and Rayburn but added that he was more than an avid student—he worked twenty-five hours every day in order to get the job done.

Senate colleagues were proud of their new leader, and they provided the press with quotable phrases that enhanced his reputation. Hubert Humphrey called his classmate of 1948 a genius in the art of legislative process. To this, Richard Russell added: "He isn't the best mind in the Senate. He isn't the best orator. He isn't the best parliamentarian. But he's the best combination of all these qualities."[3] Russell's comment was published by Albert Clark, who on his own volition concluded that if Johnson were not from "the South there's little doubt he'd have to be reckoned with for the presidency. There are those who think he might wind up in the presidency anyhow."[4]

The Senate's human dynamo even looked like a presidential candidate. General T. A. McInerney, editor of the Washington *Independent Editorial Service*, broadcast that LBJ was the second handsomest man in the upper house, trailing only George Smathers of Florida. He had tempered his Texas accent, and he now dressed like a Wall Street broker. And unlike other southern politicians who had achieved national fame, he "has never worn his hair long, worn a heavy watch-chain, and has never roared in public with stentorian tones."[5]

Beneath this calm outward exterior, however, Johnson struggled for emotional and physical health. Crisis often produced visible perspiration and skin blotches. He consumed two and three packages of cigarettes daily, and the amount of scotch he poured over ice grew ever larger. Overwork, overconsumption, and overtension reached alarming proportions by mid-1955.

George and Herman Brown, friends of the Johnson family, invited Lyndon to vacation with them in Middleburg, Virginia, over the upcoming Fourth of July. A chronic bronchial condition and the recent bout with kidney stones motivated the majority leader to accept the invitation, and he left his office on July 2 to travel to Virginia by automobile. Senator Clinton Anderson accompanied him. As the car speeded south, LBJ experienced acute stomach pains. They did not subside, but Lyndon expressed no alarm, as physicians had earlier warned him about "rich-reward foods." He attributed his distress to indigestion. Anderson, however, advised medical treatment, and perhaps this suggestion saved his companion's life. By the time Dr. John Willis Hurst could admit Johnson to a hospital, his complexion had turned ashen.

The patient did not lose consciousness, but he did go into shock. A high fever followed twenty-four hours of chills and clamminess. Johnson must have remembered through this period the long, slow demise of his father and the lingering paralysis of his grandmother. He resolved not to succumb. Dr. Hurst diagnosed the condition as myocardial infarction and recommended six weeks in the hospital and three months of rest at the LBJ ranch. The intensity of Johnson's heart attack is open to question. Hurst said he had seen people with worse conditions recover and lighter ones die. Yet Johnson told friends his was "as bad an attack as you can have and still live."[6] He stopped smoking and substituted Fresca soda for vintage scotch. Juanita Roberts, a staff member who had been trained as a dietician, prescribed a low-calorie diet.

The late summer of 1955 found the stricken man in Texas,

managing his recovery as he had guided the Senate. He relished the news stories published about him, but some seemed more like obituaries than progress reports. Holmes Alexander of the Boston *Herald* called Johnson the "best-liked political person in Washington."[7] He added that the Eighty-fourth Congress was simply the elongated shadow of this great American. Legislative leaders visited the ranch to discuss the pros and cons of upcoming bills and to wish the majority leader a speedy recovery. A November 15 speech delivered in Whitney, Texas, took Johnson out of the presidential race. He had not seriously considered running, but favorable press coverage had given rise to speculation that he would. Thereafter, announced candidates for the Oval Office dropped in for advice and consultation. The attention was flattering, and some thoughts about making the race in 1960 must have crossed the senator's mind.

In January, Johnson was back at his post in the nation's capital. His first speech reviewed the Senate's accomplishments of the previous year with great pride. One thousand three hundred twenty-five bills had been passed and signed by Eisenhower. This same group had acted on no fewer than forty thousand presidential appointments. Much unfinished work remained, however. Top concerns for 1956 included tax and social security revisions; improvements in medical research programs; restoration of 90 percent farm parity; housing reform; highway and water bills; changes in immigration and naturalization laws; passage of a measure to outlaw the poll tax; and federal aid to education. This last seemed a small item on the agenda, yet the subject opened a Pandora's box that is still a matter of debate.

As it turned out, prolonged debate on federal aid to schools did not materialize until 1957. The 1956 presidential election made it impossible to plow new ground, and much time had to be devoted to old issues, especially recent domestic recessions and Cold War strategy. President Eisenhower provided some lukewarm support for a bill to provide schools with funds for classroom construction, but it did not pass. Many Americans equated federal aid with creeping socialism. During the Korean conflict, for example, a Johnson constituent had written him that funds should not be used in this manner. He concluded his note by saying: "I hope that you take an active part in defeating any such legislation, which, in my opinion, is simply another way to get federal control of our public school systems and colleges and to inject more socialism into our way of life."[8] There were many similar letters.

The complacency of the United States toward education received a shattering blow on October 4, 1957. Leaders of the Soviet Union announced that for the first time scientists had succeeded in launching a satellite that orbited the earth about every hour and a half. This development pushed politicos into action on education as well as on defense matters. Sputnik did not surprise Lyndon Johnson; it obtained more receptive audiences for him, however. Not long after the news from the Soviet Union, he delivered to the Dallas chapter of the American Jewish Committee a speech entitled "We Need Not Lag Behind." This satellite, he told his listeners, "represents one of the greatest feats in the whole history of mankind. . . . For the first time, humanity literally escaped from the earth."[9] American schools would have to be upgraded in science, he prescribed. Quoting statistics gathered by Clarence B. Lindquist and delivered to a subcommittee of the House of Representatives, Johnson warned that Russia was producing two mathematicians and physicists for every one produced by the United States. "We must go down to the local level—to the elementary schools and the high schools. We must kindle in our people an enthusiasm for learning and an enthusiasm for science."[10]

Johnson's thoughts at the end of this address are not a matter of record. But he must have mulled over in his mind how lonely had been the road to federal aid for education. Just the March before, for instance, he had suggested the formation of a "High School Students' Government Participation

Program," a suggestion that had fallen on deaf ears. Earlier he had correctly forecast that *Brown* v. *The Topeka Board of Education* would spell trouble and embroil schools in controversy. Nevertheless, he supported desegregation as solidly as he had once favored segregation. One did not quit because of a setback. In May of 1954 he explained: "In my state, on the basis of the 'separate but equal doctrine,' we have made enormous strides over the years in the education of both races. Personally, I think it would have been sounder judgment to allow that progress to continue through the process of natural evolution. However, there is no point crying about spilt milk." [11]

As far back as 1951, Johnson had connected national defense to education. He consistently strove to lessen Cold War pressures so that citizens of the United States and the Soviet Union could get to know each other. It was far better, he thought, that they study about each other in the classroom than fight each other on the battlefield. He presented one of the most important speeches in his career on this subject just prior to the launching of Sputnik. It was entitled "The Open Curtain" and would evoke discussion for several years. Atomic power, if used in combat, could destroy the civilized world, Johnson explained. "With such weapons in a divided world, there will be little choice. We will return to the caves of our remote ancestors and burrow underground like the prairie dogs of West Texas." [12] Instead, a crusade for disarmament was needed. "We must create a new world policy. Not just of open skies, but of open eyes, ears, and minds, for all peoples of the world." [13] Then the tall Texan suggested that the United States and the Soviet Union permit their leaders to appear on television in the other country.

John Foster Dulles, secretary of state, liked the "Open Curtain" speech. He had supported radio and television exchanges with Russia since the Big Four ministers met at Geneva in October 1955. No immediate action had taken place then because of the antagonism caused by the Hungarian revolt. Now, however, the timing was better. Nikita

Khrushchev had spoken on the American television program "Meet the Press" without adverse results. Dulles also felt that technical information as well as filmed speeches ought to be exchanged. He even wondered if perhaps American scholars should be permitted to go behind the Iron Curtain to work with Soviets on nonmilitary research projects. Such programs, though, cost money, and inflation had taken a big bite out of school budgets.

Johnson followed his "Open Curtain" speech with another, in which he stated that America's "school systems are in grave peril." [14] Local school budgets could not keep pace with rising expectations and costs. Congress had attempted to help by voting funds for impacted districts: schools located near defense plants and military installations were compensated for temporary population influxes. This assistance, however, aided only a few institutions. Such communities floated bond issues, but interest on them had increased "25 percent faster than the direct general expenditures for education." [15] The United States faced a crisis in education. Only the federal government, so believed Johnson, had the power and resources to do something about the situation. And he resolved that barriers would be broken down without delay.

No federal aid to education bills of consequence passed Congress in 1957. In December, the Senate majority leader spoke in Dallas at an appreciation day held in his honor, and he elected to use this occasion to outline education legislative priorities for 1958. "This is no time for either hysteria or a siesta—for either panic or complacency. We must take a cold, hard look at the situation and determine effective, prudent steps that will assure our future," he warned. [16] He then detailed four needs: (1) scientists who were working for our national security should be supported; (2) scientists should work ahead rapidly, but without waste and inefficiency; (3) new goals must be set for education; and (4) fresh and imaginative ways of teaching must be found. Specifics, LBJ promised, would be determined in the next session.

Meanwhile, various groups were attempting to collect data on where education should proceed in the future. President Eisenhower appointed two major national committees. The first, the White House Conference on Education, headed by Neil McElroy, conducted a series of community, state, and national meetings that involved almost a half-million people. Devereux Colt Josephs chaired the other, the President's Committee on Education Beyond the High School. The House of Representatives Committee on Education and Labor conducted extensive hearings. And the Senate, not to be outdone, commissioned Johnson's Subcommittee on Preparedness to investigate the educational implications of Sputnik. This group studied the situation for 110 days, heard seventy witnesses, interviewed two hundred experts, and sent questionnaires to leaders in education, industry, and government. Altogether, the committee gathered seven thousand pages of information.

When Congress reconvened on January 3, 1958, the Senate majority leader, armed with data gathered in the House and Senate, forecast that federal aid to education would be voted that year. One phrase in his opening address to the Senate suggests that he had found a formula for justifying such expenditures. There was, he said, no adequate defense for the United States except in the reservoir of "trained and educated minds." Four days later, he wrote to a constituent that definite "plans to bring about the necessary improvements in our educational system have not yet been spelled out in detail, but it is a matter which is receiving close attention from the Senate Preparedness Committee, of which I am Chairman." [17] Nevertheless, Johnson had a specific bill in mind, H.R. 13247, popularly called the National Defense Education Act. NDEA proposed to train young men and women in science and mathematics by providing fellowships to students who were working in areas critical to American security. Liberal or conservative, who could oppose a concept like this?

As it turned out, both groups had strong objections. The

liberals were alienated first. Senator Karl Mundt of North
Dakota introduced an amendment that called for individuals
and organizations receiving federal money to sign loyalty
oaths. Colleges and universities opposed oaths on the grounds
that they impinged on freedom of thought. Academicians
sought friendly politicians to see if they could effect a change
in the proposed legislation. Former Secretary of State Dean
Acheson presented the Yale point of view. He stated that
nobody could object to taking an oath of allegiance to the
Constitution. But an affidavit of loyalty was another matter.
"This is a silly, futile, and insulting affidavit to require of
young people engaged in preparing for their future life's
work." [18]

Harvard responded in the same vein. One of its graduates,
John F. Kennedy of Massachusetts, introduced a bill the next
year to delete Section 1001. Harry McPherson, the resident
liberal in the Johnson camp, attempted to persuade his boss to
bring this measure to a vote. LBJ refused to do so. In a nose-
to-nose conversation with McPherson he explained by saying
that liberals "want me to set the Democratic party into a
national debate: Resolved: That the Communist party is good
for the United States, with the Democrats taking the affirmative. I'm not going to do it." [19] That settled the issue, at least as
far as the majority leader was concerned. The loyalty oath
controversy finally had to be resolved by the Supreme Court.
It would tear colleges and universities apart, making many
suspect that federal aid to education had its dangers.

Those on the opposite ideological side were as unhappy as
the liberals. Ralph W. Gwinn, a New York congressman,
presented the conservative case on the floor of the House of
Representatives. His most notable speech in this regard was
delivered on July 30, 1958. "For the past several years," he
began, "the halls of Congress have swarmed with advocates of
Federal appropriations for school construction, teachers' salaries, vocational education, guidance, scholarships and fellowships, and student loans." [20] He personally opposed federal aid

to education and so did others, including Dwight Eisenhower, John Foster Dulles, Marion B. Folsom, Harry Byrd, and the present or past governors of Texas, Utah, Wyoming, South Dakota, Illinois, Ohio, Mississippi, South Carolina, Indiana, and Alabama.

Representative Gwinn's own words make his point best. He told his colleagues in the House that:

> The possibility of Federal control of education cannot escape us when we see how many federal programs incubate and seldom die. It is not enough to insert a line or paragraph in any bill which states that the federal government shall not control education, regardless of the federal funds alloted to the purpose. No such inclusion is a guarantee. We must bear in mind the blunt fact that wherever there is federal appropriation, there must be federal control.
>
> Do we want a central education agency? May God forbid. It is the future and not alone the present we must think about. What assurances can we have against the possibility of some future administration that would seek to conform our youth to its particular way of thinking? There is an old saying that powers lodged in some hands will be respected, but if the same powers are inherited by other hands, they can be destructive. [21]

Gwinn's culprit in this conspiracy was the United States Office of Education. He wrote President Eisenhower: "The U.S. Office of Education is at it again. For forty years it has been propagandizing to get federal money and federal influence in our education." [22]

Gwinn and others, such as Roger Freeman, who wrote a book entitled *School Needs in the Decade Ahead* (Washington: Institute for Social Science Research, 1958), also deplored the attempt to secure federal aid to education by claiming that national emergencies demanded such funds. They felt that statistics were doctored or manufactured to garner support. "Each idea for federal direction of education," said Gwinn, "is couched in terms of an emergency. Each one is inevitably adorned in the trapping of a special situation. . . . We are almost literally asked to believe that the United States will decay in the likeness of ancient Rome unless a Washington bureaucracy assumes command of education."[23] This was what congressional supporters of H.R. 13247 were using to obtain enough votes for passage. It was an old saw, he said, but not a new scarecrow.

Besides federal aid to education, the second session of the Eighty-fifth Congress had many other difficult problems to solve. Johnson pulled many rabbits out of the hat for Eisenhower. Douglas Dillon, undersecretary for economic affairs, was astonished at the passage of a complicated tariff bill. McElroy, secretary of defense, nodded approvingly at the budget he received for the following year. He also secured permission to effect certain organizational changes in the Pentagon. James Reston, a reporter for the *New York Times*, lauded Johnson's work. In August, he praised the majority leader at a period when there was not sustained strength in the White House and complimented him on his ability to use intellectuals to define goals and compromise legislation. Reston wrote that Johnson would return home to Texas after this session with broader support than he had ever had. His "cheering section now runs from John Foster Dulles to Dean Acheson and from Hubert Humphrey to Herman Talmadge, and that is quite a distance."[24] Other Senate leaders, he continued, with large majorities and powerful presidents have pushed through more legislation, but it had seldom, if ever, happened that so much controversial legislation had gone through a divided government with so few cuts and bruises.

On August 13, the day after Reston's column appeared in the *Times*, Lister Hill, chairman of the Committee on Labor and Public Welfare, paid tribute to Johnson's educational leadership. "There is no man in America who has done more to try to strengthen education, to strengthen the national defense and to insure the survival of our nation than has the distinguished senator from Texas," he said.[25] Hill, who served with LBJ on the Subcommittee on Preparedness, had been most impressed with the way in which the chairman had handled this group's hearings on education. He had presided over the testimony of men such as Detlov Bronk, president of the National Academy of Science; Edward Teller, member of the Manhattan Project; and Wernher Von Braun of NASA, a part of the team that had developed the Explorer satellite. Their ideas would have much to do with shaping future education legislation.

If Johnson had any thoughts about resting on his laurels, an event that occurred during the summer months made him double his efforts to succeed and did much to temper the egotism which almost inevitably arises in those who gain fame too quickly. He returned to Texas after Congress adjourned in August to spend his birthday with Rebekah. The birth anniversaries of Rebekah and Lyndon were always special, and this time even more so: Johnson had been informed prior to the visit that his mother had cancer and that her condition was grave. Rebekah lingered until September 12, 1958. She died with courage and with her dignity intact. Her firstborn grieved deeply, but temporary depression subsequently gave way to a fresh resolve to live up to the promise that Rebekah thought he had always possessed. Lyndon became calmer, more confident, and less brash than he had been in the past. When crises developed in the future, thoughts of Rebekah Baines Johnson flashed through his mind; she inspired in death as she had in life.

In the fall, after Congress reconvened, the Senate passed the National Defense Education Act. Jim Murray and Mike Mansfield, both from Montana, spearheaded passage in the Senate by citing statistics that indicated the United States lagged behind the Soviet Union in science and related areas. They presented some shocking data: Mansfield revealed that only one in three high school students in the United States took a chemistry course, one out of four took physics, one out of three took intermediate algebra, and one out of eight took trigonometry or solid geometry. In 1957, 100,000 seniors graduated from high schools where no advanced math was taught; sixty-one thousand students attended institutions that did not offer physics or chemistry; and fourteen states permitted graduation without a single required class in science or math. Soviet requirements were much more stringent by comparison. But attempts by the U.S. Office of Education to study Soviet instruction were impeded because its employees did not read or speak the Russian language. For example, the commissioner obtained thirty textbooks from the U.S.S.R.; the books lay untouched for ten months, however, since no one in the USOE could translate them.

The National Defense Education Act had several titles. In general, scholarships were awarded to provide substantial assistance to individuals and states in order to ensure trained manpower of sufficient quality and quantity to meet the national defense needs of the United States. Science, mathematics, foreign languages, and low-cost loans were the major budget items. The bill, too, had a disclaimer stating that nothing in the act permitted the federal government to control administration, personnel, or curriculum in any institution of education or school system. Unfortunately, however, for proponents of federal aid to education, the bill did not mean that traditional roadblocks had been lifted. The favorable vote on NDEA came because it was tied to the security of the United States. More battles would have to be fought in the future to establish a clear precedent for federal aid to education.

Lyndon Johnson received much credit for the passage of the National Defense Education Act. But others had also helped to pave the road for this measure. President Eisenhower progressed to the point where he felt some aid to the schools was desirable, and he spoke in favor of the concept many times. Moreover, several outstanding critics of education had written voluminously to urge changes. James Conant, former president of Harvard University, toured the United States and lambasted curricula and teacher training in a series of books.

Arthur Bestor, of the University of Washington, compared American schools to wastelands. Hyman Rickover, sometimes called the father of the nuclear submarine, deplored the quality and quantity of science offered in the schools. These men were soon joined by Richard Hofstadter, a Pulitzer prize-winning historian who taught at Columbia University. He detailed America's widespread anti-intellectualism. All of these individuals had in common a desire to reduce the "life adjustment" educational philosophy that had been pioneered by the educational progressives of the 1920s. In short, this approach advocated teaching citizenship at the expense of academic excellence.

Johnson, always one to strike while the iron was hot, did not feel that his responsibility to the schools ended with the passage of the National Defense Education Act. He introduced a bill in late 1958 to provide low-cost loans to students, realizing that no formal action could probably be taken until 1959. He considered, too, a second measure—one to provide special training for exceptional American youth in the area of government. This idea grew out of a feeling that Texas high school and college students were not fully aware of how the nation's political system worked. He wrote to a constituent:

> I thought about holding a "seminar" at my ranch in central Texas at which distinguished representatives from the legislature and executive branches of our government might talk with some of our state's more exceptional graduates—student body presidents, school editors, and other campus leaders. Because of a number of interruptions—most notably the "Sputnik" investigations . . ., this idea really never got beyond the planning stage.[26]

In 1959, when Senator Ralph Yarborough and others introduced Bill 730 to establish a Foreign Service Academy, Johnson expressed sympathy for the concept. LBJ didn't forget these two ideas, and one day they would result in the creation of a unique organization designed to train the best and the brightest of the West for national service.

Education continued high on the agenda of the United States Senate until the next presidential election. On September 4, 1959, Johnson personally introduced Senate Bill 2710, which dealt with federally insured loans for college and university students. It called for a one hundred percent risk guarantee of loans made by private financial institutions to deserving students. As originally proposed, an individual could borrow up to $4,000 over a four-year period to subsidize his or her college education. Johnson knew it was too late to expect passage in 1959, but he wanted his colleagues to think about it over the fall recess. Senator Jacob Javits, a New York Republican, favored the measure as well, and he promised to co-sponsor the legislation if necessary and to share statistics that he had compiled on the subject.

In bringing the bill to the floor, Johnson stated that it was "not charity in any sense. If anything, it would promote a higher degree of self-reliance and individual initiative among our people." [27] The national inflation that had struck the country at the beginning of the Korean conflict had increased tuition beyond reasonable limits. For example, he explained, fees in public and private colleges had stood in 1957 at $1,500 and $2,500 respectively. Over the next two years, these costs had increased a full 10 percent. It was difficult for the average citizen to absorb these raises. In such situations, the government had a responsibility to intervene in the lives of the people. During the New Deal, he said, Congress had established the Federal Housing Authority to guarantee home loans. Over the next twenty-five years, the federal government, under its auspices, had experienced only a .33 percent loss out of $55 billion that had been loaned. If the government could help provide housing, why could it not sponsor low-cost loans to its youth?

It proved impossible to obtain passage of the bill in 1959. But the majority leader continued to speak on educational matters to prevent a loss of momentum. In October, he appeared before the University of Texas student forum. On this day, he discussed the changing role of education in America. There had been a time, he said, when schooling had been important solely for the advancement of the individual. Diplomas and degrees had meant a rise in social status or the opportunity to earn more money. Now, however, it "has become an indispensable instrument to the survival of our country. We have reached the point in history where if we are to survive as a country, we must redouble our efforts to bring every single American to the fullest realization of his potential capacity for achievement."[28] These words reiterated a theme he had developed four months earlier in a radio broadcast, when he had said, "Ignorance is a gateway through which the Communists attack the beliefs and goals of the free world."[29]

More than anything else, the military, during World War II, had been responsible for initiating educational change. The armed forces needed electronics technicians, physicists, chemists, mathematicians, meteorologists, and language specialists. Military cram courses had temporarily solved the problem. But as America entered a new decade, the educational system had to help develop experts. Johnson ended his talk by quoting Admiral Rickover, who had earlier forecast that the Soviet Union would produce 300,000 more engineers than the United States over the next decade. To Johnson, this seemed to justify additional federal aid to education.

LBJ gave three other education-oriented speeches at the end of the year. At the dedication of a youth center, Johnson conveyed some data given him by General James Doolittle, the hero of the famous Tokyo "Shangri-la Raid." Doolittle, just appointed chairman of the Air Force Advisory Council, had recently finished a comparison study of Soviet and American education. His report was much like those statistics gathered by the Senate Preparedness Committee. Johnson delivered thoughts similar to these at a University of Texas alumni dinner. The third speech deserves more attention. At the general session of the Texas State Teachers Association, Johnson talked on the subject of "Responsibilities and Road-blocks." He put education into the context of world events for his audience in San Antonio. "We will not have the schools we need," he said,

> until we have the national purposes we need. Dynamic education can exist only if our goal is a dynamic society, a dynamic economy, and a dynamic role of world leadership.
>
> This roadblock of static purposes must be rolled away or else we shall see American education become static education. America must grow. America must expand its capacity to meet its commitments to our own people—and to meet our commitments for free world leadership. We must accept the challenge of the battlefield of brains with the vigor we manifested on the battlefields of brawn.[30]

It was a tired leader who paused at the end of December to celebrate the end of a year and the beginning of a new decade. Johnson had now served in the Senate as long as he had in the House of Representatives. His efforts to make the nation more secure and to improve education had made his name a familiar one. The press continued to write of the tall Texan in a positive vein, likening him to some of the great compromisers of the past. But most of all, Johnson was admired by those who sat in the chamber with him. The Senate had been transformed by his leadership from a debating club of prima donnas to a reasonably efficient organization. Programs were funded quickly in spite of the divided national leadership. New vistas were pioneered, and tradition was not permitted to stand in the way of progress.

With Lyndon Johnson, then, all was well. But the same cannot be said for the general state of the American educational system. Until the 1950s, education had enjoyed broad support. The populace believed so much in education's curative powers that an English observer of the United States called schooling this country's formally unestablished church.

But the *Brown* decision, the loyalty oath controversy, mush-rooming budgets, the criticisms of people like Bestor, Conant, Hofstadter, and Rickover, and the lag behind the Soviet Union in graduating scientific specialists all suggested that American teachers were no longer infallible. These critics of education, perhaps unintentionally, because most of them were associated with the educational establishment, caused a great many to examine their own blind faith. And faith, once questioned, usually succumbs to reason. Confidence in schools and colleges would not be lost overnight, but it would diminish surely and steadily.

CHAPTER EIGHT

In the Shadow of
the New Frontier

"The vice president must understand the executive department and what is going on and must be kept up to date. He must be prepared for any eventuality because he is in the line of succession. He must also have a knowledge of the legislative branch of the government because he is constitutionally the presiding officer of the Senate and he may be called upon to break tie votes."

—Lyndon Baines Johnson, 1960

A S 1960 BEGAN, Dwight David Eisenhower looked forward to laying down his presidential burdens. Long years as a military, educational, and political leader had taken a heavy personal toll on his health and family ties. Increasingly, his thoughts turned to farming, ranching, and, of course, improving his golf swing. Even the massive library under construction in Abilene, Kansas, which would house his personal and official papers, did not greatly excite him. The most remarkable aspect of his two terms as chief executive of the nation was that he had not been tempted to expand the powers of his office. Unlike his predecessors, Roosevelt and Truman, he respected Congress and the Supreme Court and did not encroach upon the powers granted to these bodies by the Constitution and tradition. On the other hand, his biggest failure was his inability to modernize the Republican party and to reduce the rift between liberals and conservatives. He even had some misgivings about his vice-president, Richard Nixon, whom he regarded as an opportunist not to be fully trusted. Actually, Nixon possessed both ability and experience: he had served in the House of Representatives, the Senate, and had occupied the vice-presidency for two full terms. Nixon, however, was not capable of healing the wounds of the party either, and others besides Ike looked upon him with suspicion.

Lyndon Johnson had few doubts about who would represent the Republicans in the next national election, and he regarded Nixon as a most formidable opponent. The situation of the Democrats, however, was less obvious. There were still those who wanted Governor Stevenson to run again; yet he had alienated the mainstream because of his lackluster campaigning. Truman had ascended to the rank of statesman and was more interested in speaking to young people on college and university campuses about the presidency than helping Democrats select viable candidates for national offices. Johnson believed that he had a chance for the nomination himself. He had been loyal to his party and its leaders, his credentials were as impressive as those of Nixon, and his popularity stood at an all-time high. Only Jack Kennedy seemed a real threat. He had been campaigning since losing his 1956 bid for the vice-presidency. But it was hard for the Senate majority leader to believe that the nation would nominate one so young and so inexperienced. So Johnson decided to play a waiting game, hoping for a convention draft.

Late in 1959, Johnson had decided to become more deeply involved in party affairs. He had spoken to the annual Citizen Awards Division of the Democratic National Committee in Philadelphia. He appeared as a national, not a regional, politician, stating that the citizenry needed a better deal. "The people of this country want homes for their families, food for their bodies, employment for their abilities, health for their bodies, and education for their minds."[1] In May he addressed an enthusiastic crowd of five thousand who had gathered in Harrisburg, Pennsylvania, to honor Jefferson and Jackson, the founders of the Democratic party. Governor David Lawrence introduced the guest and his topic, "An America on the March." The great issue of the sixties, said the speaker, was responsibility. As America reached crisis situations in the past, it had traditionally called on Democrats. "When America needed vision, there was Thomas Jefferson. When Democracy needed a champion, there was Andrew Jackson. When peace needed courage, there was Woodrow Wilson. When men needed faith, there was Franklin D. Roosevelt. When freedom stood most in need of strength, there was Harry Truman."[2]

The principal difference between Republicans and Democrats centered on philosophy, Johnson continued. Each party was composed of honorable men and women, but Republicans seemed determined to hold back the twentieth century by overuse of the veto. The nation needed leaders, LBJ prescribed, to handle challenges in space, education, and military affairs. It was not a time to step backward. The Democratic party, Johnson pointed out, offered specific objectives: "We seek for all our people expanding opportunity, a nation without lines of class or caste, a nation where capital and labor may trust and respect their government and be trusted by it, a nation where no one is forgotten, where young have faith and the aged have hope, and the least stand equal to the greatest."[3]

An immediate call, however, did not materialize. Meanwhile, Jack Kennedy, aided by his brothers Robert and Ted and a talented campaign staff (including people such as Theodore Sorensen, Stephen Smith, and Larry O'Brien) developed strategy in Hyannis Port, Massachusetts. The Irish Mafia, as some called them, divided the nation into regions and systematically proceeded to win delegates to their cause. In spite of his youth, John Kennedy (then forty-two) was a seasoned politico. He had learned much from his father's involvement in the Democratic party over the years. And he personally had held office for almost a decade and a half. His speechmaking had two themes: he glorified America at home and lamented his nation's falling prestige in the world. A slogan for his administration, if he were elected, was taking shape. But the New Frontier would not be detailed until later. For the most part, his wit, grace, and charm were more significant than what he said. Those who met him personally became committed.

In spite of Kennedy's popularity, the summer looked bright for Johnson. In June, Barnaby Keeney, president of Brown University, presented the Texan with an honorary doctor of laws degree in recognition of his public service. Montana's Mike Mansfield requested on the floor of the Senate that Johnson's "Open Curtain" speech be reprinted in the *Congressional Record*. Nikita Khrushchev had been invited to visit the Unites States soon, and Mansfield felt that colleagues might profit from reading those sections of the speech which suggested media and cultural exchanges. Other efforts were made to package the majority leader as a man interested in the international scene. In a recent speech entitled "A Declaration of Peace," LBJ had surveyed accomplishments in space and prepared for the launching of Project Echo, a communications satellite that would allow radio waves to be reflected or bounced from its surface to the earth. This endeavor, if successful, could put Americans and Russians in close contact on a daily basis.

The Democratic convention of 1960 was scheduled to start its deliberations on July 10, 1960, in Los Angeles, California. If Johnson wanted to be a candidate, it was necessary to announce his intentions without delay. For weeks he had agonized about the future. The answer came on May 4. On that day, Sidney Yudain, editor and publisher of *Roll Call*, printed the results of a straw poll that asked 47 senators, 138 congressmen, and 585 congressional aides who they felt would be the strongest candidate for the presidency in 1960. Those polled were directed to consider the following five points in making their selection:

1. He must be a man of conviction who is willing to fight for his principles, but at the same time he must be able by conciliation and compromise to avoid fights.
2. He must be a man who is above partisan considerations.
3. He must be a man with a common touch.
4. He must be a vigorous and decisive man who can make up his mind, one who can get things done, and who will not be pushed around by other people, especially the Russians.
5. He must be a man with wide experience in foreign affairs.[4]

Out of a total of 770 ballots cast, Senator Johnson received 338 votes. He far outdistanced other hopefuls, both Democrats and Republicans. The remaining votes were distributed as follows: Richard Nixon, 150; Stuart Symington, 84; John Kennedy, 75; Hubert Humphrey, 63; Adlai Stevenson, 42; Charles Halleck, 10; and Chester Bowles, 4. Three additional individuals received one vote each. Johnson's 44 percent was more than twice what Nixon obtained. The poll gave the Senate majority leader a measure of confidence that he had not had before. And on June 2, he gave Speaker of the House Rayburn permission to hold a press conference to announce the formation of a Citizens for Johnson Committee to work toward the nomination of Lyndon B. Johnson for president. Two prior groups with similar objectives had already been formed in the Lone Star state: the Ladies for Johnson club and the Johnson for President club. The Citizens organization was to be headquartered in Washington, D.C., at the Ambassador Hotel. With Rayburn at the press conference were Oscar Chapman, who had been secretary of the interior during the Truman administration, India Edwards, former vice-chairman of the Democratic National Committee, and John Connally, a former Johnson staff aide who now had a thriving law practice in Fort Worth. The purpose of the organization, according to Rayburn, was to "review" Senator Johnson's qualifications for the presidency with every delegate to the national convention. To cap off the press conference, the trio predicted that their candidate would win because of his wide experience in government.

Johnson's entrance into the 1960 presidential race stirred much reaction. George S. McGovern of South Dakota was one of the first to endorse his congressional colleague. "I regard Lyndon Johnson," he said, "as the most masterful Senate leader in our national history. . . . If events should bring Senator Johnson into the White House, he would go down in history as one of our greatest presidents."[5] Other comments were not as favorable, and they cost the majority leader some of the goodwill he had achieved over the last decade. John Herling, in an article for the *Washington Daily News*, accused him of slowing down a vote on an important labor bill for his own advantage. The sponsor of this bill was Jack Kennedy. On the eve of the Democratic convention, the *Washington Post, Evening Star,* and *News* repeated charges that Johnson had threatened to block the Forand Bill to provide medical help to the aged if Governor G. Mennen Williams of Michigan publicly endorsed Kennedy. Even constituents questioned Johnson's motives. A Dallas voter wrote to LBJ that his senator had supported education and civil rights measures to obtain votes. Angrily, Johnson retorted: "I did not support these bills because I am running for president. I supported them because I felt that I would be derelict in my duty as a United States senator and leader in my party in this body if I did not do so."[6]

In late June, *U.S. News and World Report* published an extensive interview with Johnson, and on July 10, he appeared on "Meet the Press." The first interviewer centered primarily on LBJ's role as majority leader, while the second focused on education. When asked what type of education legislation would be passed next, Johnson responded:

The kind that we passed in the Senate, the kind that went through the Senate early in February that provides reasonable amounts of funds to be available to the school districts of

America for the construction of classrooms and to relieve us of the classroom shortage that we suffer from without in any way exercising control of our schools or dominating curriculum. I would like to see a bill passed . . . that would make some of the money available to supplement teachers' salaries, because our teachers are among the most overworked and underpaid of all the professions in the country. I think the number-one problem in this country and perhaps in all the world is education, and I think we are doing too little about it too late.[7]

Through interviews like the one just quoted and by continuing to seek passage of current education legislative proposals, Johnson hoped that leaders in American education would support his candidacy for president as Texas teachers had supported him in state elections for the House of Representatives and the Senate.

Some ten days before a "Meet the Press" interview, Johnson had testified before the Education Committee on behalf of the student loan insurance bill then before Congress. Since 1959, when he had introduced the measure, the witness explained, he had "corresponded with literally hundreds of presidents and deans of colleges and universities all over the country."[8] He had received answers from a variety of distinguished people, including Nathan Pusey (Harvard), Courtney Smith (Swarthmore), F. Edward Lund (Kenyon College), Harvie Branscomb (Vanderbilt), Mary Lasker (philanthropist), John F. Morse (Rensselaer Polytechnic), Seymour E. Harris (Harvard), Rexford G. Moon (College Scholarship Service), and Russell Thackray (American Association of Land-Grant Colleges and State Universities). Comment from these individuals had helped to modify the original bill, S. 2710.

The principal differences between the first and second bills are as follows:

1. The original bill provided that the college would assign insured student loans to financial institutions in order to

replenish its student loan funds. Under the revised bill, the college would hold and administer the loans. The college in turn would borrow funds for its loan programs without assigning student notes. Both the college and the financial institution would be insured against losses.

2. The insurance premium was reduced from one-half to one-fourth, as it was assumed that the default rate would be minimal.

3. The maximum insured loan entitlement of a student was increased from $4,000 to $5,000, although the amount awarded in any single year would still be only $1,000. This brought the measure in line with the National Education Defense Act. And it gave greater consideration to those who wished to seek a graduate degree of some kind.

4. The original bill called for repayment within ten years. A borrower, upon leaving school, had a four-year moratorium and then was required to pay the full amount in six more years. As revised, S. 2710 required repayment to begin within one year after leaving school, with payments spread over ten years.

5. The original bill called for interest on the student notes at 3 percent per annum in the hands of the college with an additional 1.5 percent interest added if the note were assigned to a financial institution. The revised draft approaches the interest rate problem differently. It prescribes that the college will borrow funds at a maximum of 4.5 percent and loan them at a rate that will provide the school with a one-fourth of one percent differential to help cover the cost of administering the loans.[9]

Overall, Johnson was satisfied with the bill as revised. But he did have several concerns. First, he believed that colleges and universities should receive more than one-fourth of one percent to cover administrative costs. Second, some college executives thought that the bill overlapped NDEA. Third, a few states had laws that prohibited educational institutions from borrowing money, and Johnson hoped these restrictions would be removed. If this was not done, however, institutions of higher education, under section 303 of the act, could declare themselves nonprofit trusts, and this subagency might qualify for funds if approved by the commissioner of education. Next, LBJ forestalled some objections by declaring that he had no intention of doing away with student tuition: the individual, as in the past, would pay for his education as opposed to society at large. And last, the majority leader pointed out again that this bill was modeled after the successful FHA home loan concept.

In spite of Johnson's efforts, the education appropriations bill that passed the Senate on August 26, 1960, did not authorize federally insured student loans. But the size and scope of the Department of Education's budget must have compensated somewhat for that bitter defeat. H.R. 11390, as amended in conference, provided $4,550,921,331 in definite appropriations and $3,249,000 in indefinite appropriations. Funds were allocated for school construction, payments to school districts, defense educational activities, the teaching of the mentally retarded, teacher salary and expenses, payments to land grant colleges, grants for library improvements, and support of vocational education. A real turning point in the history of the Department of Education had been reached. It was no longer a small, sleepy government agency authorized to collect and disseminate statistics. Henceforth, the U.S. Office of Education was destined to play a major role in the school life of American citizens.

Meanwhile, Johnson's own career entered a significant new phase. His bid for the presidency had come too late. John Fitzgerald Kennedy, aided by Ivy League intellectuals and practical-minded Irish politicians, had captured enough delegate votes prior to the convention to secure his nomination. Neither Stuart Symington nor Adlai Stevenson could effect the deadlock that might have made Johnson a viable dark horse. In the midst of the disappointment, Kennedy emissaries came to the majority leader's hotel room and offered him the vice-presidency. Logic dictated that he politely refuse the offer: he was secure in the Senate, and, if he continued in his leadership post, history surely would label him as one of America's greatest. But after some quick consultations, especially with Sam Rayburn, and some personal soul-searching, Johnson accepted the invitation and later the nomination.

Many have discussed the reasons for his affirmative decision. Even the president of the United States, Dwight Eisenhower, felt that Johnson should not have accepted second place on a ticket that Eisenhower thought had little chance of winning. The GOP hierarchy agreed. Ike wrote that most "Republican leaders were convinced that the team finally selected by the Democrats was probably the weakest they could have named. . . ."[10] Eisenhower's own view was that a ticket headed by Johnson and seconded by Humphrey or Kennedy would have had a much better chance of success. In LBJ's own party, experienced politicos could not imagine that Johnson's ego would permit him to push bills through Congress for a former colleague younger than he. Those individuals, however, who knew the majority leader intimately had little doubt about the outcome. The challenge of a new and perhaps higher responsibility was too much for LBJ to resist.

Now that some perspective is possible, Johnson's decision to run with Jack Kennedy should have surprised no one. Perhaps more than any other major politician of his time, Lyndon Johnson stressed the importance of public service. Long before President Kennedy said, "Ask not what your country can do for you, ask what you can do for your country," Johnson had urged parents to encourage talented young men and women to consider politics as a career. Many of his speeches on the campuses of high schools and colleges had been directed to this same end. And later, toward the end of his own active political life, he dreamed of going back to the classroom to instill a pride of country in students. Johnson, then, had to follow his own advice. The nation needed him. And more than that, John Kennedy needed him if he was not to founder in Washington. Few men knew that city better than the prospective vice-presidential nominee.

Journalists began to assess the chances of the Kennedy-Johnson ticket shortly after the Los Angeles convention. Walter Lippmann was one of the first to detail how Johnson would help. In general, he felt the team had a highly professional motive and a good chance of winning. Johnson was a unique choice, for he could deliver the southern vote while not alienating the industrial North. Beyond this, his civil rights record could be an asset. Lippmann wrote: "Johnson is a southerner but not a sectionalist. More than any other man in public life, more than any politician since the Civil War, he has on the race problem been the most effective mediator between the North and the South."[11] Johnson's worth, in this regard, was not long in the proving. His early August kickoff dinner in Nashville, Tennessee, drew unqualified praise. He told an audience of eight thousand that the North and South could no longer live apart and that the South had to be educated for national leadership. Ralph McGill, the best of New South journalists, stated, "No more bold or intellectually honest statement will be made in the presidential campaign than that by Lyndon Johnson. . . ."[12]

On September 1, 1960, Johnson stood before his colleagues in the Senate to assess the work of the Eighty-sixth Congress. He paid particular attention to education. He lamented that the House had not passed the Student Loan Insurance Bill, yet he believed that the next session would enact it without delay. On the other hand, he took pride in the fact that another important measure affecting education had passed. The history of this measure needs retelling because it is of worth in itself, and because it reveals a side of Lyndon

Johnson not fully known. In 1959, LBJ had proposed the establishment of an International University to be located in the new state of Hawaii. He had taken a deep interest in that part of the world since WW II. Now he had committed himself to helping to modernize this area.

LBJ has been labeled a Texas provincial. Many have felt that he was especially ignorant in regard to Asia, and there is some truth in these observations. Beginning with his experiences in Australia, however, Johnson had come to regard the South Pacific and Asia as the place where important things would happen in the future. By 1958, American accomplishments in space and the growing tensions of the Cold War had turned his attention to the international scene and to the subject of international education. Early in this year, he lectured the Senate on America's provincialism. He told his colleagues that the languages spoken by hundreds of millions of people all over the earth were virtually unknown in the United States. Specifically, the Union of South Africa, the Philippines, Korea, and Pakistan all used languages in which Americans were terribly deficient. He added that our printing presses produced nothing that most of the world's population could read. The same year, student exchanges caught his attention. On August 23, he singled out the pioneering efforts of J. William Fulbright of Arkansas for praise. He said: "I sometimes think that the student exchange program which bears his name has done more to maintain the prestige and the security of these United States than all of the weapons that have been built and all of the soldiers that have been trained since World War II." [13]

In 1959, Johnson had moved to the point where he could actually criticize American foreign policy. The founding of the United Nations, the Truman Doctrine, Point Four, the North Atlantic Treaty Organization, the Berlin airlift, the Korean Conflict, and the food program for India had all come into being as responses to crisis situations. Now it was time, Johnson believed, for the country to exhibit a more positive

leadership. His solution revolved around the use of pedagogues, not pistols, to help modernize underdeveloped areas.
His first significant pronouncement on international education
was made on April 16, 1959, at a Women's Press Club banquet
for the American Society of Newspaper Editors in Washington. He entitled his remarks "Positive Steps in Foreign
Policy." John Fitzgerald Kennedy entered this speech into the
Congressional Record.

LBJ called for the development and then the further devel-
opment of American universities in the Atlantic and Pacific
Oceans to serve as bridges to Asia and Latin America.
Johnson, no doubt, had been favorably impressed by the Point
Four program outlined by Harry S Truman in his inaugural
address of 1949, in which he had proposed the creation of a
Technical Cooperation Administration to export American
technical and agricultural expertise abroad. Henry Garland
Bennett, the first permanent director of this agency (and a
former president of a midwest land-grant college), attempted
to alleviate food shortages in Europe through what he called
the great adventure in American education. That is, U.S.
universities would sign contracts with underdeveloped nations
and build new, or modify existing, universities to train agri-
culturalists and engineers. The empty stomachs of the hungry
were thought to make people susceptible to communist propaganda. The way to avoid political conversions was for democratic countries to help increase the world's food supplies.
Bennett, then, as director, encouraged American universities
to improve education and assist in communications, transportation, and especially agriculture and engineering in the Latin
American, African, and Asian nations.

Under the Eisenhower administration, the Mutual Security
Agency had replaced the Technical Cooperation Administration. Some good work continued, but Ike's personnel appointments left something to be desired: the Republicans had been
out of office for a long time, and patronage positions were
needed to repay debts to the Republican party faithful. In a

relatively short time, therefore, the MSA became embroiled in American and international politics, diminishing the effectiveness of the program. Johnson hoped to revitalize the program now that Eisenhower's term of office had nearly expired. Thus, he proposed the creation of international universities in his April 16 speech. He placed much more emphasis on Asia than had Truman or Eisenhower. His words affected much of his thinking in the future:

Why don't we foster truly international centers of learning where the world's best and mature minds can meet and exchange ideas?

We have the facilities; we have the scholars; we even have the sites.

We have recently taken a historic step in the development of our nation. A group of mid-Pacific islands will soon share all of the rights and responsibilities of the other forty-nine States of the Union.

The Hawaiian Islands lie astride the trade routes of the Pacific. Many of the people have close ties to the countries of the Far East. They enjoy advantages of a university of stature and prestige.

Why do we not establish in Hawaii an international university as a meeting place for the intellectuals of the East and the West?

Why do we not seek to attract scholars and students alike from both the Orient and the Occident?

Hawaii could be the place at which professors from Harvard, Chicago, California, and all our great universities could meet with the learned men of Tokyo, Manila, Indonesia, Southwest Asia, India and Pakistan.

The great teachers of Asia could impart their learning to students from the West. And professors from the Eastern hemisphere could lay before students of Asia the knowledge that has been gained in our part of the world.

In Hawaii, barriers of language would evaporate rapidly. People would gain new understanding and new respect for each other. And the intellectual association would benefit all of mankind.

This is a concept which I have discussed many times with the distinguished and able delegate from Hawaii, John Burns. It is a concept which we could put into actuality at a fraction of the cost of weapons which we now ship to other nations of the world.

That this is a practical idea has been demonstrated already by the University of Puerto Rico.

Under the American flag, and the wise leadership of Munoz-Marin, the University of Puerto Rico has been building a bridge of understanding between us and the people of Latin America. A door to mutual understanding has been opened.

We have learned of the vital importance of the rich Spanish cultural heritage. And the Latin Americans have learned the truth about our hearts and souls.

The University of Puerto Rico has been such a tremendous success that it has led the senator from Florida, George Smathers, to propose a university of the Americas. And it is an idea which has great appeal.

Hawaii, a bright, new star in our flag, could also become a bridge spanning the Pacific.

We must not underestimate the importance of this bridge. The Communists long ago realized that the destiny of mankind could be settled in Asia. Leon Trotsky, the bolshevik theoretician, said: "The road to Paris and London might lead through Kabul, Calcutta, and Bombay."

The Communists exiled and assassinated Leon Trotsky. But they did not exile this idea. And one of the greatest single blows that have ever been dealt against the free world was the communist conquest of 650 million Chinese—who are gaining at the rate of 13 million people a year.

Compared to the people of Asia, our population is a drop in the bucket. There are 400 million Indians increasing at the rate of 7 million a year. Eighty million people inhabit the Indonesian chain. When these are added to the millions of Japan, Korea, Southeast Asia and the Middle East, totaling 1,500 million, this means our 175 million is a very small minority in this world.

For the challenges before us, we need both new ideas and

old boldness. But our future lies not in the multiplicity of ideas, but in singleness of purpose.

That singleness of purpose must be dedication to the concept that this can be a better and freer world for all nations.

That is not a goal which can be achieved in one night or by one idea or even by one policy. But it is a goal which is attainable if America assumes not just the political and military but the moral leadership which should be ours. [14]

The proposal for an East-West center originated from the friendship between Johnson and John A. Burns, Hawaii's territorial delegate to Congress in the 1950s. Burns and the Senate majority leader had gotten to know each other as Johnson worked to get Hawaii admitted to the Union. After Hawaii became a state in August 1959, the duo continued to consult each other in regard to securing some federal financial education plums for the fiftieth state. On June 9, LBJ introduced a bill to create a "Center for Cultural and Technical Interchange Between East and West in Hawaii." An identical measure was submitted to the House of Representatives. Both failed, however, because of the loosely worded language and the fact that many congressmen still opposed federal aid to education. Johnson then devised a new strategy. He rewrote the act, this time attaching it to the Mutual Security Act. The second measure requested that the secretary of state submit an organizational plan for an East-West center to Congress by January 3, 1960. This approach worked. And the idea for the center was incorporated into Public Law 86–108, adopted by Congress on May 14, 1959. A team from the State Department was sent to Hawaii to investigate the situation in November.

These delegates and a second team consisting of Clark Kerr, president of the University of California; John W. Gardner, president of the Carnegie Corporation; Herman Wells, president of Indiana University; and Glen Taggart, director of international programs at Michigan State University, were not overly impressed with what they saw. They found a small land grant college that did not have much of a tradition for excellence. The institution had grown from a faculty of thirteen in 1907 to five hundred in 1960. In addition, the institution now had seven colleges and a student body of eight thousand, with one hundred student assistants. Quality, however, was lacking—and the organization badly required modernization. In spite of problems, the concept of an East-West center, to cost $31 million and to house two thousand students, received approval from the State Department team, in part because of Hawaii's new-state status.

The political and educational leadership of the new state realized the advantages that would accrue to the islands if the center received federal funds. Therefore, a concerted effort was made to show good faith by having Hawaii put up a significant amount of seed money. Governor William Quinn, along with Willard Wilson, the latter acting for the board of regents, corresponded with Johnson and Christian Herter, who had recently assumed charge of the State Department, to lay the groundwork. The state donated a site valued at almost $3 million, the use of a dormitory to take care of overflow until buildings could be constructed, and $40,000 to upgrade the Asian studies program. Moreover, the university president, Laurence Snyder, appointed Murray Turnbull of the Art Department and others to develop a master plan. A state advisory committee was also formed to facilitate implementation within the State Department.

When Johnson accepted the vice-presidential nomination, he became a lame-duck senator, and the East-West center ran into funding problems. Hawaii's Hiram Fong, especially, became concerned. He wrote Johnson that the attempt to reduce the amount of federal aid could delay implementation. "I am tremendously disturbed," he said, "by the attitude of the House members with respect to this appropriation. The cut which they recommend will cripple the program of the center." [15] LBJ continued to work on behalf of the project, and the necessary funds were finally obtained. President Snyder recognized his efforts, and on May 9, 1961, the University of Hawaii granted Johnson an honorary degree. Johnson, in accepting this award, repeated concepts expressed in James Michener's *The Spell of the Pacific*. The popular novelist believed that America's destiny would be determined by her relationship with Asia.

The development of the East-West center was one of Johnson's proudest acts as a public servant. He equated the accomplishment to the pride which Thomas Jefferson had in founding the University of Virginia. The center portrayed democracy at its best. The United States, he said, planted seeds of freedom while its adversaries in the capitals of communism planted seeds of division, of strife, of suspicion, of hatred, of death and destruction. The East-West center had the potential to be freedom's greatest force in "the enlightenment of the minds of our peoples." [16] America had fused a common heritage from many races, cultures, and religions, exhibiting that unity of mankind is not impossible. Unity was important because it afforded strength to combat forces from without, and it helped to attack the internal evils of poverty, illiteracy, and disease.

The East-West center was a pleasant diversion for Lyndon Johnson, since his alliance with John Kennedy was an uneasy one, to say the least. The team did win their contest for national office by the barest of margins—a popular vote of 49.7 to 49.6 percent. But the narrowness of the victory prevented Kennedy from claiming a popular mandate for change. Kennedyites blamed the vice-president for the closeness of the election. He had not delivered the South: Florida, Tennessee, and Virginia had supported Nixon while Mississippi and a part of Alabama had cast electoral votes for Harry Byrd. Johnson felt that his present position was not unlike that of Philip Nolan, the character in the short story "Man Without a Country." He had been excluded from the Senate, the inner sanctum of the presidency, the Board of Education, and he now had little to say about the direction of politics in Texas. Inaugural day was so dismal for him that he fumbled repeating the oath of office that Sam Rayburn administered.

The tone for the Kennedy-Johnson Administration had been set on the evening the former accepted the Democratic nomination for president. His address unveiled his plans for the country's future. The phrase that caught the media's attention, and later that of the public, was short. He saw America entering a "New Frontier." The 1960s would be a time, he thought, of unknown opportunities and of grave perils. On the domestic scene, the New Frontier meant legislation primarily in four areas: tax cuts were needed to stimulate the economy; an attempt would be made to pass civil rights legislation similar to Truman's proposals in 1948; free medical care ought to be provided the aged; and federal aid should be given the schools. On the international scene, he proposed in his inaugural address of January 20, 1961, to keep America strong so that the nation could protect itself against its enemies and aid those too weak to defend themselves. He challenged all people to invoke the wonders of science instead of its terrors. Walking hand in hand, it was time to explore space, water the deserts, eliminate disease, unloose resources buried in the ocean, and encourage the arts and commerce.

Education was the deepest bond between Kennedy and Johnson. The latter appreciated the fact that his superior moved into this area without delay. On February 20, 1961, a month after Kennedy took office and a week before he delivered his famous message on the formation of the Peace Corps, the president sent a message to Congress requesting a three-year federal assistance program for schools. He sought money for public elementary and secondary classroom construction and support for teachers' salaries. The first was a continuation of a bill passed the previous year, while the latter harked back to Bob Taft's efforts in the forties to provide $250 million a year for school aid for poorer states and guarantee $40 per year for each school child. Without Johnson as majority leader, the bills failed passage. Mike Mansfield, who took Johnson's place as majority leader, could not overcome the states' righters and those who feared that such aid might break down the wall that separated church from state if parochial schools got financial help.

Meanwhile, Johnson found some escape in travel to foreign countries. During his thousand days in office as second in command, he logged some 120,000 air miles. He visited Mexico, Europe, and Africa, driving his State Department escorts to wit's end by his lack of protocol and pressing demands. Then came an extended trip to Southeast Asia where he talked to leaders in Formosa, South Vietnam, Thailand, India, Pakistan, Hong Kong, and the Philippines. This trip was more to his liking. In Manila, he spoke at the commencement exercises of the University of the Philippines. He took this occasion to return to the subject of international education, making one of the best speeches of his vice-presidency. His theme was the same as that he delivered at the University of Hawaii. He told his audience that he valued education above all other values of civilization. The perils of illiteracy and ignorance bred disastrous social consequences. "It is in the soil of ignorance that poverty is planted. It is in the soil of ignorance that racial and religious strife take place. It is in the soil of ignorance that communism brings forth the bitter fruit of tyranny." [17] In contrast, "education is mankind's only hope. Education is the imperative of a universal and lasting peace." [18]

Johnson could not forget the poverty he saw in Asia. Shortly after his return to the United States, he accepted a speaking engagement at Howard University in Washington, D.C., where he reported on this latest trip. He told those assembled that they lived in days when universities must be great:

> I have just completed a long and grueling journey over a vast area of the world where the future of civilization hangs in the

balance. I have seen there the struggle of teeming masses for human rights and dignity. The outstanding fact of this part of the country is that hundreds of millions of people are determined to be free—free from poverty and disease, free from brutality and unjust discrimination, free from despotism and indignity. [19]

Such people had only two places to which they could look for help—the U.S.S.R. and the United States. And Johnson hoped that American universities would provide the leadership and technology to give Asians hope.

President Kennedy did assign Johnson some meaningful domestic jobs to keep him busy while he was in the country. He appointed him chairman of the Space Council. This move made sense because Johnson had co-authored a measure in 1957 to establish the National Aeronautics and Space Administration. The council was an advisory body to NASA; President Eisenhower, however, had never called the group into session. Johnson presided over the committee's deliberations until James Webb, a former Fair Dealer, assumed direction of NASA. Webb and reduced appropriations for the Space Council made the advisory group less important than before, and eventually Johnson was pushed out of the limelight. Perhaps his most important act was to assure Kennedy that America could put a man on the moon before Russia.

Johnson's second assignment was to serve as chairman of the President's Committee on Equal Employment Opportunity. This organization had been charged with eliminating racial discrimination from companies who held government contracts. In the past, the Committee on Equal Employment Opportunity had waited until somebody filed a complaint before taking action. Johnson changed this procedure by drafting an executive order for Kennedy's signature that would force employers to state in advance of receiving a contract that they did not discriminate against minority groups. Abe Fortas, the friend who had helped with Johnson's election problems in 1948, provided the wording for the executive order. Kennedy liked the change of direction and signed the document. Unfortunately for the vice-president, however, southern congressmen such as Richard Russell did not like the new thrust. Moreover, disputes with Walter Reuther and Robert Kennedy gave Johnson a distaste for the assignment, and meetings of the committee were called so infrequently that little of consequence occurred.

The years 1962 and 1963 marked low points in Johnson's life. He spent more and more time in Texas generating additional revenue for the television station in Austin and adding acreage to the ranch in Stonewall. His popularity had slipped so far that some of Kennedy's advisors suggested that he be dropped from the 1964 re-election bid. Even LBJ's former Senate seat was now occupied by a Republican, John Tower. Ralph Yarborough, a liberal, held the other spot. Yarborough and Johnson were of opposite minds, and the two seldom consulted with one another except when public occasions demanded it. Then came the news that Bobby Baker, who had been Johnson's right-hand man in the Senate, was being indicted for influence peddling and soliciting bribes. In the midst of these developments, President Kennedy informed Johnson that he would come with him to Texas in November 1963 to raise funds for the party and to quell dissatisfaction among Lone Star Democrats. Texas had to be kept within the Kennedy fold if the New Frontier was to have another four years to reach its objectives, and a new race for the presidency was just around the corner.

Kennedy and Johnson met in Texas on the evening of November 21, 1963, to discuss the political situation there. It is not known what else was on the agenda. Perhaps Kennedy was disappointed that his vice-president had not been more helpful in the last legislative session in Washington. Conversely, Johnson did not like some of the rumors floating throughout the country that he might be dropped from the ticket next year. In any event, they did not reach agreement on the topics, and both men departed from the meeting unhappy. There was no opportunity to make amends. A series of shots split the air in Dallas the next day and, when the confusion had ended, the New Frontier had breathed its last.

The assassination of John Fitzgerald Kennedy shocked the nation. Many citizens saw still photographs of Johnson taking the presidential oath of office, but days would elapse before they asked questions about the nature and personality of the new chief executive. The delay was heaven-sent.

CHAPTER NINE

The Education Establishment

"I would add one personal note: the circumstances which brought President Johnson to the office he has held made it inevitable that there would be speculation about strained relationships between him and my family. President Johnson was a loyal lieutenant of John F. Kennedy, who had chosen him as his constitutional successor. He campaigned long, hard and effectively for the election of Robert Kennedy and myself to the U.S. Senate. He was extremely gracious and understanding to all of us after the events of November 1963. The differences that developed later on came not from personal grievances but from the obligation of men in public life to discharge their responsibilities to the people of the United States as they saw them and from what at the time were fundamental differences over important public policies. I know that President Johnson understood this, and history will as well."

—Edward Kennedy, 1969

THE AMERICAN presidency is a curiosity among modern nations. An incoming executive finds that the promise he makes is deceptively simple: I do solemnly swear that I will faithfully execute the Office of President of the United States, and will, to the best of my ability, preserve, protect and defend the Constitution of the United States. On the other hand, the duties associated with the Oval Office are staggering. The president of the United States, unlike most of his foreign counterparts, is both head of state and chief of government. He is expected to be present when events great and small are in the making, to command the armed forces of the nation, to conduct foreign affairs, to lead his party, and to work with the Congress and the Supreme Court in carrying out the business of the nation.

The position has exacted a heavy toll from those who took their tenure seriously. George Washington and Andrew Jackson left the nation's capital exhausted; Thomas Jefferson and Harry Truman lost much of the goodwill that had earlier been theirs; Woodrow Wilson and Franklin Roosevelt destroyed their health; and Abraham Lincoln and John Kennedy sacrificed their lives. Lyndon Baines Johnson was no more fortunate than the most illustrious of his predecessors. The awesome power and responsibility he accepted upon repeating the charge administered by Judge Sarah Hughes on Air Force One in Dallas in 1963 haunted his days and nights for the next five years. The man who returned to the Pedernales River in 1969 was bent in mind and body. Johnson had wrestled more than his share of angels and devils in his forty-odd years as a public servant. In the best spirit of the Declaration of Independence, he had offered his life, liberty, and sacred honor so that his fellow citizens could have a richer life. His fortune he retained.

The single most important attribute brought by the thirty-sixth president of the United States to the Oval Office was loyalty. Reams of paper could be filled in defining all of the implications this word possessed for him. Whatever personal feeling he had for or against John Kennedy, Johnson never for a moment thought about betraying the trust that the fallen man had placed in him. His first formal duty was to proclaim November 25 as a day of mourning in the United States, and he invited others around the world who shared in the nation's grief to join Americans in rededication. The new president spoke of Kennedy as a man who did not shrink from responsibility and as an individual who possessed wisdom, strength, and peace. Moreover, "he upheld the faith of our fathers, which is freedom for all men. He broadened the frontiers of that faith, and backed it with the energy and the courage which are the mark of the Nation he led."[1] On December 6, the day before the Johnson family moved into the White House, he posthumously awarded the Presidential Medal of Freedom to Kennedy. The former vice-president spoke softly and simply. "John Kennedy is gone. Each of us will know that we are the lesser for his death. But each is somehow larger because he lived. A sadness has settled on the world which will never leave it while we who knew him are still here."[2]

At thirty-one minutes after high noon on November 27, the new chief executive of the United States addressed a joint session of Congress. He indicated that the next year would be spent in furthering the goals of the New Frontier. The most significant phrase came in the middle of the text. Johnson reminded his audience that on January 20, 1961, Kennedy had told his countrymen that the work of the country would not be done in a thousand days, nor in the life of the administration, nor even in his lifetime on the planet. But it was time to begin. To this, a magnanimous Johnson added: "Today in this moment of new resolve, I would say to my fellow Americans, let us continue."[3]

He urged legislators to enact a civil rights law and to pass a tax bill that had been lying on the table too long. The last charge to Congress was as much Johnson as Kennedy. "In short," he said, "this is no time for delay. It is time for action—strong, forward-looking action on the pending education bills to help bring the light of learning to every home and hamlet in America."[4] His course, he concluded, was to follow a middle road, putting aside fanaticism, bigotry, and bitterness.

On January 8, President Johnson returned to the same podium for his first State of the Union message. With one exception, his theme remained unchanged: the nation was to walk in the path of the New Frontier. "Let us carry forward the plans and programs of John Fitzgerald Kennedy—not because of our sorrow or sympathy—but because they are right."[5] In the midst of reviewing past shortcomings, the speaker struck on the note that would promote most of the reform domestic bills proposed to Congress over the next five years. "This administration," he said, "today here and now declares unconditional war on poverty in America."[6] He detailed programs that would touch one-fifth of the citizenry. His aim was to cure poverty as well as to alleviate its symptoms. The long arm of the federal government was to reach into city and rural slums, into the shacks of migrant workers and sharecroppers, into boom towns and depressed areas, to help young and old alike.

As president, Lyndon Johnson set his goals too high, though he strived with all his might to achieve them. His predecessor, too, had wanted to eliminate racial discrimination and poverty. But John Kennedy never believed for a minute that a utopia could be created on this earth. Basic principles did not set the two men apart: their disagreement centered on style and the means employed to reach a desired end. The difference stemmed from contrasting backgrounds. Kennedy, at Choate and Harvard, had learned to deal with abstract ideas and to experience vicariously from books and scholars. He was comfortable with men and women who made their living with their minds. Therefore, he continued a policy set by Woodrow Wilson of bringing a brain-trust to Washington for advice on policy and strategy. On the other hand, the family's money had produced the wherewithal to be at ease with all types of people.

It is a long way from Johnson City High School to Choate and from San Marcos to Cambridge. People from rural America believed that doers accomplished more than thinkers. The lessons of life were learned from experience, not from books. Moreover, as a teacher, Johnson involved himself in transmitting the best of the past to the next generation instead of creating new ideas. Social reform movements in a democratic country originated with the people themselves, he thought.

Teachers Permanent Certificate
The Department of Education
State of Texas

The student teacher became an elementary teacher at Cotulla, Texas, and later a public speaking teacher and debate coach at a high school in Houston. Years later, this man became the "Teacher President," who believed that no price could be set on the promise which might have enriched a young life, but did not — because the right teacher was not there at the right time.

Mr. Lyndon Baines Johnson

having presented satisfactory evidence of good moral character, and having fulfilled the requirements prescribed by law, is now granted this *Permanent High School* state certificate, which entitle *him* to teach in *all grades* of the public schools of Texas. This certificate is valid during the life of the holder, unless revoked by lawful authority.

te of issue *August 21, 1930*

LBJ's teaching certificate is on display at Southwest Texas State University in San Marcos.

THE PEDAGOG 1927

LYNDON B. JOHNSON
Johnson City

This photo of LBJ appeared in the "sub college" section of the 1927 Pedagog *(SWTSU yearbook).*

Photographs in this section were provided by Southwest Texas State University in San Marcos.

LYNDON B. JOHNSON
  Johnson City
B. S.; History.
B. A. Club, Press Club, Student
  Council, Harris Blair, College
  Star, Pi Gamma Mu.

        MYLTON KENNEDY
          McNary
        B. A.; English.
        Editor College Star, Yell Leader,
          Tennis, Harris Blair, Press Club,
          Pedagog Staff.

LBJ belonged to the Class of '30 at SWTSU (Pedagog photo).

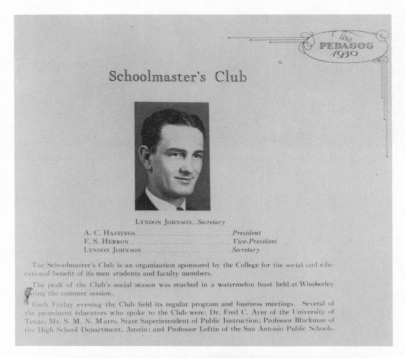

Schoolmaster's Club

The PEDAGOG 1930

LYNDON JOHNSON, *Secretary*

A. C. HASTINGS .... *President*
F. S. HERRON .... *Vice-President*
LYNDON JOHNSON .... *Secretary*

The Schoolmaster's Club is an organization sponsored by the College for the social and educational benefit of its men students and faculty members.

The peak of the Club's social season was reached in a watermelon feast held at Wimberley during the summer session.

Each Friday evening the Club held its regular program and business meetings. Several of the prominent educators who spoke to the Club were: Dr. Fred C. Ayer of the University of Texas; Mr. S. M. N. Marrs, State Superintendent of Public Instruction; Professor Blackman of the High School Department, Austin; and Professor Loftin of the San Antonio Public Schools.

Johnson was secretary of the Schoolmaster's Club at SWTSU in 1930 (Pedagog photo).

Young Lyndon Johnson sits with his debate partner Elmer Graham, left, and debate coach H. M. Greene, center.

Johnson, Graham, and Greene share a table again at homecoming celebrations in 1955.

Vice-President Lyndon B. Johnson receives an honorary Doctor of Laws Degree from Dr. John Garland Flowers, president of Southwest Texas State University, on May 26, 1962.

Southwest Texas State University President James H. McCrocklin looks on as U.S. President Lyndon Johnson signs into law the Higher Education Act of 1965. (Photo taken at SWTSU, Nov. 8, 1965.)

Samuel Ealy Johnson, Sr. (left) and Eliza Bunton Johnson (center), LBJ's paternal grandparents, join several members of the Bunton clan for a family portrait in 1914.

James Polk Johnson, one of LBJ's father's cousins, founded Johnson City, Texas.

LBJ described his mother Rebekah as "the strongest person I ever knew."

Samuel Ealy Johnson, Jr., LBJ's father, spent twelve years in the Texas state legislature.

Whenever their father was out of town, young Lyndon acted as a surrogate father to Lucia, Josefa, Rebekah, and Sam.

LBJ's boyhood home in Johnson City, Texas, was built in 1886.

Five-year-old Lyndon sits on the front porch of the Johnson home in Stonewall, Texas.

Washington Herald Staff Photo

As speaker of the "Little Congress," an organization of secretaries to senators and representatives, LBJ accepts a gavel from Vice-President John Garner in 1933.

LBJ stands with some fellow teachers in Cotulla, Texas, in 1928.

As director of the National Youth Administration in Texas from 1935 to 1937, LBJ frequently visited work project sites.

Rebekah watches her son Lyndon leave for the House of Representatives.

Rebekah and Sam visit Lyndon after his appendectomy in 1937.

This picture was one of the last taken of LBJ with his father, who died of a heart attack in 1937.

LBJ used this poster in his 1941 campaign for the Senate.

Lieutenant Commander Lyndon Johnson points to the area near New Guinea where he earned a Silver Star in 1942.

The Johnson City Windmill carried LBJ around Texas during his 1948 Senate campaign. (Photo courtesy of Earl Mercer, Navasoto, Texas.)

*President Eisenhower confers with Senate Majority
Leader Lyndon Johnson at the White House Conference
in Berlin, March 6, 1959. (Photo courtesy of Wide
World Photo.)*

*Senate Majority Leader Johnson and fellow Texan Sam Rayburn, speaker of the house, are
congratulated by Harry Truman in 1955.*

Democratic candidate John F. Kennedy poses with Senator Johnson in 1960. (Photo by Frank Muto, photographer for the Senate Democratic Policy Committee.)

LBJ visits Pope John XXIII on a vice presidential trip, Sept. 7, 1962.

Judge Sarah Hughes administers the oath of office to LBJ aboard Air Force One after Kennedy's assassination in Dallas, Nov. 1963.

As president, LBJ worked with the same intensity he displayed during his early days as a schoolteacher in Cotulla, Texas.

President Johnson addresses his fellow Americans at the time of the Gulf of Tonkin Resolution, 1964.

Robert Kennedy shared Johnson's concern for education.

Hubert H. Humphrey and LBJ watch the inaugural parade in Jan. 1965.

LBJ visits with Harry Truman in Independence, Mo., in June 1965.

LBJ sits with a teacher outside Junction School in 1965, the year when the Elementary and Secondary Education Act was signed.

LBJ talks with senators Mike Mansfield and Everett Dirksen in May 1965.

LBJ speaks at East-West Center festivities in Honolulu on Oct. 18, 1966.

Incoming and outgoing secretaries of Health, Education, and Welfare John Gardner and Anthony Celebrezze, respectively, stand outside the White House with LBJ in July 1965.

Vietnam critic J. William Fulbright strikes a skeptical pose in Jan. 1966.

Bill Moyers, Harry C. McPherson, Jr., and Joseph A. Califano served as LBJ's educational advisers in 1966.

LBJ and Lady Bird relax with remote control T.V. in the LBJ ranch master bedroom in 1968.

Daughters Lynda and Luci pose for photographers in 1963.

The First Lady poses in front of the White House in Oct. 1967.

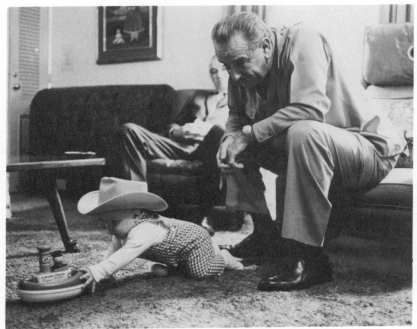

Grandpa Johnson watches young Patrick Lyndon Nugent at play, Jan. 1968.

Lady Bird and LBJ share a quiet moment at the Ranch in Sept. 1967.

American troops give LBJ an enthusiastic welcome during his Vietnam visit in Dec. 1967.

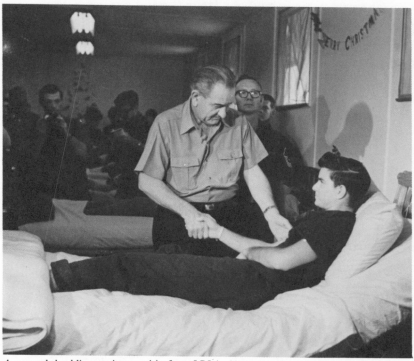

A wounded soldier receives a visit from LBJ in Vietnam, Dec. 1967.

Representatives of CBS, NBC, and ABC interview Johnson at the White House in Dec. 1967.

LBJ meets with General William Westmoreland in Vietnam in Dec. 1967.

Arizona Senator Barry Goldwater consults the president in May 1968.

President-elect Richard Nixon meets with LBJ in Dec. 1968.

Wilbur Cohen, secretary of HEW, confers with LBJ in Oct. 1968.

LBJ gives some advice to Spiro Agnew in Nov. 1968.

LBJ's Republican opposition included Dirksen and Ford in 1968.

LBJ attends the Democratic convention in 1968.

Televised broadcasts of the moon landing keep LBJ watching intently in Dec. 1968.

LBJ takes part in the Nixon inauguration in Jan. 1969.

The LBJ Library in Austin, Texas, was dedicated in June 1971.

Lady Bird and LBJ stand outside the Texas White House in 1972.

Johnson's casket lies in state at the LBJ Library in Austin, Texas, on Jan. 23, 1973.

Johnson had faith in the ability of the masses to improve their lot, and it was the duty of government to expedite the process by providing funds and programs. LBJ himself was the proof of his philosophy. Intellectuals had not assisted him in his rise to wealth and fame. He had done it alone. Therefore, he was more secure with business and military men, for, more often than not, leaders in these areas were action oriented.

A reporter from the *London Economist* clearly drove home this point at the time Lyndon Johnson retired from public life. He explained:

> President Johnson's trouble is that he is the last of his kind. He is the last frontiersman who will sit in the White House; the last real westerner born of the old west and the old south. He has the defects of the frontier breed. . . . He also has its virtues. He has roots, he is resourceful, he has courage in adversity and enough will-power for ten men. . . . The United States will never again have a president quite like Mr. Johnson, from a background like his, and with a temperament like his, because the United States has changed. It has left the frontier behind. It has bred a different kind of people. If there ever was such a thing as a log-cabin president, Mr. Johnson is the last of them.[7]

LBJ's clothes, his speech, his habits, and his mannerisms all set him apart from the urban middle-class Americans who had matured during the era of the grey-flannel suit. In addition, he came from a state that fit none of the modern regions. The Texas of his manhood was not a part of the South, the West, or the North; it was an environment unto itself.

The first challenge facing the thirty-sixth president was to deal with the staff that had been left behind by Kennedy, a group of men far more modern than he. This included the Cabinet and those who managed the White House staff. Johnson chose two strategies for dealing with Kennedy's people. First, he portrayed himself as a caretaker of the presidency for John Kennedy. Those individuals who could not accept the new executive could take some consolation in the fact that they were supporting Kennedy's program. Second, Johnson selected key figures of the Kennedy administration in whom he had confidence and dealt primarily with them. In the Cabinet, Secretary of State Dean Rusk and Secretary of Defense Robert McNamara were enlisted into the Johnson ranks. Patriots were harder to find in the area of staff. McGeorge Bundy, adviser on foreign affairs, and Larry O'Brien, the shrewd legislative liaison, were singled out for service. Walter Heller, chairman of the Council of Economic Advisers, and Kermit Gordon, director of the Bureau of Budget, provided the concept that secured cooperation from others, a projected War on Poverty. Kennedy's brother-in-law, Sargent Shriver, director of the Peace Corps, hammered out program details. The Economic Opportunity Act was the name given to the plan. It was submitted to the Congress for consideration on March 16, 1964, and signed by the chief executive on August 20.

Lyndon Johnson secured passage of some sixty education or education-related pieces of legislation while president. These bills provided federal assistance that ranged from preschool to the graduate level. During these years, the amount of money Washington invested in education almost tripled. To accomplish this, Johnson organized an education establishment that operated much like the system he had used as Senate majority leader. The team consisted of special task forces to identify needs; a group of advisers who specialized in education legislation; high officers of the Department of Health, Education, and Welfare; selected members of the Bureau of Budget; and key figures in the House of Representatives and the Senate who were known to be sympathetic to education. Six education bills were passed from Kennedy's death to the signing of the Economic Opportunity Act. These measures provided experience that was valuable in designing the so-called education establishment.

The first education bill to receive approval was entitled "The Higher Education Facilities Act." This measure was originally introduced in 1959 by Peter Frelinghuysen, Jr., in the House and by Thruston Morton in the Senate. It had the support of Dwight Eisenhower and Arthur Flemming of HEW. The bill failed passage on two counts: the opposition felt that education was the responsibility of the citizenry and that grants for construction should not be made to private institutions. The Kennedy Administration recast the Higher Education Facilities Act, but the counterproposal had some inconsistencies in it. The bill, as redrafted by the Johnson team, expanded higher education opportunities by assisting two- and four-year colleges in the construction of classrooms, laboratories, and libraries to meet rising enrollments in post-secondary education. Student numbers were expected to increase from 3.6 million in 1963 to 7 million in 1970. Loans as well as grants for public and private community colleges, undergraduate schools, and graduate schools were approved.

The amounts allocated were substantial, even though Johnson proposed a budget that would not go over the $100-billion mark. Congress authorized $1.2 billion for undergraduate facilities for 1964, 1965, and 1966. An additional provision provided $230 million annually for the same period of time for the costs of construction, rehabilitation, or improvement of undergraduate facilities—specifically in science, engineering, foreign language, mathematics, and libraries—with 22 percent of these amounts reserved for public junior colleges and public technical schools. Graduate schools would receive $25 million in 1964 and $60 million each for 1965 and 1966. Other provisions permitted the expenditure of $120 million for three years to build or modify educational structures (except those where money was charged for admission, such as athletic stadiums, or where courses were taught in physical education, medical and related schools, and programs or departments in schools of divinity).

LBJ chose the leadership for the bill in Congress carefully.

Wayne Morse introduced the Higher Education Facilities Act in the Senate, and Adam Clayton Powell of New York and Edith Green of Oregon did the same in the House. Both chambers provided a favorable vote, but they disagreed, as they had previously, on some provisions. The principal problem related to Senator Sam Ervin's request that a court test be initiated to ascertain whether aid to nonpublic institutions violated the Constitution of the United States. Minority views were expressed by Barry Goldwater and John Tower, who questioned whether a lack of classroom space existed, citing an article by Gene R. Hawes in the *This Week* magazine of November 4, 1962, entitled "The College Shortage Is a Myth." Goldwater and Tower felt that the U.S. Office of Education had withheld information and that many institutions had mounted a publicity campaign to win votes. They further suggested that colleges use buildings twelve months a year and schedule evening classes where shortages did in fact exist. Last, the two proposed an alternative: the Internal Revenue Service should grant income tax deductions for fees paid by the parents of dependents and credits for gifts and contributions made to institutions of higher education.

The IRS compromise satisfied Ervin, but the Goldwater-Tower faction could not be appeased. Nevertheless, the bill passed. When President Johnson signed the measure in the cabinet room on December 16, it was apparent that he was pleased. He praised the floor leaders and predicted that this session would be known as the Education Congress. He also called the new law "the most significant education bill passed by the Congress in the history of the Republic."[8] The Higher Education Facilities Act, he believed, would meet the demands of the economy for more skilled personnel and would enable young people to cope with the knowledge explosion, as well as help them to adjust in a time of intellectual, political, and economic complexity. Next, he urged Congress to pass other educational measures since one bill alone would not do the job. He concluded by saying that "the government is going to have to take its stand to battle the ancient enemies of mankind, illiteracy and poverty and disease, and in that battle, you are the soldier who wears the badge of honor."[9]

The second of the six bills passed two days later. Carl Perkins, a Kentucky Democrat, was selected to introduce the Vocational Education Act, which proposed to strengthen, expand, and improve vocational education in the United States. This measure revised existing legislation in four ways: (1) federal support was upped from $57 to $300 million per year by 1967; (2) the support given more closely paralleled present and future needs for skilled workers than legislation of the past; (3) experimentation was provided for youths in areas undergoing academic or socio-economic hardship; and (4) funds were earmarked for the construction of residential or boarding vocational schools along lines recommended in Kennedy's recent message on civil rights. The Vocational Education Act also provided funds for research, offered benefits to adults out of work, and provided benefits for the handicapped. In addition, the National Defense Education Act was amended to increase student loans and raise the ceiling on the number of loans educational institutions could make. It also provided aid to impacted school districts over a two-year period.

At the signing ceremony, Johnson explained that the legislation was necessary because the United States was turning out only 20,000 trained technicians per year, whereas modern demands on labor and industry required over 100,000. Senators Morse and Hill and Congressmen Carl Perkins and Powell were identified by name, making it clear that these individuals would continue to play a major role in forthcoming efforts to seek more federal aid to education. The Vocational Education Act was personally satisfying to Johnson. The president said: "Some of the most delightful years of my life were spent with the work and study program called the NYA, where thousands of young men in high school and college were brought into a work and study program, and some of these men are today the leaders of this nation." [10] Johnson's success in obtaining funds for education is apparent: in those two bills Congress had voted fifteen times more money for education than Kennedy in his last State of the Union address had proposed spending over the next four years.

The next day, Congress assented to the expenditure of $861 million for the Manpower Development and Training Act Amendment, which was sponsored by Elmer J. Holland, a Democrat from Pennsylvania. Earlier, a colleague had conducted hearings over a seven-month period on the subject of staffing freedom: that is, finding the right person for the right job. John L. Snyder, chairman and president of United States Industries, Incorporated, was among those who testified. He believed that over 200,000 jobs per year were being phased out because of automation. Holland had convinced his colleagues that the federal government had a responsibility to retrain displaced workers. The Manpower Development and Training Act proposed to offer matching grants to states concerned about this problem, to give basic literacy training to the hard-core unemployed, and to increase state unemployment compensation. It also authorized a pilot program to relocate laborers from a surplus labor market to a more desirable area, and lowered the minimum age of youth eligible for a training allowance from nineteen to seventeen. Phillip S. Hughes, from the Bureau of Budget, pointed out in a letter to Johnson that while "total unemployment in 1962 amounted to 6.7 percent of the labor force, the unemployment rate among persons sixteen to twenty-one not enrolled in school amounted to over 11 percent." [11] The president thought that the bill touched upon a crucial situation. "I believe," he said at the signing ceremony, "that the manpower revolution may have more far-reaching effects than the industrial revolution of the nineteenth century." [12]

The Manpower Development and Training Act had been conceived to help alleviate the suffering caused to those who lost jobs because of automation or those who did not have the background and skills to work with data-processing and modern copying machines. This situation, however, posed another problem, one just as pressing and just as important. The knowledge explosion was taxing the ability of the nation to keep pace. A report prepared by the first session of the Eighty-eighth Congress indicated that 18 million people did not have ready access to a public library service, and 110 million were located near libraries that were inadequate according to minimum state standards. Thirty percent of the public schools in the nation had no libraries at all, and high school and college collections were often small in comparison to student needs. This situation had been addressed by the Library Services Act of 1956, but it prohibited funding urban libraries and did not subsidize the cost of new construction. And last, the old bill had an annual ceiling of $7.5 million.

Wayne Morse introduced S. Bill 2265 in 1963 to correct this serious shortcoming. His proposal called for the expenditure of $25 million for the support of library services in 1964 and $20 million for library construction. The Library Services and Construction Act was in effect for two additional years, though no appropriations were made. Johnson affixed his name to the bill on February 11, 1964. He quoted Thomas Carlyle on the importance of books and then added his own homily: "Books and ideas are the most effective weapons against intolerance and ignorance." [13] He also pointed out that the function of libraries was changing. Such organizations today were of value to everybody, from young people curious about an exciting world to adults who needed information about jobs and how to do jobs better. "The library is the best training ground for enlightenment that rational man has ever conceived, and I am so happy that the enlightened Members of Congress and others who supported their activities can participate in this ceremony this morning, which they and their children and their children's children will always be proud of," he concluded. [14]

Landmark legislation came next, with the Civil Rights Act

of 1964. This bill was a logical legislative counterpart to the judicial positions which had been reached in *Brown* v. *The Topeka Board of Education* ten years before. Johnson deemed the bill, which he signed on July 2, important enough to address the American people on prime time national radio and television. He began with a reference to history, stating that 188 years ago that week "a small band of valiant men began a long struggle for freedom. They pledged their lives, their fortunes, and their sacred honor not only to found a nation, but to forge an ideal of freedom—not only for political independence, but for personal liberty—not only to eliminate foreign rule, but to establish the rule of justice in the affairs of men."[15] Then he went on to explain that discrimination violated the spirit of the Constitution, the principles of freedom, and the moral base of the nation. The law of the land clearly forbade such practices.

The Civil Rights Act of 1964 pertained to more than education. It provided a means for eliminating discrimination on the basis of color, religion, or national origin in voting, education, public accommodations, public facilities, and employment. Where illegal practices existed, the government could withhold federal funds. A community relations service was established to assist local groups in resolving disputed discriminatory practices. The life of the Civil Rights Commission was extended until January 31, 1968. Other provisions prohibited compilation of registration and voting statistics by race, color, and national origin, and the U.S. attorney general was given permission to intervene in jury trials where equal protection under the law seemed to be violated. Insofar as education was concerned, Title IV gave the attorney general the power to intervene "in public school desegregation cases where students or parents are unable to institute and maintain legal proceedings."[16]

John Kennedy had proposed the Civil Rights Act a full year before. The House and Senate had debated its provisions since the introduction of the measure. The shock of Kennedy's assassination, the support of Everett Dirksen, plus the moral leadership of Lyndon Johnson secured the votes needed for passage. That section of the bill permitting the intervention of the Department of Justice in voter registration procedures and in school desegregation cases was a remarkable breakthrough, something that Eisenhower had not been able to obtain in 1957. In obtaining this legislation, Johnson was able to muster a two-thirds vote in the House and Senate as well as a majority vote from Republicans and Democrats alike. The achievement stood out, even considering the special circumstances that existed in America after the assassination of Kennedy.

The Juvenile Delinquency and Youth Offences Control Act of 1964 was the last of the six education-related bills to receive passage prior to the Economic Opportunity Act. This measure, sponsored by Congressman Sickles of Maryland, extended the provisions of a 1961 bill of the same name two more years, setting back the expiration to June 30, 1966. Ten million dollars was made available to states, localities, and other public and non-profit agencies to fund demonstration projects for the prevention and control of juvenile delinquency and to train specialists in prevention and control. An additional $5 million was given the secretary of HEW for a pilot project in Washington, D.C., and for a study of compulsory school attendance laws and child labor laws in order to assess their impact on juvenile crime. The need for the legislation was detailed by a special Senate report. The compiler of this report revealed that juvenile delinquency had increased for eleven consecutive years. He explained to his readers that the "war babies" had now entered their teens and that many high school dropouts or recent graduates were not able to find suitable employment. "A million more youths reached age sixteen this year than last. As they drop out or graduate from school, many fall into the temptations of idleness for lack of available work. Youth unemployment—three times that among adults—is social dynamite." [17]

The Economic Opportunity Act was an important watershed for the Johnson Administration insofar as education legislation is concerned, and it set the tone for most future domestic reform legislation. The public initially became aware of the bill on March 16, 1964, when Johnson sent a special message to Congress proposing a national war on poverty. This measure contained many of Kennedy's ideas and became a final tribute to the thirty-fifth president. But, in addition, the proposal had some kinship to New Deal programs, especially those that employed legislation to reform society from the bottom up. Johnson, in this respect, liked to compare some provisions of EOA to New England town meetings, where communities often defined and solved problems themselves.

The specific locality that served as a model for the Economic Opportunity Act is a familiar one. In his book *The Vantage Point*, Johnson recalled:

> When I taught school at Cotulla, Texas, in the 1930s, I worked with Leonides V. Lopez, one of the leading Mexican-American merchants in town, to persuade the poor parents of my pupils to join parent-teacher associations. Such involvement was a new experience for them, but they started coming to meetings. When they came, I was able to encourage them to consider more productive afterschool hours. I had expected them to propose using afterschool time to train the children for jobs. But the parents were more interested in providing them with recreation and hobbies. I found that they had about the same hopes for their children that bankers do. So we organized a choir, a baseball team for the boys, and a volleyball team for the girls. The point is that those parents became actively involved in the life of their school, once they realized they had a voice in it. [18]

Once again, LBJ employed personal experiences to draft remedies for national ills.

"We are citizens of the richest and most fortunate nation in the history of the world," began the March 16 special message to Congress. [19] The words and phrases that followed are unique in the annals of the presidency; the chief executive asked the American people to help him eradicate poverty. One-fifth of the citizens of the wealthiest nation on earth had the gates of opportunity closed to them. Their daily struggle provided only a meager existence. Young men and women were growing up without a decent education and were being relegated to living in broken homes. They were enduring hostile and squalid environments, often in ill health or in the face of racial injustice, all of which trapped them into a life of poverty. Wealth, implied the president, was a trust, and the haves had a duty to provide for the have-nots. Listeners were not only surprised by the concept of a war on poverty, but they were also amazed at the scope of the plan.

In general, Johnson proposed tax cuts to create new jobs, thereby increasing the gross national product. Since he still possessed a strong faith in the ability of the education system to right wrongs, he advocated the strengthening of such institutions. Five specific categories of opportunities were unveiled. First, he advocated the creation of three related programs: a Job Corps, a Work-Training Program, and a Work-Study Project. The Job Corps would aid 100,000 young men by providing training, basic education, and work experience. Work-Training, on the other hand, would reach an additional 200,000 others by providing jobs. Finally, the Work-Study Project would employ 140,000 young people who could not afford to attend college. Second, a new community-action program was developed to strike poverty at its source in the streets of the city and on the farms of the countryside. This program would save the very young and the impoverished old. Local groups were to establish priorities, and then the federal government would finance up to 90 percent of the cost of program operation.

Third, the message requested the authority to recruit and train skilled volunteers to serve in the war on poverty. This plan was a domestic peace corps. Fourth, new opportunities were to be made available to the unemployed by offering loans and guarantees as incentives to businesses that would take a chance on hiring hard-core unemployed. And last, a new office in the executive department, entitled the Office of Economic Opportunity, was to coordinate the war. "If we now move forward," said the president, "against this enemy—if we can bring to the challenges of peace the same determination and strength which has brought us victory in war—then this day and this Congress will have won a secure and honorable place in the history of the nation, and the enduring gratitude of generations of Americans yet to come."[20]

Johnson and his budding education establishment took no chances with the Economic Opportunity Act. All aspects of it were thoroughly discussed and debated prior to submitting the bill to Congress. The first debate among LBJ's educational establishment centered upon whether or not the measure, once passed, would be administered using traditional channels, or if a new department should be created to oversee it. Willard Wirtz and Robert Kennedy favored the former, while Kermit Gordon and Walter Heller supported the latter. These two feared that the existing bureaucracy might bury OEO, as it represented a radical departure from the past. The establishment also hand-picked congressmen to guide its passage. Montana's Mike Mansfield introduced the measure in the Senate. After defeating an amendment proposed by the Republicans to permit state governors to veto community action programs, the bill passed by a comfortable margin, 61 to 34. Obstacles also arose in the House, but these were thwarted by a clever maneuver. John McCormack selected a high-seniority member of the Education and Labor Committee, widely known as a southern conservative, to act as the president's man. Phillip Landrum of Georgia did a superb job. He circumvented an attempt by "Judge" Howard Smith to bottle the measure in the Ways and Means Committee and then secured a 226 to 184 favorable vote.

Meanwhile, Sargent Shriver, the proposed director of the Office of Economic Opportunity, catapulted poverty into the national limelight. He solicited ideas from some one hundred fifty businessmen and politicians at every level. Shriver was aided by another former New Frontiersman, Larry O'Brien, who had earlier promised to pull this magnificent rabbit, the EOA, out of the hat. Lyndon and Lady Bird put their personal reputations on the line, as well. They entertained sympathetic dignitaries, such as Barbara Ward, and spoke to myriad groups that ranged, according to a biographer, from the Daughters of the American Revolution to the Socialist party, and from the Business Council to the AFL-CIO. The matter was also taken directly to the people, with the biggest bang coming on April 24, 1964.

On that date, Johnson visited with thousands of people and reached hundreds of thousands more via speeches, parades, and television. Both LBJ and Lady Bird, along with a large political entourage, had flown to Chicago the previous evening to meet with Cook County Democrats, including boss Richard Daley. The next morning at 5:30 A.M., a helicopter transferred the president and his wife to South Bend, Indiana, where former employees of the Studebaker Corporation heard Johnson speak to them about the war on poverty. This audience was particularly sympathetic because Studebaker had just ceased auto production in the United States. Then a fast plane flew the Johnsons to Pittsburgh, Pennsylvania. LBJ delivered two speeches there: the first to the League of Women Voters and the second to the home local of the United Steelworkers Union. Afternoon and evening speeches as well as television broadcasts were presented in and around Inez, Kentucky. It was here that LBJ drew the largest national headlines. Johnson's interview with Tom Fletcher, an impoverished local, drew attention, both friendly and otherwise.

Fletcher and his wife lived on the banks of Rock Castle Creek. The couple had eight children. Tom supported his family on an income of approximately $400 per year. Johnson told the press that these people were typical of the thirty-odd million people in America who lived in squalid poverty. Two of the Fletcher children had already dropped out of school, and the remaining six suffered from malnutrition and disease. The plight of the Dickensian urchins touched Lady Bird as well as Lyndon. The Johnsons advised Tom to keep his children in school, and in return his visitor promised that he would try to obtain help in Washington for the Fletchers and others like them. The same message was reiterated that night in short public speeches over television and radio. The return of the Johnsons to Washington was satisfying and exhilarating. The juices were flowing.

Shortly thereafter, a group of labor newspaper editors got the Johnson treatment. He told them that the poor were not going to stand by and

> see their children starve and be driven out of school and be eaten up with disease in the twentieth century. They will forego stealing and they will forego fighting, and they will forego doing a lot of violent things and improper things as long as they possibly can, but they are going to eat, and they are going to learn, and they are going to grow. The quicker you find it out the better.[21]

The newspapermen were already sympathetic to the war on poverty, and the words of the president stirred them to action. Most promised to editorialize on behalf of the cause.

Opponents of the Economic Opportunity Act came in all shapes and sizes, from all sections of the country, and represented almost all age groups. Peter Frelinghuysen, a wealthy New Jersey congressman, expressed a familiar view when he said that Americans had always fought poverty and that a poverty war was not necessary. One basic premise of the bill particularly raised his ire: he doubted that the people themselves could devise and implement viable programs to help the unemployed and the poor. If aid did have to be voted, he preferred the trickle-down theory popularized by Herbert Hoover during the early stages of the Great Depression. Hoover, for example, devised the gigantic Reconstruction Finance Corporation to keep big businesses from going under and to preserve jobs for the working classes.

Johnson countered such statements using Rooseveltian rhetoric. FDR had defended Lend-Lease during World War II by saying that if your neighbor's house is on fire, you loan him your garden hose. Johnson's adaptation of this phrase to the war on poverty was: "We have to pull a drowning man out of the water and talk about it later."[22]

In the Senate, Barry Goldwater and John Tower represented the minority view. They referred to the legislation as embodying a "Wizard of Oz" philosophy, and they charged that EOA had been sold to the American people by Madison Avenue techniques. Then, too, the solutions arrived at by the act were not visionary, but a throwback to the 1930s. "Several proposals," they wrote, "contained within the bill are, in fact, almost exact replicas of programs that were tried by the New Deal during the Depression."[23] The Civilian Conservation Corps, the National Youth Administration, and the Farm Resettlement Corporation were the most obvious models. Some House members agreed. Frelinghuysen and others lamented the fact that existing federal agencies had been by-passed, aid to religious organizations had not been prohibited, "poverty kits" had been given to supporters, and that Sargent Shriver had been made a poverty czar. A sarcastic line from the *Washington Star* newspaper was quoted by the opposition in the House minority report. It stated: "The poor will always be with us. And Lyndon B. Johnson doubtless will always be with the poor."[24]

Lyndon Johnson signed the Economic Opportunity Act in the Rose Garden. The bill substantially conformed to the proposal detailed in the special message delivered in March. The Job Corps and the Work-Training and Work-Study programs received $412 million for the first year. Community Action received $340 million. Rural and urban poverty programs were funded at the rate of $35 million and $150 million, respectively. The Office of Economic Opportunity secured $10 million to cover administrative expenses and to recruit and train VISTA volunteers. Some changes, however, were effected by Congress. These included a required disclaimer oath relating to the Job Corps, which permitted governors of states to veto certain kinds of community programs. Another provision eliminated something called the "family farm." Long-term loans to businesses to stimulate employment were also ruled out. Nevertheless, the bill was a victory. Johnson believed it would strike at the roots of poverty, and he thanked all who had struggled to make his dream come true.

The controversy over the creation of the OEO did cause some lasting damage. More than a few newspapermen believed that overkill had been employed to sell the war on poverty. They believed that the much-publicized visit with Tom Fletcher in Kentucky had been staged to obtain support. In addition, as reported by Alfred Steinberg in *Sam Johnson's Boy*, others thought that innocent individuals had been hurt by the desire to secure the largest possible majority in Congress. The man pointed to most often was Adam Yarmolinsky, a special assistant to Secretary of Defense Robert McNamara. He claimed that he had been promised a job in the Office of Economic Opportunity. When conservatives objected to this arrangement because of Yarmolinsky's known liberalism, Johnson said that he had never even discussed the matter with the bureaucrat. And reporters knew he had. Months later, a question also arose as to whether speechwriter Richard Goodwin was or was not a member of the Johnson staff. Steinberg believes that the credibility gap developed at this time. Then, too, the president's penchant for secrecy compounded the situation: increasingly, the press viewed silence in a negative context.

Enrollment of the Economic Opportunity Act provided Johnson with the time to make another important decision. Should he or should he not run for president in his own right? He toyed seriously with the idea of retiring from public life and taking permanent residence on the LBJ Ranch in Texas. Close friends advised him to run for the sake of the party. But according to Lyndon he did not resolve the dilemma until August 25, 1964, the second day of the Democratic Convention in Atlantic City. The person most responsible for his decision to run was Lady Bird. She wrote him a short note that compared him to Lincoln, Franklin Roosevelt, and Truman. She added that to step down then "would be *wrong* for your country, and I can see nothing but a lonely wasteland for your future. Your friends would be frozen in embarrassed silence and your enemies jeering."[25] Lady Bird's words left no room for doubt.

The year 1964 saw changes in the Johnson staff. New Frontiersmen had been asked to remain in service during the transition and most did. The first important member of the Kennedy-Johnson team to leave was Theodore Sorensen, who left, among other reasons, to write a history of the fallen president's thousand days in office. Shortly thereafter, Pierre Salinger, Kenneth P. O'Donnell, and Richard Goodwin exited, too. The latter was a serious loss, as many politicos regarded him as the best presidential speechwriter since the heyday of the New Deal. Arthur Schlesinger, Jr., Jerome B. Wiesner, and Ralph Dungan departed next. Perhaps the saddest loss, however, was that of Walter W. Jenkins, a longtime personal friend of LBJ's who had not been associated with Kennedy. Overwork and strain led to personal problems that made Jenkins a possible security threat. Mike Manatos, who assisted with Senate congressional liaison, became the New Frontiersman with the longest Johnson tenure. He remained with Johnson almost to the bitter end.

The Johnson staff, according to an interview published by *U.S. News and World Report*, resembled a basketball team: each person who received the ball was expected to move toward the basket. The president did not necessarily sit on top of a pyramid. Instead, in theory at least, he occupied a center circle seat with lines running to him from all directions. Staff members fit into one of five groups: special assistants, special counsel, legislative council, administrative assistants, and special consultants. The men and women who joined the administration in 1964 and '65 were remarkably young; many came from the South, and most had been involved in government service. More than a few, possibly because they had only recently graduated from college, were strongly in favor of extending federal aid to education. The average tenure in office proved to be only twenty-eight months, a relatively short term. Both the times and the demands of their leader exhausted them mentally and physically.

The personal staff of LBJ consisted of Juanita Duggan Roberts, secretary; Elizabeth S. Carpenter, press secretary and staff director for Lady Bird; and Bess Abell, White House social secretary. Special assistants to the president appointed from 1963 to 1965 not previously mentioned include: Bill Moyers, Jack J. Valenti, George E. Reedy, David Lawrence, Horace Busby, Jr., Esther Peterson, Donald F. Hornig, Robert L. Stevens, S. Douglass Cater, W. Marvin Watson, and Joseph A. Califano. Robert W. Komer, Robert E. Kintner, Walt W. Rostow, George E. Christian, Betty Furness, William Leonhart, Ernest Goldstein, and James Jones received appointments from 1966 to 1968. Fewer people served as special counsel. Myer Feldman and Lee C. White, were, as was Ted Sorensen, holdovers. Harry C. McPherson, Jr., and Larry Eugene Temple complete this list. Legislative counsel was composed of E. Jake Jacobsen and Harold Barefoot Sanders, Jr. Harry Hall Wilson, Jr., served with Mike Manatos as administrative assistants. Eric Goldman, Stan Musial, Maxwell D. Taylor, John P. Roche, McGeorge Bundy, James A. Lovell, Jr., Charles S. Murphy, and George Reedy served as special consultants. Bundy and Reedy occupied different posts and thus are listed twice.

A junior brain-trust also existed. It was composed of a seventeen-member team, some members of which later moved upward in rank. These individuals were more academic than political and more Ivy League than Texas. Only two, in fact, earned college degrees in the Lone Star state. Five sported sheepskins from Harvard, three from Yale, three from Columbia, and two from Princeton. Seven graduated with honors, six *magna cum laude*, one *summa cum laude*, four held membership in Phi Beta Kappa, and one had been a Rhodes scholar. Seven were in their late twenties, and just three had passed the age of thirty-five. The members of the junior brain-trust were: Tom Johnson, James R. Jones, Matthew B. Coffey, Ervin S. Duggan, Matthew Nimetz, William M. Blackburn, Edward K. Hamilton, Frederick M. Bohen, James C. Gaither, Larry E. Temple, Peter R. Rosenblatt, Ben J. Wattenerg, Lawrence Levinson, Richard Mosse, Stanford G. Ross, Charles M. Maguire, and Sherwin Markman.

At one time or another, most of these members of the junior and senior brain-trusts were involved in educational matters, but three individuals stand out. Douglass Cater, a graduate of Phillips Exeter and Harvard, expertly handled liaison with the Department of Health, Education, and Welfare. He had been a journalist for *Reporter* magazine prior to entering government service. Cater wrote a Johnson book in 1964 to counter Goldwater's *Conscience of a Conservative*. Joseph Califano, who studied at Holy Cross and Harvard, advised the president on domestic legislation. His steady hand and good judgment prevented many disasters. The third member of the triumvirate was Harry McPherson. He had been educated at the University of the South in Tennessee, Columbia University, and the University of Texas. His primary job related to conducting legal reviews on executive orders, proclamations and enrolled bills as well as representing Johnson on civil rights matters. Later, McPherson served as assistant secretary of state for educational and cultural affairs, making important suggestions in the area of international education. He also became one of the first Johnsonians to record his governmental experiences in book form.

From August to November 1964, Lyndon Baines Johnson became his own man with his own programs and his own staff. The last three months of 1964 were among his happiest days in the presidency. He unveiled additional plans to strengthen America internally, and he was able to keep the lid on the complicated war in Vietnam.

Great care was taken in selecting a running mate. He announced his selection, Hubert Horatio Humphrey, in Atlantic City after the Democratic convention began. Perhaps no person in high political life, with the exception of Lady Bird, understood Johnson better than the marathon talker from Minnesota. Humphrey was completely loyal, and he shared with his superior a belief that wealth in America was not static. The size of the pie, as Walter Lippmann once wrote, could be increased by organized fiscal policy to the benefit of all. Johnson and Humphrey defeated Goldwater and William Miller of New York by the largest landslide in American history to that date. Johnson viewed the election as a mandate to make a good nation a great nation, giving birth to a new reform movement in the United States.

CHAPTER TEN
The Great Society

"I pray that when historians write the story of this time, of our lives, that it may be recorded that this president tried—tried to lead his nation with justice and with compassion, and with courage; and there was faith, and there was firmness in his heart. May it further be written that the people of the United States cast out their doubts, looked with great pride on their achievements, and bravely made of this land and this world a brighter, happier place for all mankind. This is our choice. This is our decision. Let us all be greatly determined that this society shall survive and this society shall succeed. And what it should be will be for all time to come."

—Lyndon Baines Johnson, 1964

T HE MOST significant difference between the United States and Europe is that class lines in America are not rigid. All indigenous reform movements in America, in one way or another, have been designed to increase economic and/ or social mobility. Cooperation and brotherhood first began in this country when Englishmen set foot on the soil of the New World to plant permanent colonies. Neighbors banded together to ensure that friends had food, shelter, protection, and companionship. Such principles guided personal and community development as long as a seemingly endless expanse of land remained unsettled. As the continent became peopled, however, a need arose for formal associations and organizations to support the effort of individuals. At periodic intervals, then, when lack of opportunity reached unacceptable limits, citizens grouped to remedy the situation. The American Revolution, Transcendentalism, the First Reconstruction, the Populist uprising, the Progressive movement, the New Deal, and the Second Reconstruction all exemplified the belief that the political processes should be used to check undemocratic power structures, to ensure freedom of opportunity, and to help the downtrodden to live a richer life. The word used by Americans to capsule these thoughts is *decency*: that is, it is the birthright of all to earn a decent wage, to live in a decent home, and to expect others to treat them with common decency—regardless of race, creed, or color.

The slogans and symbols that presidents employ to identify their administrations reflect this point of view. The Revolution of 1800, the Jacksonian Revolt, the Square Deal, the New Freedom, the New Nationalism, the New Deal, and the Fair Deal are all illustrations of this commitment to basic decency. Lyndon Johnson's search for a personal political characterization started as early as 1963. As vice-president, he spoke to the Federated Women's Clubs in Milwaukee, Wisconsin, on June 12. He praised women for being a significant moral force in society and then proceeded to discuss the nation as a whole. Some people thought the nation "besieged and beleaguered, an America hanging at the edge of a cliff, an America already fallen into the valley of a dark shadow."[1] Such thoughts, however, were totally alien to the speaker. He hinted of things to come when he said: "On this earth, perfection has been attained nowhere. Mortal man has not yet achieved the perfect government, the perfect system—or the perfect civilization. But in no country anywhere is so much right—or so nearly right—as here in this great land of ours."[2] Six months later, Johnson, as the thirty-sixth president of the United States, moved toward something more concrete.

The U.S. Constitution, Article 2, Section 3, recommends that the president from time to time shall give Congress information on the State of the Union and propose such considerations as he shall judge expedient. George Washington and John Adams elected to deliver their comments in person before joint sessions of the House of Representatives and the Senate. Thomas Jefferson, the third chief executive, established a new trend in sending written messages to the Hill. His example lasted for almost one hundred years. Woodrow Wilson re-established the practice of appearing in person before the national legislature, and most subsequent twentieth-century leaders have followed his example; only Herbert Hoover deviated from this custom. On December 9, 1963, Jack Valenti dispatched a note to Abe Fortas, George Reedy, Bill Moyers, Dick Nelson, and Horace Busby, stating that the president wanted them to meet with Eric Goldman "to examine and search out new ideas, new proposals for the State of the Union message."[3] Thus the quest for a label quickened. It had already been decided that the president would read his speech before his former colleagues in joint session.

In the first State of the Union message there was no time to coin a popular phrase for the public. Nevertheless, it is clear that the matter was still much on LBJ's mind. On January 28, 1964, President Johnson shared his thoughts with the National Planning Committee of the Non-Partisan Political League in the room where the Cabinet usually met. "This administration," he drawled, "is going to be a *compassionate* administration. We believe in the Golden Rule of doing unto others as you would have them do unto you."[4] Then he added that the national budget was going to be trimmed in order to "have the money to take care of those who need jobs and who need education and who need a helping hand, the lame and the halt and the needy."[5] Late February still found Johnson preoccupied with the Golden Rule. A group of treasury agency heads assembled in the flower garden were told:

The best way I know to leave you this morning is to ask you to please preach the Golden Rule. Do unto others as you would

have them do unto you. Put yourself in the position of someone that may have been born a different color from what you
were born, who may have been born of a different race, a
different religion than you were born with. Ask yourself how
you would like to be treated if they were in your powerful
position and you were in theirs. Then do unto them as you
would have them do unto you. If you do that, I have no doubts
about the results.[6]

The staff had seen and heard enough of the president's mood
and rhetoric by this time so that they could follow in step.

Eric Goldman, a Princeton historian who had accepted a
position in the administration as special counsel, started the
ball rolling toward a motto in a speech he gave at Lindenwood
College. In this address, he emphasized the phrase "good
society," a term he had borrowed from a Walter Lippmann
book title. Later, Richard Goodwin made a slight, but important, modification: he substituted *great* for *good*. Johnson, now
preparing for a major speech to be delivered in May 1964 at
the University of Michigan, liked the sound of "great society,"
but decided to test the waters in advance. He asked Valenti to
use the phrase in a March speech at the annual Democratic
congressional dinner. LBJ told this audience that many things
were well in America, but that many problems existed. Some
of the difficulties, like the tip of an iceberg, were just beginning to surface, and an alert nation must solve them before a
crisis developed. On page four of a nine-page text, he made a
quick reference to the term being bandied around in and near
the Oval Office by the staff. He said, "Because of the efforts
and the achievements of Franklin Roosevelt, Harry Truman
and John Kennedy, we now have the opportunity to move not
only toward the rich society and the powerful society, but
toward the Great Society."[7]

A later section of this same speech forecast the general tenor
of the Great Society. The nation needed to increase economic
growth to meet growing needs, LBJ explained. Those barriers
that prevented a citizen from full participation in his nation

ought to be struck down without delay "to give every American a life as rich and productive as his talents and capacities will allow."[8]

In less than a week, the president was once again standing behind a lectern stating the case for assistance to the poor. This address, delivered to the United Auto Workers in Atlantic City, was important enough to have been read in advance by Willard Wirtz, Walter Heller, Jack Valenti, C. Douglas Dillon, and Horace Busby. The Great Society was not mentioned by name, but few could have missed the association. Then, too, LBJ promised to work toward his goals in an unfailing manner. "I don't know," he explained, "how history will treat me as a president. But I have set a course for myself and I intend to follow it, however much time I am given to lead this nation. I shall lead it without fear and without bias and with the sure knowledge that if I try to do what is right, our nation, in God's mind and history's imprint, will be the beneficiary."[9]

The month of April brought a short but much needed vacation. Lyndon and Lady Bird flew to the Texas white house to be in the hill country for the Easter weekend.

The pressure on Johnson since he had assumed the presidency had been intense, and he had felt the need to release some steam. One of the first things he did in Texas was to take a high-speed drive in his cream-colored Lincoln Continental, strengthened by an ever-present cup brimful of Pearl beer. Newspaper reporters who were visiting the LBJ ranch for the first time made copious notes. A correspondent for *Time* thought the politician behaved like a cross between a teenage Grand Prix driver and a back-to-nature Henry David Thoreau in cowboy boots. Johnson, however, was full of the moment. He told his visitors: "The cows are fat. The grass is green. The river's full, and the fish are flopping."[10] LBJ gave them an explicit lecture on the sex life of a bull, and he even promised to be photographed with a pig if reporters could catch one. But at sunset his demeanor abruptly changed. "Look at that sky," he moaned. "Why would anyone want to leave here and go back and fight?"[11]

Then came a trip to Chicago, the Great Lakes area, and Inez, Kentucky. On the first stop, Lady Bird spoke to Daley Democrats about the need of the poor for a decent life, and her husband quoted Aristotle, using his phrase the "good life." On May 9, the president mentioned the Golden Rule and the Great Society together in a speech given at the dedication of the JFK cultural center at Mitchell Field, New York. The same day he spoke to the Amalgamated Clothing Workers union gathered in New York's World's Fair Singer Bowl to celebrate the fiftieth anniversary of the union. Here Johnson spoke of the malignancy of poverty and prophesied that future generations would curse the present unless all available resources were marshalled to help the afflicted. The cause was great enough to make the struggle worthwhile. He told his listeners:

> I have come here this morning to ask all of you to enlist as volunteers. Members of all parties are welcome to our tent. Members of all races ought to be there. Members of all religions should come and help us now to strike the hammer of truth against the anvil of public opinion again and again and again until the ears of this nation are open, until the hearts of this nation are touched and until the conscience of America is awakened. [12]

On May 22, 1964, Lyndon Baines Johnson delivered the most important speech of his presidency. Some ninety thousand people assembled in the football stadium of the University of Michigan to observe the president receive an honorary doctorate and to hear him talk of his plans for America's future. A college setting was deliberately chosen for this speech, as Johnson believed that young people were more receptive to change. He had believed this since his experience in heading the Texas National Youth Administration. Much correspondence had been exchanged between the Johnson staff and officials in Michigan to select the right topic for the address. Letters and telephone calls had identified three themes: cities, countryside, and classroom. When the president entered the gates of the stadium, only one omen hinted that youth in the Depression had been different from youth in prosperity: a small number of young men and women gathered at the entrance to protest inadequate domestic programs and the war in Vietnam.

Eric Goldman, in his book entitled *The Tragedy of Lyndon Johnson*, traces the history of the "great society" phrase and informs his readers that the concept has deep roots in western civilization. Peasants in the English revolt of 1381 employed the term. Adam Smith made reference to it in his *Wealth of Nations*, published the year in which the American revolution erupted, and Graham Wells, an English Fabian, marketed a book of the same title in 1914. Johnson's use of the term, however, had been given flesh by Goodwin, Moyers, Cater, Busby, and Valenti. Perhaps Busby provided the clearest definition in a May memorandum in which he said that the United States "has largely succeeded in fulfilling the traditional 'American dream' of national abundance and leisure and now we must develop new vision, a new dream to guide our further efforts—this is the vision of the Great Society wrought by our next scientific and technological capabilities." [13]

It took twenty minutes to deliver the Great Society speech. The audience applauded fourteen times. Few who heard the address forgot the magic of the moment. The text as delivered reads:

I have come today from the turmoil of your capital to the tranquility of your campus to speak about the future of your country.

The purpose of protecting the life of our nation and preserving the liberty of our citizens is to pursue the happiness of our people.

Our success in that pursuit is the test of our success as a nation.

For a century we labored to settle and subdue a continent. For half a century, we called upon unbounded invention and untiring industry to create an order of plenty for all our people.

The challenge of the next half century is whether we have the wisdom to use that wealth to enrich and elevate our national life—and to advance the quality of American civilization.

Your imagination, your initiative, your indignation will determine whether we build a society where progress is the servant of our needs, or a society where old values and new visions are buried under unbridled growth.

For in your time we have the opportunity to move not only toward the rich society and the powerful society, but upward to the Great Society.

The Great Society is a place where every child can find knowledge to enrich his mind and enlarge his talents. It is a place where leisure is a welcome chance to build and reflect, not a feared cause of boredom and restlessness. It is a place where the city of man serves not only the needs of the body and the demands of commerce, but the desire for beauty and the hunger for community.

It is a place where man can renew contact with nature. It is a place which honors creation for its own sake, and for what it adds to the understanding of the race. It is a place where men are more concerned with the quality of their goals than the quantity of their goods.

But, most of all, the Great Society is not a safe harbor, a resting place, a final objective, a finished work. It is a challenge constantly renewed, beckoning us toward a destiny where the meaning of our lives matches the marvelous products of our labor.

I want to talk to you today about three places where we can begin to build the Great Society—in our cities, in our countryside and in our classrooms.

Many of you will live to see the day, fifty years from now, when there will be four hundred million Americans; four-fifths of them in urban areas. In the remainder of this century urban populations will double, city land will double, and we will have to build homes, highways and facilities equal to all those built since this country was settled.

In the next forty years we must rebuild the entire urban United States.

Aristotle said "Men come together in the cities in order to live, but they remain together in order to live the good life." It is harder and harder to live the good life in American cities.

The catalogue of ills is long: there is the decay of the centers and the despoiling of the suburbs. There is not enough housing for our people or transportation for our traffic. Open land is vanishing and old landmarks are violated.

Worst of all, expansion is eroding the precious and time-honored values of community with neighbors and communion with nature. The loss of these values breeds loneliness and boredom and indifference.

Our society will never be great until our cities are great. Today the frontier of imagination and innovation is inside those cities, not beyond their borders.

New experiments are already going on. It will be the task of your generation to make the American city a place where future generations will come, not only to live, but to live the good life.

A second place where we begin to build the Great Society is in our countryside. We have always prided ourselves on being not only America the strong and America the free, but America the beautiful. Today that beauty is in danger.

The water we drink, the food we eat, the very air we breathe, are threatened with pollution. Our parks are overcrowded, and our seashore overburdened. Green fields and dense forests are disappearing.

A few years ago we were concerned about the Ugly American. Today we must act to prevent an Ugly America.

For once the battle is lost, once our natural splendor is destroyed, it can never be recaptured.

And once man can no longer walk with beauty or wonder at nature, his spirit will wither and his sustenance be wasted.

A third place to build the Great Society is in the classrooms of America. There your children's lives will be shaped.

Our society will not be great until every young mind is set free to scan the farthest reaches of thought and imagination.

We are still far from that goal.

Today 8 million adult Americans—more than the entire population of Michigan—have not finished five years of school. Nearly 20 million have not finished eight years of school. Nearly 54 million—more than one quarter of America—have not finished high school.

Each year more than 100,000 high school graduates, with proved ability, do not enter college because they cannot afford it.

And if we cannot educate today's youth, what will we do in 1970 when elementary school enrollment will be 5 million greater than 1960? High school enrollment will rise by 5 million. College enrollment will increase by more than 3 million.

In many places classrooms are overcrowded and curricula are outdated. Most of our qualified teachers are underpaid, and many of our paid teachers are unqualified.

We must give every child a place to sit and a teacher to learn from. Poverty must not be a bar to learning, and learning must offer an escape from poverty.

But more classrooms and more teachers are not enough. We must seek an educational system which grows in excellence as it grows in size.

This means better training for our teachers. It means preparing youth to enjoy their hours of leisure as well as their hours of labor. It means exploring new techniques of teaching, to find new ways to stimulate the love of learning and the capacity for creation.

These are three of the central issues of the Great Society. While our government has many programs directed at those issues, I do not pretend we have the full answer to these problems.

But I do promise this:

We are going to assemble the best thought and broadcast knowledge from all over the world to find those answers. I intend to establish working groups to prepare a series of conferences and meetings—on the cities, on natural beauty, on the quality of education, and on other emerging challenges.

From these studies, we will begin to set our course toward the Great Society.

The solution to these problems does not rest on a massive program in Washington, nor can it rely solely on the strained resources of local authority. They require us to create new concepts of cooperation—a creative federalism—between the national capital and the leaders of local communities.

Woodrow Wilson once wrote: "Every man sent out from his university should be a man of his nation as well as a man of his time."

Within your lifetime powerful forces, already loosed, will take us toward a way of life beyond the realm of our experience, almost beyond the bounds of our imagination.

For better or worse, your generation has been appointed by history to deal with those problems and lead America toward a new age.

You have the chance never before afforded to any people in any age. You can help build a society where the demands of morality, and the needs of the spirit, can be realized in the life of the nation.

Will you join in the battle to give every citizen the full equality which God enjoins and the law requires—whatever his belief, or race, or the color of his skin?

Will you join in the battle to give every citizen an escape from the crushing weight of poverty?

Will you join in the battle to make it possible for all nations to live in enduring peace—as neighbors and not as mortal enemies?

Will you join in the battle to build the Great Society—to prove that our material progress is only the foundation on which to build a richer life of mind and spirit?

There are those that say this battle cannot be done; that we are condemned to a soulless wealth. I do not agree. We have the power to shape the civilization we want. But we need your will—your labor—your hearts—if we are to build that kind of society.

Those who came to this land sought to build more than a new country. They sought a new world. I have come here to your campus to say that you can make their vision our reality. Let us from this moment begin our work so that in the future men will look back and say: It was then, after a long and weary

way, that man turned the exploits of his genius to the enrich-
ment of his life.[14]

The Great Society speech established Johnson as a president in his own right in the eyes of the American public. Most
citizens were concerned about urban decay, suburbs too
quickly built after World War II, and decadence in schools.
The goals Johnson selected for emphasis were appropriate for
the period. Moreover, Johnson issued an imaginative challenge
to work hard rather than a promise of a safe harbor.

Many who heard the speech missed an important phrase—
creative federalism. The term would not be fully explained
until later, and, when it was defined, the Vietnam War had
reached such proportions that almost all other things seemed
dim by comparison. In general, creative federalism promised a
pragmatic approach to problems that encouraged local, state,
and regional participation in the decision-making processes of
government. One observer suggested in a newspaper interview that creative federalism might have four components:
(1) a restructuring of the federal bureaucracy to make it more
sensitive and more efficient in dealing with state and local
government; (2) a redirecting of federal grants-in-aid so that
there would be fewer requirements on how money was spent;
(3) a process permitting local and state governments to help
establish priorities in specific geographical areas; and (4) a close
working relationship with universities and private industry to
plan viable programs.

After the speech, however, it was education that the president emphasized as he took the Great Society out into the
highways and byways of the country. And he continued to
court the young, a move that was a calculated venture, a risk
suggested mostly by his youthful advisers. For example, on
May 30, Johnson delivered an address in Austin to graduates
of the University of Texas. He had originally titled his
remarks "A Confederation of Decency." Moyers, Valenti,
Goodwin, and Busby were responsible for the draft. The first

writer wanted a major address instead of hometown-boy-makes-good talk. Johnson told the graduates that they could not escape taking responsibility for their times because "the eyes of the nation, the eyes of millions in faraway lands, the eyes who love liberty are upon you. You can't get away." [15] It was apparent to those assembled that the educated elite would be instrumental in reshaping the America of the Great Society.

During the campaign of 1964, President Johnson spoke at many educational institutions and to many groups of professional educators to seek support for his dream. On June 6, he attended the commencement of Swarthmore College. At the airport in Philadelphia, he heralded this city as a center of learning and culture and predicted that it would be important in building the Great Society. Students were told, later that same day, that individuals were still important and that more "than anytime in the past, you can find personal fulfillment while contributing to the betterment of all mankind." [16] He stated that government did not stifle individual initiative, citing the ways in which programs like social security, rural electrification, ending pollution, a ban on the sales of harmful drugs, and civil rights helped to create a better life. In short, people should not fear government. He also made clear what he meant by the word *government*. "Let me state clearly what I mean by 'this government.' I do not mean just the politicians, technicians, and the experts in Washington. I do not mean only the agencies that make up the federal system, or the departments and bureaus of your state government or your local municipality. I include you. I include every citizen." [17]

Johnson could not overstress the importance of education. He told a meeting of school superintendents on July 30 that onto "my desk each day come the problems of 190 million men and women. When we consider those problems, study them, analyze them, evaluate what can be done, the answer almost always comes down to one word: education." [18] On August 13, he spoke to a meeting of state university presidents. He recounted the importance of their institutions in supplying intellectuals for the nation and praised his own education braintrust. He pointed out that four of his advisers (McNamara, Rusk, Heller, and Bundy) had been college presidents or university executives. Eric Goldman of his staff, another former academic, received high praise as one who had contributed mightily to the everyday work of running the country. In closing, LBJ urged others to take advantage of the institutions of higher education in their midst. "Through the history of our federal system," he said, "state universities have played a very special role. They were always there to serve as a brain reservoir for the governor or the legislature, for citizens' groups. If I had my one wish, I would hope that in every state capital the governor made as much use of educators and college brainpower as the president does here." [19]

More on education, particularly higher education, came on September 28, 1964. Johnson had been invited by President Barnaby Keeney of Brown University to speak at his institution's two-hundredth anniversary. "Higher Education in this Age of Expanding Knowledge" served as the day's theme. In an auditorium rich in pageantry and filled with some five thousand people, a few of whom were from the far corners of the globe, Johnson expounded at great length about the partnership of campus and country. In appropriate fashion, he also said to those who feared the intellectual and scientific revolution of the twentieth century that the "growth of knowledge is not a curse, but a cure for the ills of this age. Our concepts must change in both education and in politics." [20]

The meeting of Keeney and Johnson had a long-term impact as well as a short-term one. The former had recently chaired a commission on the humanities sponsored by the American Council on Education, the American Council of Learned Societies, the Phi Beta Kappa Honor Society, and the Council of Graduate Studies. This committee published a report urging the development of a National Endowment for the Humanities, and Keeney used the occasion to lobby on its behalf. The president was not unfamiliar with the subject, because in 1963 John Fogarty of the House of Representatives had sponsored a bill with the same purpose.

Other speeches in the fall focused on the Great Society. And some off-guard comments were generating criticism or demands for clarification. For instance, he told a convention of communications workers in Cleveland, "We are going to build a Great Society where no man or woman is the victim of fear or poverty or hatred; where every man and woman has a chance for fulfillment and prosperity and hope."[21] A Pittsburgh civic area crowd also received a little preview, as he called it: "It is the time when man gains full domination under God over his own destiny. It is the time of peace on earth and goodwill among men."[22] Lady Bird continued to support her husband's goals as well. She told an overflow luncheon group in Ohio that no one could give the people a great society. Others could shape it, but the people had to give it life. And the matter was urgent. "We are," she said in Fort Smith, Arkansas, "at a crossroads where the signs point clearly to two different philosophies: the philosophy of 'Yes, Certainly' and the philosophy of 'No, Never.'"[23]

Meanwhile, Johnson was not idle: he had specifics in mind. But he did not want details leaked prematurely. On July 2, 1964, he met with his advisers in the cabinet room. He instructed those secretaries assembled to work personally on position papers in their respective fields that could be used in the "serious business" of preparing the Democratic platform. Moyers was assigned to coordinate, and Fred Dutton was made his assistant. Cabinet members themselves were to do the job because career people did not have the political experience to make the necessary judgments and because LBJ was concerned that the administration could be criticized for using civil servants to develop a political document. The assignments were to be done quickly and without publicity. Each memoranda should include objectives, contain supporting documentation, appraise major arguments against proposals, and show the extent to which these priorities related to the 1960 platform.

It was also at this meeting that steps were taken to move the Great Society closer to reality. Johnson surprised some associates when he stated that he was appointing a number of task forces to deal with pressing problems. "The time to begin planning the administration's program for next year—and the years after—is *now*. But you and I are going to be exceedingly busy during the next four months. Therefore, as the *first* step in drawing up a 1965 program now, I am establishing a number of program task forces made up of outstanding people, from within and without the government," he explained.[24] The task forces would be small, select groups of experts who would identify major issues, analyze problems, and recommend specific programs. Their purpose was to come up with ideas, not to sell ideas to the public. The president then named task forces in the following areas: transportation, natural resources, education, health, urban affairs, environmental pollution, preservation of natural beauty, intergovernmental fiscal cooperation, efficiency and economy, antirecession policy, agriculture, civil rights, foreign economic policy, and income maintenance policy. And Johnson wanted these units to operate without publicity: "It is very important that this not become a public operation," he admonished.[25]

Bill Moyers was also placed in charge of coordinating the task forces. He was to be assisted by the White House staff, the Bureau of the Budget, and the Council of Economic Advisers. Johnson made sure that the cabinet members did not think he was circumventing them by employing outside personnel to serve on the commissions. Secretaries would be involved with reports that pertained to them, and the findings of the various groups would be discussed by the Cabinet prior to formulating legislative programs for 1965. Johnson also made it clear that there was urgency to what they did. The prospects for change were good in 1965, and he thought that the administration would have an unparalleled opportunity to make a substantial impact on the country. He reasoned:

There is every likelihood that the economy will continue to move toward greater prosperity—from an *economic standpoint* we can afford to move boldly where bold new programs are called for.

The administration's interest in economy is firmly established. The growth in revenue from economic prosperity and the savings which continuing economy measures yield will make room for new programs and (allow us) to modify or eliminate obsolete ones. The political situation in January very likely will be even more favorable—if we do our work well in the next few months—from a *political standpoint* we can afford to think in bold terms and to strike out in new directions.[26]

From 1964 to 1968, sixteen separate education task forces were appointed. Many of them included people from outside of government. Johnson did this, beyond the reasons mentioned earlier, because he was aware that the Washington bureaucracy often placed limits on the presidency. He once told Richard Nixon: "Before you get to be president you think you can do anything. You think you're the most powerful leader since God. But when you get in that tall chair, as you're gonna find out, Mr. President, you can't count on people. . . . The office is kinda like the little country boy found the hoochie-koochie show at the carnival, once he'd paid his dime and got inside the tent: 'It ain't exactly as it was advertised.' "[27]

The outside task forces, especially, were within the spirit of creative federalism, bringing in leaders from all sections of the country. Some of these individuals would serve as consultants but would not accept appointments because of the financial sacrifices involved or because they did not want to subject their private lives to the scrutiny of the Senate in the "advise and consent" process. On the other hand, the interagency task forces brought established units of government together in closer cooperation to accomplish administration goals more efficiently.

The task forces appointed were as follows:

INTERAGENCY TASK FORCE	CHAIRMAN	REPORTING DATE
1965 Task Force on Education	Dwight A. Ink	6/14/65
1966 Task Force on Education	John W. Gardner	10/31/66
1967 Task Force on Child Development	William Gorham	11/9/67
1967 Task Force on Education	John W. Gardner	11/1/67
1967 Task Force on Manpower	W. Willard Wirtz	11/28/67
1967 Task Force on Administration and Science	Charles L. Schultze	10/22/68 12/4/68
1968 Task Force on Education	Wilbur Cohen	11/29/68

OUTSIDE TASK FORCE	CHAIRMAN	REPORTING DATE
1964 Task Force on Education	John W. Gardner	11/14/64
1965 Task Force on International Education	Dean Rusk	11/65
1966 Task Force on Manpower for State and Local Governments	William D. Carmichael	12/17/66
1966 Task Force on Early Child Development	Joseph McHunt	1/4/67

1966 Task Force on Career Advancement	John W. Macy, Jr.	1967
1966 Task Force on Education	William C. Friday	6/30/67
1966 Task Force on Urban Employment Opportunity	George P. Schultz	7/14/67
1966 Task Force on Gifted Persons	Champion Ward	6/30/68
1967 Task Force on Urban Educational Opportunities	Paul A. Miller	7/17/68

The most irritating problem faced by the task forces was the necessity for secrecy. Califano or Gaither would kick off a group, and from that time on, according to Gaither, everything was completely "off the record; the membership was never publicly released."[28] Work sessions met unannounced, and the only telltale physical sign was the name of the chairman on an office door. More than one congressman complained about the procedure. Robert H. Michel from Illinois, for instance, told Califano that since "the field of education is in no wise to be considered a matter of national security, why has it been necessary to cloak the White House efforts in education in secrecy? Isn't it the principal purpose of education to open the doors to knowledge rather than to close them? Why should the American people be deprived of the names of those who strongly influence the president's education proposals?"[29] Nevertheless, the policy continued, and LBJ defended it to the end of his administration.

Sometime in late 1968, the president drafted a memorandum in which he once again explained his reasoning on secrecy. He wrote:

This has been one of the most controversial characteristics of the entire Task Force operation, but I personally feel that it is probably the most important characteristic of the operation and one that is essential to its effectiveness. My reasons for taking this approach did not involve any desire, as some have suggested, to operate in secrecy. Instead, I was prompted primarily by a desire to obtain the most candid, objective advice possible. I strongly believed then, and I believe now, that when a group or individual is preparing a document for public consumption, they will be far more cautious and concerned about their public image, and far more reluctant to be critical of others than they are when doing a job on a confidential basis.[30]

In addition, Johnson increasingly grew more wary of the press, and he did not think task force members should be subjected to journalistic harassment.

The first task force to deal with education was appointed in 1964. Its chairman, John Gardner, did his work efficiently, and the force reported its findings and suggestions before the year was out. The Gardner Commission was important for two reasons: it made some important recommendations in regard to obtaining federal aid for elementary and secondary schools, and it served as something of a model for subsequent study groups. For example, the experience of the 1964 Task Force on Education pointed out the need for appointing a staff liaison officer to determine whether an interagency task force should follow in its wake and to ascertain just how the Bureau of the Budget should be involved. Gardner's performance was impressive, and when Anthony Celebrezze resigned in 1965, the chairman of the task force took over as secretary of HEW. He left government service two years later, having established himself as a dedicated civil servant and a man who had an exemplary interest in the affairs of the nation.

Meanwhile, the national elections were nearing, and Johnsonians worked feverishly to push more education bills through Congress. Five measures secured passage in the waning months of the year. The first, entitled the "National Arts and Cultural Development Act of 1964," was introduced by New Jersey's Frank Thompson, Jr. The purpose of H.R. 9586 was to establish a national council on the arts that would stimulate cultural development. This legislation permitted the president to appoint a full-time commission chairman, one who would be aided by twenty-four councilmen serving on a part-time basis. The secretary of the Smithsonian Institution would serve as an ex-officio member of the organization. One hundred and fifty thousand dollars was authorized in a lump-sum appropriation to fund the commission.

A National Council on the Arts was much needed. The National Education Defense Act had strengthened science, leaving the arts and humanities to founder because of a lack of proper financial support. The specific charges given to the National Council on the Arts included: (1) recommending ways to maintain and increase United States cultural resources; (2) proposing methods to encourage private initiative in the arts; (3) advising and consulting with local, state, and federal agencies on means to coordinate existing resources and to foster artistic and cultural endeavors; and (4) studying and recommending methods to encourage and promote creativity, higher standards, and increased opportunities in the arts. Then, too, the chairman of the commission had a responsibility to report on federal activities in the arts to the president. This legislation was signed on September 3.

The Nurses Training Act of 1964 was enacted one day later. Representative Kenneth A. Roberts from Alabama brought the bill to the attention of his colleagues. The purpose of the measure was to increase opportunities for the training of nursing professionals. The act provided funds for grants to support the construction of college and hospital schools of nursing, loans to students enrolled in degree programs, and grants for upgrading instruction and defraying the cost of maintaining nursing schools in hospitals. H.R. 11241 also extended the opportunities for working nurses to train for administrative and teaching roles. The funding level recommended was for some $233 million, divided roughly as follows: $90 million for construction; $17 million for curriculum enrichment; $41 million for hospitals that had nursing schools; and $85 million for student loans. A student could receive up to $1,000 per year, and the entire debt would be cancelled if that person worked as a nurse for ten years.

In October, Senator Harrison A. Williams of New Jersey introduced S. 2180, a bill to provide long-term loans to students of optometry. This legislation extended the loan provisions of the Health Professions Educational Assistance Act to optometry students. Previously, only those studying dentistry, medicine, or osteopathy were eligible. Secretary Celebrezze had some reservations about the bill, but he did execute its provisions, entering into agreements with public and other nonprofit schools to establish loan funds for worthy degree candidates. Students could borrow up to $2,000 a year, with repayment beginning three years after graduation. Loans were repayable over a ten-year period.

The final education act of 1964 passed Congress on October 16. Senator Morse introduced the measure entitled National Defense Education Act amendment. The original bill, it will be remembered, had been drafted partially by Johnson while Senate majority leader. In general, the amendment to NDEA extended federal support to education in the sciences and continued payment of impacted area support. The 1964 bill gave NDEA additional years; made students of business, technology, nursing, and library science eligible for loans; increased the number of fellowships for doctoral candidates; and offered aid to teachers of English, history, geography, and civics who wanted to upgrade their credentials. Funding came in the following amounts. The numbers represent millions of dollars.

	1965	1966	1967	1968
Student loans	163.3	179.3	190.0	195.0
Counseling	24.0	24.5	30.0	30.0
Language Development	13.0	14.0	16.0	18.0
Curriculum Improvement	100.0	100.0	100.0	100.0
	300.3	317.8	336.0	343.0

This one bill provided over a billion dollars for federal aid to education over the next four-year period.

Lyndon Johnson signed the National Defense Education Act amendment in the East Room. He again singled out for recognition the Eighty-eighth Congress, and he stated his pride in extending a bill that he had helped to draft while in the Senate. Under the original act, over 3,000 men and women had been assisted in becoming college teachers, and 5,000 more individuals were receiving help at the time he spoke. Sixty thousand students had obtained loans to complete their college education. On the other hand, Johnson was convinced the nation had not gone far enough fast enough. For example, he estimated that 100,000 fully qualified students were not going to college because of a lack of funds. Universities should not turn away students in a time of world crisis, he said. Britain had a new prime minister; a new government had recently been formed in the Soviet Union; and the Chinese had just detonated a nuclear bomb. The solution, Johnson said, was a wellspring of education. He concluded with a quotation he often used to emphasize the importance of learning. He said: "A great president of the Republic of Texas once said, and I have repeated it so much that I hope my colleagues in the Senate will indulge me, that 'the educated mind is the guardian genius of democratic government, of democracy. The educated mind—it is the only dictator that free men will ever recognize. And it is the only ruler that free men desire.'"[31]*

Only days before these comments, the president had made education a national issue in his campaign for re-election, the only chief executive of the nation to do so. As he recalled in *The Vantage Point*, "I made a personal decision during the 1964 presidential campaign to make education a fundamental issue and to put it high on the nation's agenda. I proposed to act on my belief that regardless of a family's financial condition, education should be available to every child in the United States—as much education as he could absorb."[32] His viewpoint was reaffirmed in a press release dated November 1: "I believe," he said, "that every child has a right to as much education as he has the ability to receive. I believe that this does not end in the lower schools, but goes on through technical and higher education—if the child wants it and can use it."[33]

Except for material written by the contestants and by Theodore White, not much of worth has been published about the 1964 presidential campaign. Johnson, as had Jack Kennedy before him, believed that Arizona's Barry Goldwater would carry the standard for the Republican party. Goldwater was a personable man, and, with some professional packaging, he could have been a most attractive candidate. By the time he reached the Cow Palace in San Francisco, California, in the summer of 1964, he had secured enough delegates to assure him of the Grand Old Party's nomination. If, in his acceptance speech, Goldwater had been more gracious to Republican liberals such as Nelson Rockefeller of New York and William Scranton of Pennsylvania, the November elections might have been closer. Unfortunately—for him, his party, and all con-

---

*LBJ was referring to Mirabeau LaMar, second president of the Republic of Texas, who held that office from 1838 to 1841.

servatives—Goldwater refused to be charitable to the other wing of his party. His speech hurt him in 1964 and prevented him from being a viable candidate in the future.

Later, Eisenhower and Nixon persuaded Goldwater to soften his extremist stance. But it was too late: LBJ had already tagged him with an extremist label, and the identification was to haunt Goldwater until election day. He never had a chance, then, to offer the people a "choice" instead of an "echo." Goldwater attacked the welfare state at a time when it was still popular, and his hard-line pronouncements on the war in Vietnam frightened an already skittish public. While Goldwater flopped and foundered, Lyndon Johnson whistle-stopped the country, speaking to large, enthusiastic crowds. The summer and fall of 1964 marked LBJ's last and greatest campaign. It was his time, and he soared like an eagle.

In January 1965, Lyndon Johnson delivered his first State of the Union message since he had been elected president of the United States in his own right. This address, against the advice of Richard Goodwin, did not give enough stress to education. Goodwin complained to Cater: "It seems to me that the education section has gotten short shrift,"[34] when compared in length, for example, to the one on natural beauty and pollution. No changes were made, however. The address given on the fourth provided Johnson with a touching experience, for he must have remembered how he had felt almost thirty years before as a freshman congressman from the Tenth District of Texas. He detailed three general concerns: the nation must be kept prosperous, opportunity must be opened to all people, and the quality of American life must be improved. In the third section, Johnson mentioned education and hinted at a new program that would cost $1.5 billion.

The State of the Union message closed on a personal note. He told those assembled that the burdens of the presidency were so great that only a chief executive could comprehend the burden. His hardest job, he said, was not working with Congress or keeping a tight appointment schedule: the biggest challenge did not lie in doing what was right, but in knowing what was right. Where, he asked rhetorically, did one look for answers? His response was that he sought inspiration in the hill country where he was born. The land had once been barren. The hills were lined with scrub cedar and a few live oaks. There was little that would grow in the harsh caliche, and the Pedernales would flood each spring and overrun the valley. But the people had a dream. They endured. And they built a community where a living could be made, children could be raised, and a better life obtained. Johnson, as had his ancestors and friends, hoped to build a more perfect union.

CHAPTER ELEVEN

A Wellspring
of Education

"Man's most notable enterprise is the work of education."
—Lyndon Baines Johnson, 1965

A VIRTUAL WELLSPRING of educational legislation flowed through the United States Congress in 1965 and 1966. Much of it involved landmark bills that touched many individuals and institutions, but perhaps no single agency was affected more than the United States Office of Education. The first commissioner of that office, Henry Barnard, was appointed in 1867 by Andrew Johnson. He saw his primary duty, in accordance with federal statute, to be the collection and dissemination of knowledge to help in the creation and "maintenance of efficient school systems, and otherwise to promote the cause of education."[1] The data he uncovered were published in the now defunct *American Journal of Education*. The Office of Education originally found a home in the Department of the Interior. It remained there until 1939, when New Dealers transferred it to the Federal Security Agency. Dwight Eisenhower later elevated the office to cabinet status and made it a part of Health, Education, and Welfare. Oveta Culp Hobby headed the new behemoth and became the second woman to hold full secretarial rank.

The growing importance of education can be judged from

the fact that ten individuals served as commissioner from 1867 to 1949 and six from 1949 to 1966: the demands of the position decreased tenure from an average of eight to three years. On the whole, with the exception of Barnard and William Torrey Harris, the position had little impact at home or abroad until World War II. Personnel associated with it were mostly academicians who were satisfied to operate within their narrow specialities, letting others establish philosophical objectives. Then, too, few heads of government bothered to consult with the commissioners of education on national or international policy.

In 1956, the annual budget of the Department of Health, Education, and Welfare approximated $200 million. But the passage of legislation in the Eisenhower and Kennedy-Johnson years catapulted the number of dollars ever upward. Ten years later, for instance, Anthony Celebrezze was to be responsible for supervising a budget of $1.5 billion. Lyndon Johnson's commitment to additional programs caused concern in Washington, because many feared that the Office of Education was not ready for the task. Douglass Cater later investigated the situation. On April 2, 1965, he wrote Mike O'Neill, a reporter for the *New York Daily News* who covered HEW, to ask if he thought the organization could survive additional strains. O'Neill responded that the agency's "high command structure is an administrative mess . . . and will collapse completely under the weight of its new Great Society responsibilities." [2] Other observers felt the same way.

In 1965, therefore, Johnson initiated a twofold attack to modernize the Department of Health, Education, and Welfare and the Office of Education. First, he changed the command structure, replacing Celebrezze with John Gardner. The replacement was sympathetic to the Great Society, and his service with the Carnegie Foundation and as chairman of the Education Task Force of 1964 had provided him with valuable background experience. He was succeeded in 1968 by another capable individual, Wilbur Cohen.

The men who occupied the commissioner of education's office were equally astute: Francis Keppel and Harold Howe II, though markedly different in temperament, often bordered on genius in devising strategy, securing legislation, and implementing programs. These men, in concert with staff aides, task force personnel, and key members of the House and Senate (such as John Brademas, Edith Green, Adam Clayton Powell, Carl Perkins, Wayne Morse, and John Fogarty) steadily pushed education to the forefront of American life.

The second part of the president's plan was to reorganize the U.S. Office of Education. He created a task force, headed by Dwight Albert Ink of the Atomic Energy Commission, to study the organization for thirty to sixty days. Herbert Jasper of the Bureau of the Budget and Nicholas Oganovic of the Civil Service Commission assisted. The way for these men was prepared by removing longtime Deputy Commissioner Wayne Reed and naming Henry Loomis, the director of the Voice of America program, in his place. Ink, Jasper, and Oganovic urged sweeping changes in structure and organization. And, as a result, many bureaucratic faithful were terminated or placed elsewhere in government. The Ink Commission shocked and stunned, but in the end one document was not enough to undo the traditions of a century. Fright, however, did increase productivity.

The flood tide of educational legislation in 1965 and 1966 initiated another problem, one still not fully resolved. Should education be made a separate department? As early as January 6, 1965, Barnaby Keeney wrote the president that he had learned that Congressman Fogarty intended "to introduce a bill to raise education to cabinet rank."[3] This action generated considerable discussion. Steven Bailey, in a scholarly paper entitled "The Office of Education: The Politics of Rapid Growth," delivered in September 1966 to the American Political Science Association meeting in New York City, dramatically revealed that USOE was unprepared to administer expanding budgets. Another analyst, Rufus E. Miles, Jr., in an essay called "The Case for a Federal Department of Education," suggested that education could never gain stature of the first class until it became a department in its own right. Secretary Gardner, in the future, would suggest a compromise. He felt that HEW ought to be divided into two sections: health and a department of individual and family services. Other pressures and priorities, however, were surfacing, and little action was taken on the last two proposals.

Johnson believed that he should proceed full speed ahead in sending additional education legislation to Congress. Time was of the essence. Jack Kennedy's educational program had languished because *Brown* v. *The Topeka Board of Education* had made a national issue of race. If LBJ's ideas on federal aid to education were to be salvaged, something had to be done without delay; Johnson determined to put old and new ideas into an omnibus bill and push for passage. Prospects were favorable at that time because the Democratic majority in Congress had increased in the last election. Commissioner Keppel later remembered that the president came into a meeting in the Fish Room and said, "Look, we've got to do this in a hurry. We got in with this majority in the Congress. . . . It doesn't make any difference what we do. We're going to lose [voters] at a rate of about a million a month, and under those circumstances, get your subcommittee hearing going. I want to see this coonskin on the wall."[4]

In a message to Congress on January 25, 1965, Johnson told the House and Senate that the improvement of education should be the nation's first priority. "It is our primary weapon in the war on poverty and the principal tool for building a Great Society."[5] Then he proposed a budget that would more than double the programs of the Office of Education. The Eighty-eighth Congress had done much, he said, but the job needed completion. In particular, he wanted to obtain federal funds for elementary and secondary education—something that had never been done before. "Such aid," he pleaded, "is

vital if we are to end the situation in which children are handicapped for life because they happen to live in communities
which cannot support good schools."⁶ Johnson also requested
expansion of present support levels for academic research and
science education. The National Science Foundation, for
example, was scheduled for a 25 percent increase.

Johnson's proposal to open the nation's purse strings to
extend federal aid to elementary and secondary schools
threatened to awaken some sleeping dogs. A conservative bloc
in Congress had always believed that federal funds should not
be allotted to grade and high schools because it was dangerous
as well as unconstitutional. Conservatives feared that the
national government might attempt to interfere with policies
set by local school boards; they objected, too, to the proposal
to give federal funds to help private and parochial schools as
well. They resurrected, then, the age-old question of separa-
tion of church and state. Aid to common and high schools also
posed some racial problems, for the *Brown* decision had motivated white supremacists to establish alternative schools to
avoid integration. Therefore, if funds were to be voted for
institutions of learning below the college level, somebody
needed to find a formula or to forge a compromise acceptable
to opponents of federal funding.

But before a vote could be taken on this matter, one other
bill passed quickly through Congress. The Appalachian
Regional Development Act of 1965 had been recommended by
a presidential commission that had studied the 165,000 square
miles of territory that stretched from northern Alabama to
northern Pennsylvania. This area encompassed some 17 million residents, many of whom had not achieved the prosperity
of the industrial Middle West and the thriving Eastern Sea-
board. Public Law 89–4 established a regional commission and
a federal-state coordinating and planning body and modified
certain existing programs so that Appalachia could receive
special help for its economic problems. The act allocated
$1.0924 billion for highway construction and program devel-

opment, of which $16 million was earmarked for vocational education. The bill passed easily, but opponents issued a sharp minority report charging another Tennessee Valley Authority-type plan was being created. Johnson signed the measure on March 9 and commended Congress for helping to alleviate poverty in a depressed section of the United States.

Kentucky's Carl Perkins introduced H.R. 2362, a piece of legislation designed to strengthen and improve educational quality and educational opportunities in the nation's elementary and secondary schools. In general, the Elementary and Secondary Education Act of 1965 proposed to provide a better education for disadvantaged youth, to improve teaching technology, to make more hardware available to teachers, and to strengthen state departments of education. The initial appropriations level called for the expenditure of some $1.25 billion. Aid to impacted school districts (Public Law 874) was extended through the 1967–68 school year, and new programs under five titles received funding. Title 1 authorized a three-year program to support the educational needs of children from low-income families. Title 2 provided $100 million for library resources and instructional materials. Title 3 supported the development of community supplementary educational centers to assist local schools. Title 4 established regional education laboratories, organizations that would focus on the capabilities of institutions of higher education to conduct educational research. The last, Title 5, launched a five-year program to strengthen leadership resources of state educational agencies. This item, though funded at the level of only $25 million, was most important because state agencies often were less effective than community school systems.

In spite of widespread fears within the government, the Elementary and Secondary Education Act passed by a wide margin. The House voted 263 to 153 and the Senate 73 to 18 in favor of the legislation. But the lopsided vote was not the biggest surprise: the most amazing aspect of the bill was that it became law in less than three months.

The quick passage, however, was far from a miracle. A twofold strategy had been employed. First, Johnson and members of his staff—or others supporting the measure—met with individuals and groups who were interested in the outcome. The president provided an example by personally inspecting the Office of Education on February 25. Francis Keppel was delighted. He wrote Jack Valenti the next day: "Nothing in the world could have done our cause more good, or raised morale higher, than the president's visit to this office yesterday."[7] In the same vein, educational professional organizations were encouraged to lobby for the bill to their congressmen or senators. Monroe Sweetland, a regional representative for the National Education Association, for example, wrote Douglass Cater that Johnson stirred his group to action, and, in return, the organization had made sure that "nearly every congressman was hearing from the home front school people regularly."[8] He also pointed out that formal sessions were being held with freshman, pro-education, liberal Democrats. The National Democratic Committee also had been helping schools and other organizations to get their congressmen back to the district for education discussions.

Second, Johnson encouraged the leadership of the U.S. Office of Education to package the bill so that what Stephen Bailey called "Red, Religion, and Race" problems could be resolved. Francis Keppel and Wilbur Cohen acted as brokers, bringing pressure groups, legislators, staff aides, and task force personnel into close contact so that a formula could be devised to satisfy even the most skeptical. Title 6 of the Civil Rights Bill of 1964 no longer made it advantageous for southern whites to oppose federal aid to education. The Red issue had many ramifications, but the provisions calling for "loans" of equipment to private and parochial schools by *state* departments of education alleviated this potential stumbling block. If states were administering aid, how could one then charge the federal government with interference? The religious issue, too, was ingeniously solved. The bill decided how much aid would be given individual states by tying this money to the numbers of disadvantaged students residing in any particular entity, regardless of the type of school they attended.

The major breakthrough in aid to common and high schools was devised by the 1964 Task Force on Education. Its report suggested that federal funds to elementary and secondary schools not be given on a "general aid basis, as earlier plans had specified, but on a selective formula related to the poverty of an area."[9] Later, as Johnson recalled in *The Vantage Point*, Celebreeze, Cohen, Wayne Morse, Keppel, and others sought to develop a mathematical formula to express the basis for federal aid. The latter found the answer. He suggested a simple equation: $\frac{A}{2} \times B = P$. "In that formula," said Johnson, "*A* represented a state's average expenditure per pupil, *B* the number of poor schoolchildren in a local school district, and *P* the payment to that district. The formula was based on an old concept familiar to the Congress: aid to impacted areas."[10] Thus, in laymen's terms, the states received grants on the number of impoverished children in an individual school district in the amount of one-half the average expenditures of the state per school child.

The signing ceremony for this bill was held in the old Junction school near the LBJ ranch and the birthplace of Lyndon Johnson. Miss Katie Deadrich, his former teacher, was invited as well as former school classmates, and local, state, and national political leaders. On Palm Sunday, Johnson affixed his signature and spoke in a folksy fashion to his audience. He said that he felt that this act was the most important he had ever signed: he hoped that these education benefits would break the poverty cycle in America. The president had also come to Texas to be refreshed. He told those gathered in the dust of the school that "I felt a very strong desire to go back to the beginnings of my own education—to be reminded and to remind others of that magic time when the world of learning began to open before our eyes."[11] Moreover, the moment renewed in him the desire to re-enter the classroom when his presidency had been completed.

The passage of the Elementary and Secondary Education Act of 1965 again revealed the importance of the education establishment and forced an assessment of the concept of the task force. The principal strength of the task forces was that they promoted fresh ideas, but the memberships were of little use in getting legislation enacted. Of them, Frank Keppel said: "They've been rather exaggerated in their influence, if I may be frank about it." [12]

It was not the task forces but the education establishment that had saved this bill from extinction. Members had worked with Emanuel Celler of New York to obtain a judicial interpretation that helped to avoid some cumbersome bottlenecks. John Brademas and Hugh Carey had sold the distribution formula. Adam Clayton Powell and Carl Perkins had handled their respective congressional committees in a deft manner. Phillip Landrum had won some key southern votes by soft-pedaling the race issue. And Wayne Morse, an ever-growing thorn in the side of Johnson over Vietnam, nevertheless rose to one of his finest hours to back the act.

Lawrence O'Brien and Douglass Cater also deserve much credit. The former had acted as legislative liaison and dealt with the congressional leadership when problems had developed or a strategy had to be decided. Cater played a major role in hearings conducted by subcommittees. Together, these men decided which Republican amendments could be permitted to pass and which ones had to be bottled up or tabled. All members of the education establishment were elated with the victory, because the Elementary and Secondary Education Act opened new vistas.

In preparation for what was to come, Johnson, on the day he signed the bill, also affixed his signature to a document that would reorganize the Office of Education. A committee headed by Dwight Ink was authorized to begin its investigation. The Ink Commission reported on June 14, 1965, forwarding a document some forty pages long. It was divided into eight sections: personnel administration; financial administration; planning and evaluation; management reporting and information systems; contracting and construction activities; evaluating contract and grant proposals; organization of the office of education; and follow-through. It was brilliant on paper, a model of its kind. Yet many in the office resented its formation and secretly determined to checkmate its influence.

During the time remaining in 1965, Congress approved fourteen additional education measures. Most of these bills simply extended or modified previous legislation. On April 26, the Manpower Development and Training Act Amendments Bill was passed. It had originally become law in 1962, and now Johnson wanted to bring it into harmony with the Great Society. The next act came in the summer. A small amount of money was involved—some eight million dollars— but the bill touched the Johnsons personally. Mary Thornberry, the mother of Congressman Homer Thornberry (who had replaced LBJ as congressman from the Tenth District of Texas in 1948), had acquainted the president with the needs of Gallaudet College in Washington, D.C., an institution that worked with the deaf. H.R. 7031 established a National Technical Institute for the Deaf to be administered by Gallaudet. The recommendation came from an advisory committee appointed by the secretary of HEW. Thousands were helped as a result of this legislation, and Johnson made no secret of his unabashed support in the signing ceremony.

Two more bills were ready for the president's signature in July. The first, Amendments to the Juvenile Delinquency and Youth Offences Control Act of 1961, extended the original legislation for two years and provided funding for one year, to the tune of $6.5 million. In its final form the measure authorized the secretary of HEW to make grants to demonstration projects for the control and prevention of delinquency as well as to subsidize the training of additional professional personnel. The second, Public Law 815, pertained to the construction of school facilities for children in Puerto Rico, Wake Island, Guam, and the Virgin Islands, places that were not being accommodated by regular local schools.

In August, following the signing of the medicare bill, which provided free medical care for the aged, Congress enacted legislation to provide construction funds for the building of mental retardation facilities and mental health centers. This bill amended two titles of Public Law 88–164, providing $73.5 million for staffing health centers and for expanding teacher training and research and demonstration projects for handicapped children.

The subject of health had been of interest to Johnson since he entered Congress in 1937. He thought that legislation in this domain was particularly beneficial to his section of the country, since states below the Mason-Dixon line had not been progressive in either prevention or treatment of disease. Moreover, the citizenry as a whole were concerned about their well-being; so, Johnson reasoned, health bills ought to increase his popularity at the polls. At the signing ceremony for Public Law 88–164, Johnson made a pledge to the people on health as he had earlier on education. His goal was to increase longevity. He said: "We presently have a life expectancy of seventy years. I have a prediction—and I am not in Drew Pearson's business and don't want to compete with him—but I tell you now we want to raise that goal: it is not going to stay at seventy; it is going to go up." [13] Here again, perhaps personal experience played a part in his concern: Johnson's ailing gall bladder would soon be removed at Bethesda.

Only one education bill completed movement through Congress in September, but it was a bill that pleased a heretofore sadly neglected segment of the academic community. Senator Claiborne Pell of Rhode Island sponsored an effort to establish a National Foundation on the Arts and Humanities. Each of these two agencies would make grants and promote progress and scholarship. The signing ceremony was held in the Rose Garden. The president, in a philosophical mood, stated: "We in America have not always been kind to the artists and the scholars who are the creators and the keepers of our new vision. Somehow, the scientists always seem to get the penthouse, while the arts and humanities get the basement." [14] Approximately one year later, Johnson was present when Barnaby Keeney, formerly of the University of Rhode Island, assumed the chairmanship of the humanities division. On this occasion, the president made several references to the works of Carl Sandburg and wished his friend good luck in his new position. The theme for the day was that America should help its best minds find the time, as Sandburg said, to reach "for lights beyond . . . for keepsakes lasting beyond any hunger or death." [15]

No less than five education bills found their way through the House and Senate in July. The Economic Opportunity Act of 1964 received some adjustments, doubling the budget of the war on poverty by providing $1.785 billion. The signing was a jubilant occasion, marred only by the fact that funding had been provided for just one year. That meant going back to Congress for funds a year earlier than Johnson expected. One more bill passed on the nineteenth and three more on the twenty-second. The first provided money to develop captioned films for the deaf while the others authorized a system of loan insurance for vocational students (up to $75 million), extended the Health Professional Education Assistance Act ($585 million), and amended the Public Health Service Act so that money could be provided to help medical libraries keep pace with the knowledge explosion. To support this bill, Johnson ventured that published research in medicine doubled every ten years.

Two bills in November brought 1965 education legislation to a close. The first bill, introduced earlier by Congressman William Ford of Michigan, received approval. H.R. 9022 amended Public Laws 81, 815, and 874 so that financial assistance could be granted for the construction and operation of public schools in disaster areas. The Elementary and Secondary Education Act also was amended in a minor fashion. Ford's measure carried an allocation of $40 million. The second bill, H.R. 9567, entitled the Higher Education Act of 1965, was signed by the president in the Strahan Gymnasium, on the campus of Southwest Texas State Teachers College. It did for higher education much of what the Elementary and Secondary Education Act had done for the common and high schools. Several titles strengthened university extension, library improvement, support for developing institutions, student loans, equipment purchases, money for construction of graduate facilities, and the creation of a National Teacher Corps.

Johnson estimated that a million students who otherwise would not have made it into higher education at the college and university level could now attend. It took a stroke of genius to get the bill passed without undue lobbying. Edith Green, who had given the administration trouble while the Elementary and Secondary Education Act was under consideration, was asked to serve as sponsor, preventing future trouble. She got the act passed and secured some $22 million in funds in the bargain. The opposition felt that this amount was excessive. William H. Ayes, who composed the report for the minority, wrote: "If legislation affecting education continues in this atmosphere the federal involvement is going to be completely chaotic." [16]

President Johnson invited many old and trusted friends to the signing ceremony. It was a sentimental moment as he gazed on the face of Cecil Evans, former head of San Marcos; Jesse Kellam, who had worked with him in the National Youth Administration; and Tom Nichols, a former student friend at college. On days like this, his thoughts turned back to the hardships of his own pupils at Cotulla. "I shall never forget," he said, "the faces of the boys and girls in that classroom in that Mexican school, and I remember even yet the pain of realizing and knowing then that college was closed to practically every one of those children because they were too poor." [17] He added that he had made up his mind then and there that he would never rest while the door of knowledge was closed to any American. And now, no doubt, he fully believed that this goal had been accomplished.

The end of 1965 evidenced a transition in Lyndon Johnson. The old-style back-slapping politician was laid to rest, and he once more became a pedagogue. From his podium in the White House, he wrote lectures for his students, the people of the United States. Most of his thoughts were on the importance of teaching and learning. In March 1966, he told the delegates to the annual convention of the American Alumni Council that history would honor those who worked for the education of youth. A film strip script to explain the various provisions of the Elementary and Secondary Education Act said that freedom was fragile if the needs of the citizenry were neglected. LBJ also called for three T's to accompany the three R's. The nation needed teachers who were superior; techniques, so that instruction could be modernized; and thirst, the urge to place education first in all of our plans and hopes. When Richard E. Klinck, a sixth-grade teacher at Wheat Ridge (near Denver, Colorado), came to Washington to be honored as Teacher of the Year, Johnson added: "This year we put education where it belongs, as the number one priority at the top of our national agenda." [18]

He also looked with great pride on his efforts to aid the American Indian. Their problems, too, he thought, could be solved with more education, better health care, and assistance in finding employment. In a speech concerning the work of the National Science Foundation, the president expressed his hope that scientists at developing institutions should play a larger part in setting standards of excellence. In a bill related to the war on poverty, he spoke of five- and six-year-old children as the inheritors of poverty's curse, and he praised a measure that would give young boys and girls a better foundation for education. He called the measure Project Headstart. It was, to him, the "most stirring . . . of any peacetime program within memory." [19] The month of May found him telling the students of Howard University that the number of black Americans attending institutions of higher education had almost doubled in the previous fifteen years. Days later, he informed men and women at Gallaudet College that humanitarianism was the nation's most precious resource. "Strong and successful as America is," he continued, "we cannot allow any of our human potential to be wasted or neglected. This conviction motivates us now in all that we do in the field of education." [20] A summer address to the National Education Association unveiled plans for a new White House Conference on Education. This meeting would bring influential citizens from every state to discuss the question, How can a growing nation in an increasingly complex world provide education of the highest quality for all of its people?

Many people in the country missed the transition in Johnson. One who did not was the head of the Department of Philosophy at the University of Texas, the controversial John R. Silber. He correctly captured the essence of what was happening in an essay entitled "Lyndon Johnson as Teacher," which was published by *The Listener* magazine on May 20, 1965. The article was motivated by Silber's ten-year-old daughter, who had announced one day at breakfast that she did not want Johnson to run for the presidency again in 1968 so that he could come to Austin and teach school. Professor Silber agreed that this possibility would be a logical end to a long career as a civil servant. As he reflected further on his daughter's comments he felt that more people ought to think of Johnson not merely as the consummate compromiser, cajoler, conniver, and manipulator of men and movements. It was more illuminating to view him instead as a teacher with a variety of teaching methods. In fact, Silber concluded, the thirty-sixth president had added a new dimension to the office of the presidency by showing that in modern times the position had a teaching mission to fulfill.

The year 1965 had been an important one for the nation. Johnson hoped that 1966 would build upon the work of the previous twelve months, and thus he took much time in preparing his annual State of the Union message to the joint houses of Congress. The speech delivered on January 12 seemed much like the discourse of a professor laying the groundwork for a new class. It touched upon both the domestic and international situations at present. The initial section was devoted to the Great Society. He told his audience that the nation was "mighty enough, its society healthy enough, its people strong enough, to pursue our goals in the rest of the world while still building the Great Society at home."[21] He asked Congress to continue the war on poverty; to support a foreign aid program that would make a maximum attack on hunger and disease and ignorance; to expand trade among the United States, Eastern Europe, and the Soviet Union; to attack the wasteful poisoning of water in America; to deal with crime in the streets; to extend civil rights protection; and to authorize a new cabinet position to deal with transportation problems. He also proposed a constitutional amendment to extend the term of congressmen from two to four years. A total budget of $112.8 billion was proposed, which would have only a $1.8 billion deficit.

The Great Society road, Johnson hoped, would lead in three directions: growth, justice, and liberation. Growth in the economy was necessary to generate revenue to help the nation's unfortunate. By equal justice Johnson meant changes in the judicial system, repealing the Taft-Hartley Law for labor, funding the teacher corps provision of the Higher Education Act, and forming community development districts. Education came under the heading of liberation. "A great people flower not from wealth or power, but from a society which spurs them to the fullness of their genius."[22] He challenged legislators to improve the health and education programs of the previous year as well as to extend special opportunities to the young men and women who wore the uniforms of the armed forces.

Johnson announced that his administration had five major objectives in foreign policy. First, the nation needed to be kept strong at home by holding down expenditures and getting value out of dollars to keep the economy sound. Second, he promised that he would work toward controlling, reducing, and ultimately eliminating modern engines of destruction. Weapons control and limits on nuclear proliferation were prime concerns. Third, in the spirit of Franklin Roosevelt and Harry Truman, he would make an effort to strengthen world associations to which America belonged, especially the Alliance for Progress, the unity of Europe, the Atlantic community, and regional organizations associated with developing continents. Fourth, he made a pledge to push the goals of the Great Society abroad. The Marshall Plan had been a sign of America's compassion, and now this concept should be expanded to "conduct a worldwide attack on the problems of hunger and disease and ignorance."[23] He recommended health and education acts to help neighbors overseas. And last, in Wilsonian terms, Johnson stated that the most important principle of the United States should be the right of each people to govern themselves and to shape their own institutions.

The last section of LBJ's speech dwelt upon a theme that was receiving increasing attention—the burdens of the presidential office. The weight of the position was beginning to have some telling personal effects. War, he said, was a sign that madness still existed in the world and that leaders had to deal with it. It was difficult for a president to order the guns to fire on the battlefield. Vietnam had been causing him sleepless nights and long days. Additional pain came to Johnson because every bullet that was spent shattered a cherished domestic dream, for "we have children to teach, and we have the sick to be cured, and we have men to be freed. There are poor to be lifted up, and there are cities to be built, and there is a world to be helped."[24] At times, Johnson must have felt like a man in a whirlpool; he knew what had to be done, but his dwindling strength prevented him from freeing himself from the maelstrom.

Educational legislation continued in 1966 at a furious pace. Johnsonians did find that money was growing more difficult to come by, and sometimes the education establishment had to be satisfied with modifying what had been done instead of pioneering. Just one measure passed Congress from January to July, a bill entitled the Veterans' Readjustment Benefits Act of 1966. Its purpose was to provide a permanent program of education assistance, in addition to home and farm loans, hospitalization and medical care, job counseling and placement services, to those who had served in the armed forces after January 31, 1955. The funding level was pegged at $2.5 billion. It was more than Johnson wanted to spend, but he recognized that the citizenry thought well of congressmen who took care of their sons and daughters, so he did not voice his objections.

Johnson gave careful attention to the speech he delivered at the signing ceremony in the East Room of the White House. World War II and Korean War veterans had profited from the two public laws that aided them in the return to civilian life, he said, and now benefits should be offered to those who fought in Vietnam. The nation had a moral obligation to help veterans; the bill, however, also made good economic sense. The first two G.I. bills had cost $21 billion and had returned, said economists, $60 billion in federal taxes. Moreover, the average educational level of veterans was a full two years above that of nonveterans. The World War II and Cold War G.I. bills had also contributed to the development of leadership in the United States. Johnson said: "One hundred sixteen members of the House of Representatives, in our Congress, received training under the G.I. bills, as did eleven United States senators, twelve of the governors of our states, three members of the president's Cabinet, six of our astronauts, and five of the president's special assistants here in the White House." [25] The president stated that he would sign this bill even though it spent more than he thought necessary, since it was for education. He took the occasion, too, to point out that his administration had increased education expenditures for the general public. In 1964, Washington spent on education $4.75 of every $100 taken in from taxes, and that now the rate had risen to $10.02. To put it another way, the administration currently spent $10.2 billion per year, as opposed to a previous level of $4.75 billion.

Only one bill, the Library Services and Construction Act Amendments of 1966, passed in the summer. Congressman Roman Pucinski of Illinois served as sponsor. This measure assisted the construction of new buildings as well as supporting interlibrary cooperation at the local, regional, state, and interstate levels. For fiscal years 1967 through 1971, a total of $700 million was authorized.

Then four bills moved through Congress in October and five in November, saving what might have been a disastrous setback for the administration. On October 11, Johnson signed Public Law 89–642, the Child Nutrition Act of 1966. This bill extended and expanded nutrition programs administered by the secretary of agriculture: it enabled the government to offer milk subsidies, hot lunches, and a breakfast program for children whose parents' income was assessed at poverty level. At the signing ceremony Johnson stated that twenty-one years had elapsed since Truman had signed the National School Lunch Act. And again, he told his audience in the cabinet room that his bill fulfilled a promise he had made as a young man. He said:

> I know what it is to teach children who are listless and tired because they are hungry—and realize the difference a decent meal can make in the lives and attitudes of school children. It can be a heartbreaking experience if there is nowhere to turn for help when your child is hungry. This was just one more situation that I saw when I was a very young man that I have been trying to do something about and have determined to do something about ever since.[26]

The three other October bills were: The Marine Resources Education and Research Act; the International Education Act of 1966; and the Model Secondary School for the Deaf Act. The first, sponsored by Congressman Paul Rogers of Florida, authorized the National Science Foundation to make grants and contracts to initiate and support programs of education and research in fields relating to the development of marine resources. The International Education Act will be discussed later, but it should be stated now that Johnson signed this measure on Asian soil. Time and circumstances had not diminished his interest and personal commitment in this part of the world. The last of this trio of bills was introduced by Congressman Hugh Carey of New York. This measure authorized the Secretary of HEW to enter into an agreement with Gallaudet College to create and operate a model high school for the deaf.

During the first week of November, 1966, five bills passed as Congress began preparation for adjournment. On the third, a measure introduced by Congressman Harley Staggers of West Virginia, entitled Allied Health Professions Personnel Training, passed. Its purpose, simply stated, was to increase the supply of trained personnel in the health profession. Students now eligible for federal grants-in-aid included physical and speech therapists, laboratory technicians, dental hygienists and assistants, and others. Funding levels were: for 1967, $51.25 million; for 1968, $66.76 million; and for 1969, $37 million. The same day another Edith Green-sponsored bill, this one entitled Higher Education Amendments, became law. It adjusted the Higher Education Facilities Act of 1963, the Higher Education Act of 1965, and the National Defense Education Act of 1958. Johnson had outlined certain problems related to these three bills in a special message to Congress sent on March 1. The first amendment scaled construction funds from $200 million in 1967 to $400 million in 1968 and 1969. The second extended title III of the Higher Education Act, which dealt with developing institutions, and set funding in 1967 at $30 million and at $55 million in 1968. The last amendment modified loan forgiveness to teachers who worked with the handicapped and to fulltime teachers in the Trust Territory of the Pacific Islands. The amount of money available for school equipment in certain crucial areas increased from $100 million to $110 million.

On November 7, Congress approved some recommendations that had been made by the Committee on Public Higher Education in the District of Columbia. This group had recommended the creation of a two-year and a four-year college in the nation's capital. Johnson sent his views on the subject to Congress on March 18, 1965. The result was that $350 million was allocated for what would become Federal City College and the Washington Technical Institute. Congress made one significant change in the legislation: the administration had wanted one board of regents for both institutions, but those on the Hill decided upon two governing agencies. The same day, the Manpower Development and Training Act Amendments of 1966 received passage. This bill brought the Manpower Act into harmony with the Great Society by extending broader services to the disadvantaged in order to make them more employable. Greater program efficiency and skill shortages received attention as well. The last education bill of the session, the Economic Opportunity Amendments Act of 1966, passed the next day. The 1964 legislation was extended for another three years and funded at a level of $1.75 billion.

With the exception of some important pronouncements in the field of international education, 1966 had been a quiet year, without much change in Johnson's rhetoric. He continued to push aid to education, especially pointing out, for example, that small colleges as well as full institutions required support. He continued to maintain that support for research should not detract from the teaching mission. In this he had the backing of HEW. The secretary of that department wrote that: "I intend to urge all federal agencies supplying research funds to colleges and universities that they should be alert to the dangers of administering these funds in such a way as to diminish the emphasis on teaching."[27] In a speech at Princeton University the president illustrated once more that he relied on an educated elite for assistance. He said: "The 371 appointments I have made in the last two and one-half years collectively hold 758 advanced degrees."[28]

On October 7, Johnson spoke in Newark, New Jersey. Clearly education was the concern of the day. His remarks on this occasion once more illustrated that the partisan politician image was giving way to a new character formation. He told his audience: "I am not speaking as a politician, I am speaking as an historian."[29] He added: "I am a free man first; an American second; a public servant third; and a Democrat fourth—in that order."[30] The President continued by saying that he was proud of the record that he and the Eighty-ninth Congress had compiled in legislating federal aid for education. This combination had, in fact, outdone all of the previous administrations combined in providing aid to education. Johnson said:

> When I took the oath in November 1963 as president, there were six education acts on the books—six in more than one hundred sixty years. Abraham Lincoln had the first one passed back in the 1860s. Woodrow Wilson got the second one passed during his administration. Harry Truman got the third one passed during his administration. President Eisenhower passed the other three. That made a total of six bills in more than one hundred sixty years to educate your children.[31]

On the other hand, the Eighty-ninth Congress had passed more than eighteen education bills. Dollars, too, proved the point. When Johnson became president, the national government spent $2 billion per year on education. Now the figure had jumped to well over $6 billion.

In 1967, however, delays in getting some of the education bills through Congress indicated that LBJ's honeymoon with Congress was almost over. Some old allies—such as Jacob Javits, Wayne Morse, and Ralph Yarborough—were beginning to question the high expenditure rate. To compensate, in July Joe Califano announced some new procedures to thirteen members of the staff, which would provide two more days for planning congressional support. He ordered that congressional information henceforth would be reported on Saturday instead of Monday and that Henry Wilson and Mike Manatos would make condensations and immediately inform the president. "It is essential," said the same memo, "that these procedures be followed to coordinate the flow of congressional information, to decrease the amount of reading material now required of the president and to obtain the maximum results from our efforts to enact the president's legislative program." [32]

A team effort in late summer and early fall had produced results. But it was almost time once again for another State of the Union message. Rampant inflation and an escalating war necessitated the review of priorities and the formation of new tactics. Some dissension, too, had started within the administration ranks. Long work periods, divided allegiances, and a troubled, impatient president brought tempers to the boiling point more frequently than in the past. Some aides decided that they had been expended beyond reasonable limits and made no bones about wanting to resume their private lives. In the future, Johnson would appoint older and more experienced personnel to replace members of the major and minor braintrusts. Danger signals here and there, such as the cooling of Congress to LBJ's education legislation, suggested that it would be impossible to do much toward expanding the Great Society at home. This meant that if new departures were to continue the emphasis would have to be worldwide—not national. In short, LBJ was faced with the question, Could the war on poverty be exported to distant horizons?

CHAPTER TWELVE

A Distant Utopia

"This year I propose major new directions in our program of foreign assistance to help those countries who will help themselves. We will conduct a worldwide attack on the problems of hunger and disease and ignorance. . . . We will aid those who educate the young in other lands, and we will give children in other continents the same head start we are trying to give our own children."
—Lyndon Baines Johnson, 1966

THE UNITED STATES became a world power in the dawning of the twentieth century. Events just before and after the "Splendid Little War" with Spain brought recognition as a mature nation. The Open Door policy of Secretary of State John Hay advertised an interest in China and Manchuria, and the Spanish-American War itself hastened the annexation of Hawaii, fostered a curious relationship with Cuba under the Platt Amendment, and brought Puerto Rico and the Philippine Islands under the Star-Spangled Banner. Monied interests and missionaries sped across the oceans to build railroads, sign trade agreements, and save souls. The disillusionment of the 1920s and '30s stemmed the tide of zealous expansionists, and America turned isolationist almost as quickly as it had moved toward imperialism. World War II, however, brought new realities and President Harry Truman

in his inaugural address of 1949 stated that the United States
would once more venture beyond its borders. But this time
benevolence, not greed or passion, would motivate. The
fourth point of his speech announced that the country would
now "embark upon a bold new program for making the benefits of our scientific advances and industrial progress available
for the improvement and growth of underdeveloped countries."[1] So began, among other things, a great adventure in
American education. College and university personnel
traveled in large numbers to other lands, especially South
America, India, and Africa, to build schools, write textbooks,
recruit students, and modernize educational thought and
practice.

President Dwight D. Eisenhower slowed this trend, but his
successor, John Kennedy, obtained international publicity for
his imaginative Peace Corps. Young and old from many walks
of life were trained to help individuals and villages in deserts
and jungles with grass roots problems. Lyndon Johnson
wanted to follow in the footsteps of Franklin Roosevelt's Good
Neighbor Policy, Truman's Point Four Program, and
Kennedy's Alliance for Progress and Peace Corps, but he
inherited a war in Southeast Asia that had drained America's
leadership and economic surplus almost from the beginning of
his administration. Up to 1964, Johnson, and his predecessors,
had looked upon Vietnam as an aberration—something to be
dealt with, but a minor conflict where one simply reacted to
events as they occurred. The so-called Gulf of Tonkin Resolution passed by the United States Congress changed the nature
of America's participation and ended a decade of peace.

The Gulf of Tonkin Resolution charged that the communist
regime in Vietnam had violated the principles of the charter of
the United Nations and had repeatedly attacked naval vessels
of the United States in international waters. Moreover, the
government of North Vietnam had been waging war against
its neighbor to the south, and America had joined South Vietnam so that the latter entity could be left in peace to work out

its own problems. The Tonkin Resolution stated that Congress believed that peace in Southeast Asia was vital to the self-interest of the United States, and authorized the commander-in-chief "to take all necessary measures to repel any armed attack against the forces of the United States and to prevent further aggression."[2] The resolution was to expire when the president determined that the security and peace had been reasonably assured. Members of Congress debated the Tonkin Resolution for eight hours before passing the measure. Only two senators cast negative ballots, and the House of Representatives voted for it 416 to 0. If ballots can be considered a mandate, surely Lyndon Johnson had one.

The lopsided vote produced no victory celebration in the White House. Johnson, like Woodrow Wilson, wanted to be a reformer, and the Gulf of Tonkin Resolution was clear evidence that the situation in Vietnam had to be given concerted attention. Moreover, the chances of beating communist Vietnam and its allies were slim, Johnson knew. A no-win situation was at hand. To a biographer, Johnson declared:

I knew from the start that I was bound to be crucified either way I moved. If I left the woman I really loved—the Great Society—in order to get involved with that bitch of a war on the other side of the world, then I would lose everything at home. All my programs. All my hopes to feed the hungry and shelter the homeless. All my dreams to provide education and medical care to the browns and the blacks and the lame and the poor. But if I left that war and let the Communists take over South Vietnam, then I would be seen as a coward and my nation would be seen as an appeaser and we would find it impossible to accomplish anything for anybody anywhere on the entire globe.[3]

In retrospect, perhaps the situation was not as desperate as Johnson believed. But it appears that he took the advice of his Joint Chiefs of Staff and others, and plunged into murky waters on faith.

That Johnson admired Woodrow Wilson, who found himself in a similar situation, is not debatable. Yet Johnson forgot another important pronouncement. In the negotiations that preceded the Treaty of Versailles, Wilson, as one of his Fourteen Points, had said that one future principle ought to be to arrive at covenants of peace openly. The thirty-sixth president, unfortunately for his good name, often operated in a secretive manner. There was, of course, much precedent for so conducting himself in a military situation, but times had changed. The world was tired of war, the press regarded secrecy as deceitful, and large segments of the American people were restless. Then, too, Vietnam presented a political opportunity for those who regretted that the heir to Camelot was a brash Texan instead of a leader with more style. Such people could not attack the Great Society, as it was in harmony with the New Frontier. War, however, was a different matter. Thus at home and abroad the hounds began to bay—a president had been treed and the killing time was imminent.

Lyndon Johnson made two major mistakes in administering the Vietnam War. Both of them were more errors of the heart than errors of judgment. First, Johnson had no real interest in conducting a war. On March 15, 1965, he said:

> I do not want to be the president who built empires, or sought grandeur, or extended dominion. I want to be the president who educated young children to the wonders of their world. I want to be the president who helped to feed the hungry and to prepare them to be taxpayers instead of taxeaters. I want to be the president who helped the poor to find their own way and who protected the right of every citizen to vote in every election. I want to be the president who helped to end hatred among his fellow men and who prompted love among the people of all races and all regions and all parties. I want to be the President who helped to end war among the brothers of this earth.[4]

These remarks certainly suggest the possibility that the president was reluctant to use his executive talents on a wasteful war. He, as an old spiritual put it in another day, "did not want to study war no more."

Second, it is clear in retrospect insofar as Vietnam is concerned that LBJ retained too many New Frontiersmen on his staff after the death of Jack Kennedy. Some of these individuals remembered the futile invasion of the Bay of Pigs in Cuba and felt that Kennedy should have given air cover to the frogmen and soldiers who wanted to replace Fidel Castro. Americans who were captured by Castro had cost the country millions of dollars in medical goods and agricultural machinery. The United States had been embarrassed by Kennedy's indecision in the matter, and the nation lost prestige abroad. The Cuban Quarantine was more successful, but it did not erase the earlier widespread humiliation. In the case of Southeast Asia, New Frontiersmen believed that the United States could regain some of what had been lost in Cuba by escalating and winning in Vietnam. Johnson, preoccupied with a smooth presidential transition and with instituting his domestic reform programs, followed the advice of others—to the detriment of his place in history.

Then, too, it must be remembered that the situation in Vietnam worsened from 1961 to late 1964 and early 1965. When Kennedy took office, nobody believed that North Vietnam could capture South Vietnam. Just the opposite was true four years later. David Trask, in his perceptive book *Victory Without Peace*, later wrote that "the Viet Cong, controlling most of the Vietnamese countryside, was likely to achieve victory in the absence of even more American assistance."[5] In this light, Secretary of Defense Robert McNamara urged Johnson to escalate. The precise advice of Dean Rusk, secretary of state, and the Joint Chiefs of Staff is not yet public. But there is no reason to believe that their suggestions were contrary to what had been proposed by McNamara.

And so Johnson escalated. The process of increasing troops and supplies began in 1964 and did not stop until March 31,

1968. In 1964, the president requested $125 million in economic and military aid from Congress. Six months later, on July 27, he sent an additional 5,000 military advisers to Vietnam, bringing the total American troops there to approximately 21,000. The attack on U.S. military personnel in the Gulf of Tonkin and the subsequent Gulf of Tonkin Resolution produced even more escalation. From 1965 to 1968, the number of Americans in Southeast Asia increased each year, reaching a high of some 450,000 under Johnson. Simultaneously, the war spread from the ground and sea to the air. The air force, with LBJ's permission, moved from retaliatory air strikes to Operation Rolling Thunder, a policy which ultimately permitted the bombing of any strategic military target in North Vietnam.

The president's decision to escalate did not end the war, nor did it win him any public support. Hawks wanted cities and harbors bombed as well. Doves felt that the United States should simply pull out. The military establishment was not happy either. On the eve of the bombing halt, General William Westmoreland wanted an additional 250,000 troops. The lack of unity in Washington confused the man on the street. Gradually American citizens came to question the sense of sending their sons and daughters into a situation where even the leaders could not agree on what should be done. This, then, resulted in numerous demonstrations.

Within this context, Johnson moved to do something that no other American president had ever done. He attempted to modernize South Vietnam at the time military personnel were fighting a war. His country assistance program was designed to show America that some good could come out of evil. He also, of course, could work more enthusiastically on an objective like this than on issuing orders that resulted in death and destruction.

LBJ's time in the South Pacific, as has been stated before, was responsible for his deep interest in Asia. In 1959, for example, when the East-West center was much on his mind,

he told a group of Texans that all freedom-loving nations
ought to have full universities. His own words illustrate that
his effort to export American educational know-how predated
his presidency. He said:

> If we, of this generation, are to insure greatness for our nation,
> survival for our freedoms, and honor for ourselves, we must
> make provision in our land—and in all lands where men are
> free—for education of the first class on all levels.
>
> The fights we have made against poverty, against illiteracy,
> against disease, against injustice, against frustration—these are
> the fights other men now need to make, and they will follow
> those who provide the strongest leadership in these endeavors.
>
> Of all the oppressors with which we wrestle now, the first
> and greatest is ignorance. Freedom has no real meaning in this
> world until we give it meaning in terms of *enlightenment and
> education.*
>
> A century ago, when the founding fathers of Texas made
> provision for a "university of the first class," they were think-
> ing of the great institutions of New England—of *Harvard* and
> of *Yale* and *others.*
>
> *Today we must make other comparisons.* In our world there are
> universities of the first class. Not only at Cambridge and New
> Haven. There are universities of the highest calibre at *Moscow*
> and *Peiping*—and on throughout the world, on every continent
> and in many lands. Wherever we look, men who want to build
> *strong nations*—whether their purpose be good or evil—are
> *starting first* where our forefathers started *more than a hundred
> years ago.* [6]

Several of the speeches Johnson gave after his vice-
presidential trip to Asia in June 1961 reflected a knowledge of
world events and a faith in the curative powers of education.
For instance, he told students at East Kentucky State College
that satellites had made the world much like a neighborhood
community. Courageous Asians were building schools to
alleviate suffering and social injustice. Five years after he made
the dedication speech at the East-West center as president, he

returned to Honolulu to re-emphasize what he had said before. LBJ said on October 18, 1966, that he looked at that state and the center as a cultural bridge between the East and the West. He also made it clear that America's involvement in world affairs was not selfishly motivated. He began:

> In centuries past, men of the West went to Asia for many reasons.
> Some made the long ocean trek in search of wealth.
> Others went as the agents of governments that wanted colonial possessions. Still others went to teach; to treat the sick; to spread the gospel; to aid the farmers; to help build factories; to advise officials; to translate Western works of literature and technology.
> Much that was good and constructive and abiding came from those efforts.
> But it is a fact we must understand and recognize that these movements from West to East were also disturbing and revolutionary in their effect. The West entered the industrial revolution earlier than the East. By this accident of history, the West commanded the tools of modern science and technology sooner than the East. Through colonialism and by other means the West intruded its then superior power into the East. And there was a reaction.
> That reaction has taken many forms, some peaceful and some violent. It should not surprise us that scars—sometimes deep scars—have remained in men's minds and hearts.[7]

Asia had now, Johnson continued, reached a turning point in its history. The United States, he said, should at this time help nations in this area to remain stable, in order for them to have time to decide their own destiny. A new spirit was being born. The Asian and Pacific Council and the Asian Development Bank, for example, were cooperative in nature. In addition, the United States had to form a better relationship with Asian nations which had become adversaries. Of China, he said: "We do not believe in eternal enmity. All hatred among nations must end in reconciliation."[8] He added that America's role in the future should be that "of a neighbor among equals—a partner in the great adventure to bring peace, order, and progress to a part of the world where more than half the human race lives."[9]

The periods LBJ spent in Congress, as vice-president, and as president, had made him a specialist in national defense. His mind bulged with statistics on population, capabilities of conventional and atomic weapons, communications satellites, and space exploration. This information was almost always tied to other nations. Nonetheless, he was not an advocate of war. Yet if a war did have to be fought, he thought, perhaps the destruction could be alleviated by working for progress at the same time. Therefore, he began to compile data on South Vietnam in 1965.

Johnson learned that the average life span in that part of the world was thirty-five years, that the average annual per capita income was less than $100, and that no fewer than twelve thousand people had been killed in the first year of his presidency. These figures suggested the possibility of doing something to raise economic and educational levels in Vietnam's secure areas. Johnson then decided to use the Agency for International Development, the current name for Truman's Technical Cooperation Administration, to help make life better for the Vietnamese. In May 1965, he told an audience of American school administrators gathered in the Rose Garden, "We have gone in there and we have doubled their rice production, we have doubled their pig production, and we have multiplied the children going to school five times, from 300,000 to 1.5 million."[10] Because many military and State Department records still remain classified, it is impossible at present to verify these figures. But it is evident that the president wanted to fight simultaneously a war on poverty in the South and a hot war against the North.

He also hoped that these humanitarian actions would quiet the voices of some leading doves, such as Senator Wayne Morse, who had cast one of the two votes against the Gulf of

Tonkin Resolution. Another outspoken critic was J. William Fulbright, but his soft spot was an educational exchange for American students and professors so that they could study and teach abroad. Johnson outlined the pacification effort in Vietnam and some new proposals in international education in the State of the Union message in 1966. In part, these programs were designed in such a manner as to capture the loyalty of Morse and Fulbright. In this speech, the president promised to help South Vietnam to protect itself from aggression. Then he said that the United States would "continue to help the people care for those that are ravaged by battle, create progress in the villages, and carry forward the healing hopes of peace as best they can amidst the uncertain terrors of war." [11] This made the policy public and quasi-official.

There are many people who must bear some guilt for America's hasty entrance into this military conflict. But one reason not often discussed is that the United States had an appalling ignorance of Asia. Perhaps the man on the street can be forgiven for this omission, but the intellectuals cannot. United States leadership in the twentieth century had been oriented to Europe at the expense of Asia. Many U.S. citizens discovered the complexity of the social, economic, and political state of Vietnam for the first time in Frances FitzGerald's *Fire in the Lake: The Vietnamese and the Americans in Vietnam* which was not published until 1972. Had this book been available ten years earlier perhaps more caution would have been exercised prior to making a military commitment to a nation that already was in rack and ruin.

On March 6, 1966, Lyndon Johnson appointed a task force to examine the health and education needs of the South Vietnamese. Membership included: John Gardner, secretary of Health, Education, and Welfare; Oveta Culp Hobby, the first HEW secretary; Frank Keppel, assistant secretary for education; William H. Stewart, surgeon general for the Public Health Service; and Douglass Cater, among others. This group was instructed to leave for Vietnam on March 12 in order to plan an intensified attack on hunger, disease, and ignorance. The impetus for the formation of the task force came from a conference with Vietnamese officials in Honolulu. John Gardner, who served as spokesman for the team, informed the public what was on the president's mind. He said: "The president has made it clear that the United States has a twofold objective in Vietnam—not only to help the Republic of Vietnam win its war against aggression, but also to lay the groundwork for a meaningful and durable peace by helping the government of Vietnam build a better society for its people." [12]

Of principal concern here is what the "education specialists" attached to the task force had to say about the situation in Vietnam and what type of recommendations were forwarded to the White House. Max A. Braude, Russell Davis, Edward J. Meade, James Earl Rudder, and Howard S. Turner wrote individual reports, and a composite document was shaped later.

Braude looked into the refugee situation, investigating particularly the operations of a new post, the commissioner of refugees, which had been created just prior to the arrival of the team. Before this, the Ministry of Social Welfare and the Ministry of Rural Construction had handled problems related to displaced people. The refugee report was not optimistic about the future: fluctuating security and unstable political conditions inhibited temporary as well as permanent planning.

Russell Davis proved more encouraging in his analysis of the educational system. He felt that an infrastructure had been established that put South Vietnam ahead of other nations in Southwest Asia. About two-thirds of elementary-school-aged children were being accommodated. However, the French overlay on a Mandarin base made schooling in Vietnam more of a cultural acquisition than a formal education. In his report, entitled "Toward a Strategy of Human Resource Development in Vietnam," Davis detailed efforts to use television to teach classes in a three-hundred-mile circle that had Saigon as the center. One hour per day of instruction was in the Vietnamese language and three hours in English.

Edward J. Meade, Jr., a program associate for the Ford Foundation, wrote the longest analysis. His introduction revealed that he had investigated generally into educational affairs, with a special emphasis on teacher training and vocational and technical education. He believed the idea of replacing Viet Cong terror with a new form of political, civic, social, and educational instruction in hamlets was a risk—but a risk well worth taking.

Earl Rudder commented on agricultural and higher education. His insights were most valuable. First, Vietnam did not have a well-defined educational system; one could, however, identify primary, secondary, technical, and higher education as recognizable divisions. Without question, primary and secondary levels were the most advanced. Second, Vietnam, like the United States, had a pluralistic educational system, including public, semi-public, and private schools. Enrollment in these institutions had increased from 663,720 in 1956–57 to 1,622,828 ten years later. Third, the new textbooks written in the Vietnamese language seemed to be having a good effect, and he estimated the literacy level at about eighty-five percent. Last, while some progress was evident, there were some real problems: school attendance was not mandatory; some students enrolled in educational institutions to evade the draft; there was little cooperation or coordination among schools; and agricultural education remained woefully weak—Vietnam had no specialized libraries in this area and what books did exist on the subject were printed in French. The latter was a real tragedy, as most of the people in Vietnam made their living from agricultural pursuits.

The report of Howard S. Turner centered on school construction. In the next fiscal year, Secretary Gardner prepared a document that followed up the Vietnam task force. His report suggested that real progress in terms of numbers had been made. Using U.S. funds, the country assistance program had been instrumental in strengthening the hamlet schools. In

1966, 2,157 schools had been built in the villages, as compared to 1,430 in 1965. The former figure represented a 49 percent increase. Vietnam now had approximately 6,291 classrooms, and 3,323 new teachers had been certified in 1966 alone. This translated into a 33-percent rise in the number of teachers over the previous year; the total number of available teachers in 1966 approximated 8,720. Projected goals for 1967 were 3,000 additional classrooms and 4,000 new teachers.

Other developments were also in the making. For example, thirty education chiefs in the provinces had been brought to the United States for a ninety-day study-observation tour of American elementary education. More education advisers were now based in Vietnam. Fourteen million American-authored textbooks were currently in use. Twenty percent of the forty-six provincial education chiefs had been supplied with motor vehicles so that they could inspect school operations in their respective districts. Contracts had been made for the construction of additional normal, engineering, and agricultural schools. Great strides were being taken to make schools more efficient, and special teams were in the process of establishing a materials center to lend instructional equipment to instructors and students. Also, efforts were underway to make Vietnamese high schools more comprehensive, and radio broadcasts were being used to give language instruction to teachers. A model American secondary high school was being built in Saigon as a contrast to the French lycée pattern and the construction of a modern multi-purpose university was projected to help modernize existing social and economic institutions in Vietnam when peace arrived.

Johnson personally spoke on behalf of the pacification program and offered support to others who wrote on the subject. On May 13, 1965, he addressed the Association of American Educational Cartoonists with a speech entitled "Vietnam: The Third Face of the War." He explained:

> Education is the keystone of future development in Vietnam.
> It takes trained people to man the factories, to conduct the

administration, and to form the human foundation for an
advancing nation.

This, then, is the third face of our struggle in Vietnam. It
was there when the war began. It will be there when peace
comes to us—and so will we—not with soldiers and planes, not
with bombs and bullets, but with all the wondrous weapons of
peace in the twentieth century. [13]

In 1966 and 1967, Ruth Sheldon Knowles did the research for
an essay called "The Three-R War in Vietnam," which she
planned to publish in the *Reader's Digest*. She wrote to Johnson
for a quote that she could use in her article, stating that the
people were hungry to hear some positive news about the war
instead of getting only "blood-mud-and-politics." Johnson
complied, forwarding the above quotation.

The escalating war in Vietnam drew criticism at first from
abroad. Thus the administration searched for ways to develop
a more positive world image in the area of foreign affairs.
Consequently, in 1965 the president began to think about
making education a part of American foreign policy and to
create goodwill by offering leadership in international education. Help came from several quarters. John Gardner had been
chairman of the United States Advisory Commission on
International Education and Cultural Affairs prior to serving
as secretary of HEW. The U.S. Office of Education under his
leadership took more interest in implementing and coordinating international education. And last, Johnson's appointment
of Charles Frankel as assistant secretary of state for educational and cultural affairs was a brilliant move. Frankel had
just finished a book on American cultural policy when he
joined the administration in 1964 and this made him a natural
to advise in international education. Frankel was reluctant to
accept the appointment, but conversations with Fulbright and
John Kenneth Galbraith turned the tide. Galbraith told the
New York philosophy professor: "This president's an old
schoolteacher. He ought to like the kind of thing you repre-

sent. Maybe you can give him something more constructive to think about than Vietnam."[14]

Other people, too, had an interest in international education. William Fulbright and Wayne Morse had been zinging Johnson relentlessly of late, and LBJ thought that a foray into international education might bring them closer to the administration. In 1965, the president told Doug Cater to prepare a special address on the subject. This speech was to be presented at the Smithsonian Institution in September. The presentation was heard by a large number of Americans as well as by representatives from almost one hundred foreign countries. In a meeting just prior to the speech, Cater met with Gardner, Frankel, and Joseph Laitin in the Fish Room. He said the president considered education as "the number-one work of the nation for quite some time. He has been indicating that he did not regard this interest as stopping at the water's edge. So, he had charged in this speech a task force that is to be set up, growing out of these initial works, to come up with a plan for international education cooperation."[15] Cater then posed some questions: How could the federal government do a better job in international education? How could American educational institutions, including the Smithsonian, be more effectively brought in on the international program? How could the private sector of the economy contribute? How could America find better ways of cooperating with the efforts of other countries in this field? The task force on international education was to report in January 1966.

LBJ delivered the Smithsonian speech in sweltering heat, and it did not get the attention it deserved from the audience. Moreover, the *New York Times* newspaper was on strike, so that the public at home and abroad did not get customary coverage of a major policy pronouncement. Johnson initially paid homage to Smithson, an English scientist who bequeathed his entire fortune for the "increase and diffusion of knowledge among men" in a country that he never visited. Smithson, Johnson thought, had left a threefold legacy: the notion that learning respects no geographic boundary, the concept of a partnership between government and private enterprise serving the greater good of both, and the idea that the growth and spread of learning must be the first work of a nation that desires to be free. The second section of the speech was titled "Ideas, Not Armaments." Here Johnson stated that the founders of the United States believed in the revolutionary power of ideas. A middle passage suggested: "In my own life, I have had cause again and again to bless the chance events which started me as a teacher. In our country and in our time we have recognized, with new passion, that learning is basic to our hopes for America. It is the taproot which gives sustaining life to all of our purposes." [16]

Near the end of the Smithsonian speech, the president announced that he was forming a new task force "to recommend a broad and long-range plan of worldwide educational endeavor." [17] Dean Rusk would chair the group, with Gardner assisting from the sidelines. This new and noble adventure would assist education efforts in developing nations and regions, help American schools to increase their knowledge of the world and the people who inhabit it, work to advance exchange of students and teachers, to increase the free flow of books, ideas, art, and science, and "assemble meetings of men and women from every discipline and every culture to ponder the common problems of mankind." [18] The conclusion quoted Alexis de Tocqueville and stressed the need to banish strangeness and ignorance everywhere. The president's words this day not only initiated the two hundredth anniversary celebration of the birth of James Smithson, but they also proclaimed a new endeavor in international education.

The Task Force on International Education reported more than a month ahead of schedule, on November 9, 1965. Its membership included: Rusk, Cater, Frankel, and Keppel, and David Bell (administrator, Agency for International Development), Leland J. Haworth (National Science Foundation), Leonard Marks (director, United States Information

Agency), Harry C. McPherson (special assistant to LBJ), Henry R. Rowen (assistant director, Bureau of the Budget), Sargent Shriver (director of the Peace Corps), Harold Howe, II (executive director, Learning Institute of North Carolina), James A. Linen, III (president, Time Inc.), Pauline Tompkins (general director, American Association of University Women), Mrs. Arthur Goldberg, and numerous representatives of colleges and universities, such as Harvie Branscomb, Margaret Clapp, John Fischer, John Hope Franklin, Charles Odegaard, Harry Ransom, and Herman B. Wells. William Marvel served as special adviser to the chairman, drawing praise from Rusk for his hard work and insight.

The report summarized what had been done in international education in the past, what was being done today, and listed recommendations for future action. The most important items in the latter category were as follows: The United States should establish within the Department of Health, Education, and Welfare an Institute for Educational Cooperation. This organization would then review and oversee the total government effort in international education. It would provide clearinghouse services, act as a manpower headquarters, administer research funds, create and sustain dialogue with foreign countries, and offer guidance in foreign relations. Next, the commission suggested the creation of a corps of education officers that would serve in American missions abroad. That is, an education officer would be assigned to embassies to coordinate recommendations of the committee on international education. This individual would be responsible to the ambassador of the country in which he resided. And, finally, it was decided that international education in the United States should be upgraded and that binational education commissions ought to be strengthened.

The early submission of the report enabled President Johnson to send a message to Congress on February 2, 1966, in time for the House and Senate to consider passage of the International Education Act in the current session. He included most of the recommendations of the task force. He began his message by saying that education "lies at the heart of every nation's hopes and purposes. It must be at the heart of our international relations."[19] There was little doubt that the IEA was a part of the Great Society scheme and that Johnson wanted to make education a central focus in the development of foreign policy. The implications of this were unprecedented in presidential history. And the consequences were large: Harold Howe once wrote to Douglass Cater that the presidential election of 1968 might be the first time in the history of the United States in which national policies on education might truly become a crucial issue.

Leadership for the IEA was chosen with care. Frankel, at the request of the administration, asked Fulbright to sponsor it in the Senate. Fulbright declined, stating that since most of the funding went to domestic institutions it was outside the purview of the Senate Committee on Foreign Relations. The offer next went to Wayne Morse, who accepted, though he really wanted to discuss Vietnam. John Brademas of Indiana assumed responsibility for the measure in the House of Representatives. He also took some convincing, because sensational news disclosures in the recent past had reported that the Central Intelligence Agency had conducted some covert activities within the Asian Foundation and the National Students Association. Brademas extracted a promise from Johnson that the International Education Act would not be subject to such activities.

The IEA ran into trouble in Congress from its inception. John Rooney, congressman from Brooklyn, New York, held the first budget hearings. A colorful man who made many shudder when they had to appear before him, Rooney ranted and raved when this latest grandiose plan, as he called it, was presented. The Brademas Committee proved more friendly and even suggested that the budget be increased. In the Senate, Morse stated that he believed the bill was too loosely drawn, and he threatened to rewrite it himself. A number of congressmen and senators opposed, because some believed that the administration was simply getting too much of its own way at the expense of Congress. Even the Bureau of the Budget put up an obstacle. It prevented HEW from controlling funds for the Education Corps proposal. This decision was reached in spite of the fact that Rusk and Gardner had discussed the bill and reached a mutual agreement that decreed otherwise. Furthermore, the only subject Congress really wanted to discuss with the president was Vietnam and the Gulf of Tonkin Resolution.

As usual, with a major bill pending, Johnson took to the banquet circuit. He spoke with fervor in February 1966 to the delegates of the American Association of School Administrators. He spoke of the Great Society. Vietnam was mentioned. He defended the International Education Act. And then he turned his words toward education in the future. This subject was now one of the few things left that LBJ really felt like pushing. As Richard Nixon later wrote in his presidential memoirs, Johnson increasingly became discouraged with press coverage of his administration and he quit fighting for programs in public. IEA, however, was an exception. He said:

Tomorrow's schools will reach out to the places that enrich the human spirit: to the museums, to the parks and rivers and mountains.

It will ally itself with the city, its busy streets and factories, its assembly lines and laboratories—so that the world of work does not seem an alien place for the student.

It will be the center of community life, for grownups as well as children: "a shopping center of human services." It might have a community health clinic, a public library, a theater and research facilities. It will provide formal education for all citizens—and it will not close its doors at three o'clock. It will employ its buildings round the clock and its teachers round the year. We cannot afford to have an eighty-five billion dollar plant in this country open less than thirty percent of the time.

In every past age, leisure is a privilege enjoyed by the few at the expense of the many. But in the age waiting to be born, leisure will belong to the many at the expense of none. Our people must learn to use this gift of time—and that means one more challenge for tomorrow's schools.

I am not describing a distant Utopia, but the kind of education which must be the great and urgent work of our time. By the end of this decade, unless the work is well along, our opportunity will have stepped by.[20]

This clarion call, however, did not stir support for pending bills, nor did it generate esteem and enthusiasm for the tall Texan who had done so much for education in America.

The lack of support by educational leaders is surprising, but it can easily be explained. Much of the criticism aimed at Johnson by pedagogues can be traced to the campuses of American colleges and universities. In the 1950s, Northern college youths had gone south to help blacks end segregation and register to vote. The unfair treatment that they saw accorded black Americans radicalized them, and when they returned to school, they politicized their campuses. At first, they protested that their degree programs were not relevant: their courses, they claimed, were aimed more at transmitting the cultural heritage than studying the world around them. Then they moved to the point of calling institutions of higher education autocratic organizations. To get attention, they marched, demonstrated, and shouted obscenities. After all, the Right had purged colleges in the early fifties. Could not the Left do the same?

Vietnam intensified protests on college campuses. It was time to attack the national president as well as college presidents. They were probably all in league anyhow, the anti-establishment activists reasoned. During the Johnson administration, organized protests broke out from Cornell in New York to Berkeley in California. A new generation of college faculty, some up from the working ranks as a result of obtaining academic credentials through the World War II and Korea G.I. Bill of Rights, knew the horrors of war firsthand.

Many of them were sympathetic to student demands, and on occasion they marched and picketed with their charges. College presidents, who obtained state and federal funds on the basis of head counts, were afraid to expel students in large numbers. In this atmosphere, it was dangerous to praise Johnson for his education legislation. Their silence was interpreted as dissatisfaction, leaving the president to wonder if he had any friends at all.

It was not only the educational community that deserted their president. In 1966, momentum rushed downhill as rapidly as it had risen earlier. Johnson's prediction that he would lose a million voters a month after the election in 1964 had come true. The month of April brought the loss of a trusted adviser when Francis Keppel resigned his post. The president wrote to this key member of the educational establishment, "I accept your resignation with regret. Over the last four years we have fought many battles together in the cause of education. You have been a valiant warrior and you will be sorely missed."[21] Nevertheless, the IEA had to be passed. Cater worked with Senator Morse, who was having trouble getting a quorum for his subcommittee. And he talked at length with Yarborough, Randolph, and Robert Kennedy to prevent troublesome add-ons. The opposition, mostly Republican, felt that clarification was needed to distinguish between the International Education Act, National Defense Education Act language programs, the role of the Agency for International Development, and the Fulbright exchange program.

The IEA did pass, on October 29, 1966. But it was not funded. Some $140 million had been requested for the next three fiscal years: $10 million for 1967, $40 million for 1968, and $90 million for 1969. The absence of financial support was disappointing, yet a half-loaf was better than no loaf at all. Johnson, as he had promised, signed the measure on Asian soil, choosing Thailand University in Bangkok. "I think," he said, "it is fitting and appropriate to sign this program into law here today on this stage of this great university in a land where international cooperation has become a national byword."²² In the same speech he quoted the prominent transcendentalist philosopher Ralph Waldo Emerson, who had written that the true assessment of a nation was in the kind of man a country turns out. "That is the meaning," Johnson continued, "of my legislative program in the United States—the creation of a Great Society where each American has the opportunity to pursue excellence—to be the best that is within him to be."²³

The battle over funding continued into the next legislative session. In January 1967, when Congress reconvened, the death of John Fogarty, chairman of the Health, Education, and Welfare subcommittee, on the opening day signified that the prospects for money were exceedingly slim. John Rooney bore down hard on Frankel in April. He said that the International Education Act was the camel's nose in a tent, that a whole new bureaucracy was being planned and that he wanted no part of it.

Paul Miller of HEW and Frankel continued to lobby. The odds, however, were against them. An article in *Ramparts* magazine concerning the infiltration by the CIA of educational organizations abroad caused widespread concern and reaction. Moreover, some unfavorable newspaper criticism of federal grants given to war-protesting academicians produced some genuine embarrassment to Johnsonites. Also, the group in Congress that had always been opposed to federal aid to education was now growing in strength, and such people could not be steamrollered as they had been in the past. At the same time, overzealous bureaucrats were striving to give the outward appearance of unity within the administration. One such individual, who was never named, called Charles Frankel and asked why his programs should be supported when he was not one hundred percent in favor of the war. He also wondered whether Frankel's lack of enthusiasm could be attributed to the fact that the Vietnamese people were not of the right color. After all, the caller said, Fulbright did not favor the war because he was a white supremacist, and Frankel and the senator from Arkansas were friends.

Not long afterward, at a Senate hearing, John McClelland stated that he had had enough of this international business. His outspoken comment signaled the end of the effort to fund the International Education Act. The bill became a dead letter on the books. And so did Frankel. He resigned his post and returned to his teaching duties in New York. He did, however, take time to record his personal governmental experiences in a book entitled *High on Foggy Bottom.*

Concurrent with his attempt to pass and fund an international educational measure, Johnson tried to develop an imaginative program related to the use of television as an instructional device. On May 19, 1965, Douglass Cater sent a long memorandum on the subject to President Johnson. He reminded his boss that he had recently spoken to the National Association of Broadcasters on the future of educational television. That group had established a study committee and now requested that a national commission on the subject be appointed. The United States at this time had over one hundred educational television stations and over three hundred educational radio stations in operation. Most of these organizations were funded by the Ford Foundation. The support, however, was not strong enough to ensure even programming. Cater discussed the matter with Wilbur Cohen and Keppel later, reaching the conclusion that either the government or the Carnegie Corporation should indeed create a national commission.

By September, discussion of instructional television entered the international arena. Harold Rosen, assistant manager of the Space Systems Division at Hughes Aircraft Company, wrote Leonard Marks of the United States Information Agency a memorandum. He hoped that Johnson would help establish an educational television system in Latin America through the use of communications satellites. In the past, Rosen had approached Fulbright, who had not been receptive to the idea. The president, as everybody knew, was a television fan and interested in international education. So Rosen hoped his idea might germinate in the White House. Meanwhile, Donald B. MacPhail, acting assistant administrator for technical cooperation and research, joined in the endeavor. He detailed the uses of television that the Agency for International Development had been making. His report stated that there were some two hundred and forty transmitters functioning at present in some thirty underdeveloped countries. For example, the Washington County School Board of Hagerstown, Maryland, had a contract to assist the nation of Nigeria to solve some instructional problems in Africa. The Peace Corps, in conjunction with the Agency for International Development, was working in Brazil and Colombia to build transmitters and improve reception and classroom instruction. Other areas needed help, but lack of electrical power and language difficulties were holding back progress. In Africa alone, the best estimates suggested that Nigeria had one hundred and fifty different indigenous languages, Ghana fifty, Tanganyika one hundred, and Sierra Leone sixteen.

The big advantage of educational television was that it could reach large numbers of students at a minimal cost. Prospects in this area seemed worth further exploration. In late 1966, therefore, Johnson appointed a new task force, the White House task force on educational television in less-developed countries. He selected Leonard Marks to serve as chairman. Paul Miller, Cater, Frankel, and others were to assist. The membership met in December 1966 and in January, February, and May 1967. Specifically, the group was charged with assessing the effectiveness of television as an educational and nation-building tool in less-developed countries. Then, too, it was to determine what resources were presently available, what would be needed in the near future, and how big a role the United States should play in assisting other countries. There is much evidence to suggest that Johnson himself established these priorities and sent them to Cater.

The experiment that served as the major model for using educational television as an instructional tool was being instituted in American Samoa, in the South Pacific. In August 1965, Clifford H. Block of AID visited the project and wrote a report detailing how television there was the basis for almost all instruction. The United States had administered American Samoa since 1900. This "nation" consisted of six islands, of which the main one, Tutuila, had a population of some 18,000. The Manu'a group of three islands about seventy miles from Tutuila had 4,000 inhabitants, while the neighboring islands of now Independent Samoa contained 100,000 people.

Distance and sparse population posed severe problems. Moreover, the islands contained different cultures. The major one, of course, was Polynesian, but a genetic mixture of Japanese, American, and East Indian existed as well. The United States had not been generous with money. A magazine article entitled "Samoa: America's Shame in the South Seas" stated that little had been done to modernize the area until H. Rex Lee assumed control in 1961.

Governor Lee, once he had assessed the situation, concluded that the core of the education system was forty-three village elementary schools which served about fifty-five hundred students. The teachers were generally ill-trained, by American standards: most had only a fifth-grade education. The textbooks in use were culturally oriented to the mainland. Schoolrooms were barren. And money was scarce—so scarce that it was impossible to upgrade the system in a traditional manner. It was decided, therefore, that educational television was the only practical way of modernizing. By 1965, eight television schools, all elementary, were in operation. Expansion would be continued until seven thousand schools were involved. Samoa, then, became the only place in the world where resident teachers were ancillary to those who instructed via the airwaves.

Block, after his visit to the South Pacific, reported favorably on the Samoan experiment to the White House Task Force on Educational Television in Less-Developed Countries. Recent inroads into communications satellites like Early Bird, the first commercial communications satellite launched over the Atlantic Ocean on April 6, 1965, made the idea even more intriguing. Could television be used to export the Great Society abroad? Johnson thought that it could indeed. On March 3, 1966, he told Congress that dynamic developments in "communications and transportation are fundamental for the achievement of the aims of the Great Society for the people of our land and other lands."[24] Early Bird could become a new force in the world. "This historical space bridge will be enlarged. Satellites scheduled to be launched later this year are to span the Pacific and expand coverage over the Atlantic," LBJ promised.[25]

Johnson's new discoveries meant more speeches had to be given to promote his plans. He discussed educational television at length in an address to the World Conference on Education, held on October 8, 1967, in Williamsburg, Virginia. His initial comments focused on the trillions of dollars then being spent on the machinery of death and war. The world needed to concentrate on other things, he said. In this, the richest age the world had ever known, there were regions where eight out of ten people were illiterate. People died without knowing how to spell even the simplest words. Such a situation was lamentable, LBJ said, and many were now crying, "Shame on the world, and shame on its leaders."[26]

History was once more on the president's mind. Clio's disciples had written of the world's elite instead of the common man. Thus citizens were not aware of the lot of the poor in America or the poor of the world. Johnson identified himself as one astute enough to see the inequity that had been committed, and he thought he should be given some credit for rising to the challenge. "If future historians . . . should seek a name for this period in America, I hope they will give consideration to calling it the age of education."[27] After all, his administration had increased expenditures in this area from $4.7 billion in 1964 to $12.3 billion in 1967.

In the middle of his Williamsburg address, Johnson in dramatic fashion took up the matter of educational television. Progress in traditional education was being made, he said, but at a slow pace. It took too long to make boys and girls into teachers. What could be done? Johnson said:

I can see no reason in the world why modern technology cannot, for example, permit the best professors in the world to teach students all over the world in a field where vocabulary and the concepts and the standards are uniform; and this is true of many fields, I think—science, natural and social.

Moreover, our capacity to produce microfilm and distribute information should make it possible for a young scholar or researcher at any place in the world to have the same basic library facilities that are available in the British Museum, the Library of Congress, or at one of the great university libraries.

Therefore, I would like to suggest to you this evening some consideration be given to some of these challenges: How can we use what we already know about educational television to accelerate the pace of basic education for all the children of the world? How can we use modern technology to economize on that most essential and that most needed educational resource, the good teacher?

How can we make the good teacher available to the maximum number of students in the world through television?

How can we make the best scholars and teachers in the world available to all universities—wherever they may be—through satellite communications?[28]

Then, as was so characteristic of Johnson in recent months, his thoughts drifted back to his own roots—humble roots, he would likely have said. "So often," he remarked, "have I thought of the wonders that could have been brought to those young, struggling minds with warped bodies that I taught back when I was in that little rural school on the United States-Mexican border if we had had satellite communications, and the best scholars and best teachers had been able to invade those classrooms, to expose those Mexican children to the English language."[29]

The next month, the president signed the Public Broadcasting Act in the East Room of the White House. He called television a revolutionary invention that could make America a replica of the ancient Greek marketplace, a place where public affairs could be conducted in front of the nation's citizens. On February 5, 1968, a tired executive provided a disinterested nation with what could be a fitting epitaph for his administration. In a message to Congress, he recalled the four freedoms that Franklin Roosevelt had identified in his January 6, 1941, inaugural address—freedom of speech, freedom of worship, freedom from want, and freedom from fear. He reminded those who worked on the Hill that America had stood for these principles at home and overseas. To these, he added a fifth freedom: freedom from ignorance.

Regardless of political consequences, LBJ would now have his say. Perhaps he should have spoken of intellectuality, but he preferred to discuss literacy. Perhaps he ought to have been more concerned with Europe than Asia. Perhaps it would have been more chic to disdain rather than support education. Perhaps it was unwise in this sophisticated age to talk about dreams out loud. But he said what he felt was true, and damn the consequences.

> The fifth freedom is freedom from ignorance.
> It means that every man, everywhere, should be free to develop his own talents to their full potential—unhampered by arbitrary barriers of race or birth or income.
> We have already begun the work of guaranteeing that fifth freedom.
> The job, of course, will never be finished. For a nation, as for an individual, education is a perpetually unfinished journey, a continuing process of discovery.[30]

More education bills would be passed by Congress in the

time that remained of the administration of Lyndon Johnson. The great victories, however, had been won.

The war in Vietnam adversely affected international as well as domestic educational programs. Guns and butter do not mix. And LBJ had difficulty in understanding the contemporary generation. No man in public life in the United States had ever done so much for the poor, nor had anybody worked harder for civil rights. His legislation in education was more than had ever been done before, and it is unlikely that the level he achieved will ever be approached again. Despite great personal abuse, LBJ had not retaliated against the opposition. He did not publicly chastise critics, nor did he withhold federal funds from protestors. Research grants, for example, went to the most deserving person, regardless of his or her politics. Perhaps the most he did in a public sense was to quit ordering newspapers that were violently against him and his policies. Nevertheless, the hurrahs shouted for him were as faint as they were infrequent.

CHAPTER THIRTEEN

The Cross
of Leadership

"The presidency is a lonely, awesome job. Decisions of historic impor-
tance must be made every day and events will not wait. Have we
rewarded the men who shoulder this load with loyalty, with trust?
Have we given them credit for good motives? In times of trouble do we
give them the benefit of any reasonable doubt? The answer, for many
Americans, must be no. Our record is a sorry and non-partisan one
which will indict Americans of both political parties and all shades of
opinion. Every president and important national leader of modern
times has borne the same heavy cross."
                                            —Morris K. Udall, 1963

A S HE SAID SO MANY times in his last years in office,
Lyndon Johnson wished the twilight of his presidency to
be known as the "Age of Education." He hoped that reason
would overcome emotion in the daily business of making
democracy work. Men and women, young and old, regardless
of economic circumstance, creed, or color, he wanted to uplift
toward the Great Society. America, too, was to be a model of
a kind, a "city on a hill" to be imitated by others in faraway
places. In 1964–1965 everything seemed possible, but in 1967–
1968, nothing seemed right. The nation had turned topsy-
turvy. Youth rebelled against the church, the educational system and the government. The president was taunted with
jeers like "Hey, hey, LBJ. How many kids did you kill

277

today?" The next older generation was infected with what a popular rock-and-roll artist would later call "middle-aged craziness." Prosperity disintegrated American families at an alarming rate, and increased leisure created a lingering rest-lessness. Many in this category dropped out of society, imitat-ing the hobo, and the beatnik of previous decades. The old were scared by inflation, shocked at the attacks on patriotism, and amazed by the depths of social alienation. The crime rate rose to disturbing proportions while racial unrest bred in long, hot summers. Rapid change evoked a number of emo-tions—frustration, anger, rage, fear, and even violence of two types. The first was exemplified by the war in Vietnam and the assassination of political leaders such as Martin Luther King and Robert Kennedy. The second type of violence related to rhetoric: obscenities, racial slurs, and slander. That old adage, "Sticks and stones may break my bones, but words can never hurt me," was simply not true. Words, and words alone, could cut as sharply as a knife.

It is impossible to estimate how many people in America believed in the dreams of the Great Society. But when rising expectations were not immediately fulfilled, the nation experi-enced an enormous depression. The intellectuals and the press combined to discredit the man in the White House and to search for someone with more acceptable credentials. The man on the street lashed out blindly, sometimes suspecting that a conspiracy was corrupting the present leadership.

Morris Udall, a Congressman from Arizona, wrote of this phenomena in an essay entitled "We Abuse Our Leaders," which he published in his newsletter shortly after the death of John Kennedy. He was shaken by the hate mail that poured into his office. One letter written on the day of the funeral characterized national leaders and the programs of the federal government as "a . . . hypo of 'Jew deals' by the Christian-hating Zionist Mongolian Marxist satanic perverted Jews who control every phase of our once great Republic. And the Marxist Jews move 'Jew-stooges' like you and your brother [Stewart] around like checkers on a board."[1]

All immediate past presidents of the United States, Udall continued, had suffered similar abuse. A talented, kind, and distinguished Herbert Hoover had been blamed for causing the Great Depression. An imaginative, courageous Franklin Roosevelt had been charged with almost every vile act possible. "If there is a foul word," Udall wrote, "not applied to him, I don't know it."[2] An unassuming Harry Truman had found himself frequently subjected to sneers and cruel jokes. And Dwight D. Eisenhower, a fighter for his country in war and peace, had to face accusations of being a communist agent.

Though Udall did not write about him, Lyndon Johnson received similar treatment in the final months of his presidency. He was portrayed as crude in speech, vulgar in dress, a southern demagogue, a liar, a religious hypocrite, an inept commander-in-chief, insincere, a second-rater who did not understand urban life, a charlatan who had stolen public office, and an innocent who still believed in copybook maxims. Congressman Udall closed his 1963 newsletter with words that were more appropriate in 1968. "The greatest need in America today is not fear or suspicion. The greatest need is *trust*. We need to trust and respect and support the leaders our people have elected."[3]

It was a patient and tolerant Lyndon Johnson who walked down the aisle in January 1967 to deliver the annual State of the Union message to Congress. In spite of all the evidence to the contrary, the president still believed in the goodness of America, and he had no doubt that reason and logic would return when peace provided the time for perspective. He spoke to the country over television not with the prose of a Richard Goodwin, but with the directness of a father talking to children. "I have come here tonight," he began, "to report to you that this is a time of testing for our nation."[4] The big question at home, he went on, is whether or not we want to continue working for better opportunities for all. The big question abroad is whether we should stay involved in a costly war when the objective is limited and the personal danger to individual Americans is remote. Johnson, of course, answered these queries himself. Neither the Great Society nor the war in Vietnam, he thought, should be abandoned. In the first part of his address, the president reviewed government spending since his last annual report to the House and Senate. The next section spelled out future domestic concerns. Progress was to be continued by *programs, partnerships, priorities, prosperity,* and *peace.* The previous three years had been a process of trial and error as new *programs* for social advancement had been forged. Much of value had been learned. Now a number of administrative changes were needed to gain a higher degree of efficiency. For example, LBJ proposed that the Department of Commerce and the Department of Labor fuse into something called the Department of Business and Labor. *Partnership* referred to creative federalism, though the concept was not identified by name. Specifically he advocated that the federal government work in concert with city, county, and state agencies to achieve desired ends. Under *priorities,* the president outlined urban and rural needs as well as advocating the strengthening of education. Headstart required attention, Social Security benefits needed to be raised, and a model-cities program was outlined to combat urban decay. A domestic war on crime in the cities needed to be launched as well. In the section entitled *prosperity* LBJ urged that attention be given to the economy to prevent unnecessary inflation. And last, he asked both Republicans and Democrats to work toward *peace.*

LBJ next turned his attention toward the international situation, specifying problems in Latin America, Africa, the Middle East, Western Europe, the Soviet Union, and Eastern Europe. He made some interesting comments in regard to the communist world, identifying U.S. relationships with Russia and Eastern Europe as in a period of transition. He explained: "We have avoided both the acts and the rhetoric of the Cold War. When we have differed with the Soviet Union, or other nations, for that matter, I have tried to differ quietly and with courtesy, and without venom."[5] In fact, significant efforts were underway to reduce the tensions of the Cold War and reach for detente. In the recent past, agreements had been made with the United Nations for the peaceful use of space. Direct air flights to the Soviet Union had been approved, commercial credits were being extended to Hungary, Bulgaria, Czechoslovakia, Romania, and Yugoslavia, and arms control was under discussion. Johnson concluded this section of his speech by saying, "Every member of the world community now bears a direct responsibility to help bring our most basic human account into balance."[6]

In the next section, Johnson turned his attention to Southeast Asia and the war in Vietnam. He promised a more detailed report to Congress in the near future. For now, he simply stated that the United States was in Vietnam because this country and its allies were committed by the Southeast Asia Treaty Organization, Congress had voted to intervene, and the people of South Vietnam wanted us there. This, however, was not what was causing controversy in the United States. Diminishing support for the war had resulted from the fact that not all available men and weapons were being employed to achieve a total victory. (Disillusionment over the war itself would come later.) LBJ made no false promises. America had 500,000 troops in Vietnam, and yet the end of the war was not in sight. Moreover, the pacification program had run into trouble. Johnson said: "While I cannot report the desired progress in the pacification effort, the very distinguished and able ambassador, Henry Cabot Lodge, reports that South Vietnam is turning to this task with a new sense of urgency."[7] The speaker left no doubt that he would rather rebuild Vietnam than destroy it. "The moment that peace comes, as I pledged in Baltimore, I will ask the Congress for funds to join in an international program of reconstruction and development for all the people of Vietnam—and their deserving neighbors who wish our help."[8]

Johnson's State of the Union address for 1967 was apt. The sixties were a time of testing and a time of transition. The president explained that such periods were difficult ones:

"The transition is sometimes slow; sometimes unpopular; and almost always painful; and often quite dangerous."[9] He did not stress education, though he would sign eight new bills before his next annual message. (Most of these measures would amend acts that had been passed earlier.) Yet he did not neglect the Great Society. "Let us be remembered," he closed, "as a president and a Congress who tried to improve the quality of life for every American—not just the rich, not just the poor, but every man, woman, and child in this great nation of ours."[10]

All eight education bills received approval late in the session. The first, the Teacher Corps and Educational Personnel Training Act, extended the Teacher Corps through 1970 and amended Title 5 of the Higher Education Act of 1965. Funding levels were set at $33.1 million for 1968, $385.2 million for 1969, and $492.2 million for 1970. New Mexico's Senator Joseph Montoya sponsored the Veterans' Pension and Readjustment Assistance Act of 1967. Payments to veterans and their dependents were increased, and wartime benefits were extended to the men and women who had served in the armed services since the passage of the Gulf of Tonkin Resolution. Costs the first year were expected to reach some $285.6 million. This bill was signed the last day of August.

In September, President Johnson added his signature to Public Law 90-82, which amended the college work study program. The number of hours students could work was raised, while the federal government's share of matching money decreased, falling from 90 percent in 1966, to 85 percent in 1967, to 80 percent in 1968, and to 75 percent in 1969. Festivities for the measure were held in San Antonio, Texas. There the president pointed out that over 300,000 students had been helped since 1964 and that next year the federal government would spend $164 million to send students through college. Johnson had high hopes for such bills. In this case, he said: "The student who works to pay for his education does more than help himself financially. He builds resources of character, self-reliance, and independence that make his degree even more valuable to himself and to the country. And every student in the program contributes importantly to his college and his community."[11]

November saw the passage of three new pieces of legislation. Senator Jennings Randolph of West Virginia introduced the Appalachian Regional Development Act, which passed without prolonged attention or debate.

Warren Magnuson, from Washington, sponsored a measure to establish a Corporation for Public Broadcasting. This legislation created a nonprofit private corporation to facilitate the development of noncommercial educational radio and television broadcasting. The president would appoint a fifteen-member board with the advice and consent of the Senate. Major political parties could have no more than eight members of their party represented on this board. Appointees had to be U.S. citizens and prominent in education or the arts, and this board as a whole was to be broadly representative of the various regions of the country.

The Corporation was authorized to: (1) contract for the production of high-quality programs for distribution to educational radio and television stations; (2) provide funds for noncommercial educational broadcast stations to assist them in programming and operating costs; (3) assist in the establishment and development of one or more *systems* of noncommercial educational radio or television stations throughout the United States and to help in interconnecting facilities for distribution and transmission; (4) encourage the creation of new stations; and (5) conduct research, demonstrations or training on matters related to noncommercial educational television or radio broadcasting. Last, the corporation could not own or operate a station, nor could it support a political party or candidate for public office.

The Corporation for Public Broadcasting Act, and other related national and international measures, qualifies Lyndon Johnson as a pioneer in the communications revolution of this century. He knew full well the importance of the measure when he signed it. He viewed the legislation as an aid to teaching and learning. "I believe the time has come," he said, "to stake another claim in the name of all the people, stake a claim based upon the combined resources of communications. I believe the time has come to enlist the computer and the satellite, as well as television and radio and to enlist them in the cause of education." [12]

Fourteen days after he made these remarks on November 7, he also signed a bill to amend the Library Services and Construction Act of 1964.

Two additional bills were enacted in December. The fourth day of that month brought passage of an extension and expansion of the Mental Retardation Facilities and Community Health Centers Construction Act of 1963. The plight of the mentally retarded had always struck a soft spot in Johnson. He explained in his remarks that facilities for such people had been deficient for some time. Most were cared for in dilapidated buildings that were more than fifty years old. Johnson believed that the government had a responsibility to help those with deficient minds and to save them from "the culture of poverty, physical or spiritual poverty, into which they were all born." [13]

On December 23, the Economic Opportunity Act was amended. Public Law 90–222, sponsored by Clark of Pennsylvania, provided $4.16 billion over the next two years to the Office of Economic Opportunity. Funding for two years instead of one was a significant breakthrough for Johnson. And the total allocation was slightly more than the figure he had suggested earlier. In its final form, however, PL 90–222 instructed the General Accounting Office to investigate OEO programs and report its findings to Congress by December 1, 1968, letting LBJ know that he could not count on the House and Senate to sign any blank checks in the future. Nevertheless, OEO, the heart of the Great Society scheme, did obtain two more years of life.

Although 1967 had not produced startling education legislation, the president believed that what had been done was important in and of itself, and perhaps it also prevented an armed revolution at home. He commented to this effect on December 9, 1967, in a television interview with three well-known reporters—Ray Scherer of NBC, Frank Reynolds of ABC, and Dan Rather of CBS. Much of the questioning pertained to Vietnam. Rather, however, did ask him why Americans, especially blacks who lived in crowded, impoverished, and substandard areas, should not follow an extremist leader and revolt. LBJ had responded to this question many times before, but he went through the appropriate rhetoric once again:

> I told you the reasons why: because revolt and violence are unlawful. It is not going to be allowed. It doesn't solve the problem. It is not the answer to the conditions that exist.
>
> The answer is jobs. The answer is education. The answer is health. If we refuse to give those answers, people are going to lose hope, and when they do, it is pretty difficult to get them to be as reasonable as we think they should be.
>
> But there is every reason why they should not. Violence is not going to produce more jobs. Violence is not going to produce more education. Violating the law and taking the law into your own hands is not going to produce better health or better housing. It is going to produce anarchy. That cannot be tolerated. [14]

The events that occurred in January 1968 set the tone for LBJ's last full year in office. These twelve months someday will stand out as one of the most difficult periods in the history of the country and the presidency. In the third week, Johnson was informed that the North Koreans had captured an American ship, the *Pueblo*. Almost simultaneously, another message indicated American B-52s had drifted over the Cambodian border and that four U.S. planes had been lost. Shortly thereafter, two American aircraft were charged with violating Chinese air space. Then, too, the Tet offensive began in South Vietnam. This attack was so strong that the United States suffered a major military setback, and Tet convinced many Americans that the United States had no further business in Vietnam. Also, Tet stalemated peace talks. In February and March of 1968, a run on the dollar abroad threatened the stability of currency back home. In this atmosphere, Lyndon Johnson went before Congress to give his next State of the Union message.

He delivered his speech on the evening of January 17, 1968, like a man resigned to his fate. Public opinion had been running against him, and Congress was treating his programs with a new independence. His first words forecast that he had a job to do and that it would be done regardless of the consequences. He said: "I was thinking as I was walking down the aisle tonight of what Sam Rayburn told me many years ago: The Congress always extends a very warm welcome to the president—as he comes in."[15] There were few new departures. The war in Vietnam was the first important item on his agenda. Johnson reiterated that he continued to search for peace under what had become known as the San Antonio formula: the bombing of North Vietnam would stop when meaningful talks began and assurances had been made from the other side that advantage would not be taken of America's restraint. Progress in foreign relations, however, had been achieved elsewhere. Trade barriers had been broken, Vice-President Humphrey had visited Africa, and the telephone hot line between Washington and the U.S.S.R. had been used to discuss the June 1967 Arab-Israeli war. The Glassboro Conference had brought Johnson and Chairman Alexis Kosygin into a personal meeting.

The United States continued its efforts to improve the world, Johnson reported, in spite of the lack of success in Vietnam. Food had been shipped to the hungry and medicine to the sick. Ocean research continued, contributions were being made to the International Development Association and the Asian Development Bank, and millions of dollars had been contributed to help avoid the terror of famine. Johnson continued to believe that rich nations could survive only if resources were shared with the poorer nations. He put world problems in human terms. Uncontrolled and dangerous overpopulation in undeveloped countries remained a constant fear; it had to be reduced. Moreover, those who already had life needed assistance. Johnson explained that "we must also improve the lives of children already born in the villages and towns and cities of this earth. They can be taught by great teachers through space communications and the miracle of satellite television—and we are going to bring to bear every resource of mind and technology to help make this dream come true." [16] To the bitter end of his administration, Johnson believed that national and world problems could be resolved.

Next, Johnson examined the domestic situation. Americans in 1968 were as prosperous a people as the world had ever known, and the government was doing more for its citizens than had ever been done before. There was a restlessness in the land, however, that prevented enjoyment. Why, Johnson asked, this restlessness? He answered his own question with a metaphor: when a great ship cuts through the sea, the waters are always stirred and troubled. The American ship now was moving through troubled waters toward new and better shores, and these new shores created questions. Employment was at record heights, but how could we get it higher? How could violence be decreased? How could wages and income for the rural worker be increased? How could decent shelter be given to every family? What steps could be taken to improve health care for all? How could rivers and air be cleansed of impurities? "We have lived with conditions like these for many, many years," Johnson stated. "But much that we once accepted as inevitable, we now find absolutely intolerable." [17]

The Great Society and other reform movements had done much, but they had also created a feeling that all problems could be solved for all time. It was a mood that Europeans would have branded as unrealistic and utopian. Many of Johnson's problems with the public came not because he had given too little, but because he had given too much.

Still, the president took time to ask Congress for additional funds to combat crime, to provide more housing, to reverse civil rights injustices, and to attend to other social matters. He singled out the Higher Education Act and the Juvenile Delinquency Act as the most important educational items on the congressional agenda. LBJ ended his State of the Union address with a detailed analysis of his budget requests and a reaffirmation of the idea that mutually agreed-upon goals could be accomplished:

> If ever there was a people who sought more than mere abundance, it is our people.
> If ever there was a nation that was capable of solving its problems, it is this nation.
> If ever there were a time to know the pride and the excitement and the hope of being an American—it is this time.
> So this, my friends, is the State of our Union: seeking, building, tested many times in this past year—and always equal to the test. [18]

Such a State of the Union address was not easy to deliver. And no doubt the president was not eager to face the Congress again in the near future. But strange times produce unusual events.

The intensity of the war did not diminish. And the Tet offensive continued to shake Americans hard. So hard, in fact, that Johnson found himself in political trouble. He made a poor showing in the 1968 New Hampshire primary, and this spurred him to take more direct action. He had earlier told friends that he would not run for a third presidential term. Now he had to make a definite decision. He had powerful opponents for the nomination, including Eugene McCarthy, Minnesota; Robert Kennedy, New York; George Wallace, Alabama; and more. On March 31, he announced his decision over television. At nine o'clock in the evening, while seated in the White House, he laboriously reviewed the situation in Vietnam and then explained that to bring peace and American troops back home required all of his energy. What followed was a surprise at the time, but in retrospect LBJ's announcement made sense. He closed his speech by stating:

Throughout my entire public career I have followed the personal philosophy that I am a free man, an American, a public servant, and a member of my party, in that order always and only.

For thirty-seven years in the service of our nation, first as a congressman, as a senator, and as vice-president, and now as your president, I have put the unity of the people first. I have put it ahead of any divisive partisanship.

And in these times as in times before, it is true that a house divided against itself by the spirit of faction, of party, of region, of religion, of race, is a house that cannot stand.

There is a division in the American house now. There is a divisiveness among us all tonight. And holding the trust that is mine, as president of all the people, I cannot disregard the peril to the progress of the American people and the hope and the prospect of peace for all peoples.

So, I would ask all Americans, whatever their personal interests or concern, to guard against divisiveness and all its ugly consequences.

Fifty-two months and ten days ago, in a moment of tragedy and trauma, the duties of this office fell upon me. I asked then for your help and God's, that we might continue America on its course, binding up our wounds, healing our history, moving forward in new unity, to clear the American agenda and to keep the American commitment for all of our people.

United we have kept that commitment. United we have enlarged that commitment.

Through all time to come, I think America will be a stronger nation, a more just society, and a land of greater opportunity and fulfillment because of what we have all done together in these years of unparalleled achievement.

Our reward will come in the life of freedom, peace and hope that our children will enjoy through ages ahead.

What we won when all of our people united just must not now be lost in suspicion, distrust, selfishness, and politics among any of our people.

Believing this as I do, I have concluded that I should not permit the presidency to become involved in the partisan divisions that are developing in this political year.

With America's sons in the fields far away, with America's future under challenge right here at home, with our hopes and the world's hopes for peace in the balance every day, I do not believe that I should devote an hour or a day of my time to any personal partisan causes or to any duties other than the awesome duties of this office—the presidency of your country.

Accordingly, I shall not seek, and I will not accept, the nomination of my party for another term as your president.

But let men everywhere know, however, that a strong, a confident and a vigilant America stands ready tonight to seek an honorable peace—and stands ready tonight to defend an honored cause—whatever the price, whatever the burden, whatever the sacrifice that duty may require.[19]

In these dramatic words, the thirty-sixth president of the United States ceased to be a politician and made the full transition to statesman. He sought not to pick a successor, and he eventually made himself available for advice to both major parties' nominees, Hubert Humphrey and Richard Nixon.

Reporters who interviewed the president after the speech could not fully believe what they had heard. Was this one more Johnson attempt at deception? Were there qualifications? Would he accept a draft? Did he plan to support another candidate? One can only speculate on the reaction of those who watched their television sets at home, but it must have been clear to some that an era was ending. The reform impulse started by Franklin Roosevelt back in the days of the Great Depression had almost run its course. Then, too, the Lyndon Johnson on the television screen was no longer the vibrant, enthusiastic, strong leader that had come to the attention of the public during the two terms of Dwight Eisenhower. The Oval Office had taken a frightening toll on him—such a heavy one, in fact, that most people probably forgot that Johnson had risen to power on a consensus platform and on promises of domestic reform. His actions should not have shocked—but they did.

Meanwhile, he had work to do. In the days and months ahead, his love of history and his desire to be remembered as the architect of the Great Society led him to order government agencies to chronicle the Johnson years in departmental histories. Moreover, he assented to the appointment of a prominent Texas historian to take temporary residence in Washington to make oral history tapes with leading lights of the administration. He also invited a young, ivy-league political scientist, Doris Kearns, to view him at close range, grooming her for assistance later when he would write the story of his presidency and perhaps a full autobiography.

Present members of the staff began to resign, while former associates now in civilian life cranked up their typewriters to get memoirs into print as fast as possible. Most of these had seen this leader close at hand, for they were often with him day and night. Johnson, unlike Kennedy, did not have friends outside of the political establishment. Perhaps the men and women of the Great Society saw too much of LBJ and were too close to him to form balanced judgments, because most of the initial books on him and his administration are negative in tone. Professor Kearns, for example, has stated that she herself may have rushed to judgment too soon. In early 1979 she wrote: "Surfeited with such rich, dramatic material, I wish I could have waited to write my book for ten or twenty years, so that I could really understand and convey its human value. But I was a young professor at Harvard; I had to publish."[20] By waiting, she added, she might have composed a much richer tale.

Besides producing personal and institutional "inside" histories, LBJ's legislative program needed votes. One education bill had passed prior to Johnson's March announcement that he would not seek the presidency again. On January 2, 1968, Johnson signed Enrolled Bill 7819, entitled Elementary and Secondary Education Act Amendments. It modified the 1965 measure and extended the legislation through 1970, altered slightly the impacted areas program, gave additional life to the Adult Education Act of 1966, provided for a study of school-bus safety, and established a new program for the special needs of children for whom English was a second language. The signing ceremony was held in the shadows of the old Junction school. In his speech, the president listed the educational accomplishments of his administration and then stated proudly that "we also celebrate that the great programs passed by the Eighty-ninth Congress have come of age. They have been tested in practice. They are working. They have begun to improve life for millions of Americans."[21] Some people had predicted, LBJ said, that the Ninetieth Congress would eliminate reform legislation of the past. "But," he added triumphantly, "not one Great Society measure was repealed."[22]

The next bills to pass Congress had to wait until the month of June. On the eighteenth, a measure to amend and fund the National Foundations on the Arts and the Humanities for fiscal years 1969 and 1970 became law.

The following day, Johnson added his signature to the Omnibus Crime Control and Safe Streets Act of 1968. This was, according to many, a bad bill—perhaps the worst he signed as president. Attorney General Ramsey Clark wrote LBJ that the eleven titles and 110 pages of text "barely resembles the Safe Streets Bill we sent to the Congress with such high hopes and ardent pleas. This bill is far more a reflection of the years, frustration and politics of the times than an intelligent, carefully tailored measure to meet the urgent need to professionalize police, coordinate criminal justice and effectively protect the public."[23] Harry McPherson also sent similar comments. In the end, however, Johnson felt he had to accept the measure. The public wanted some visible assurance that those who broke the law would be apprehended and punished. This bill was stronger than Johnson liked, but he thought that perhaps it could be toned down later. At the customary ceremonies, he struck a positive note, calling the bill a pioneer in legislation of its type, offering forgivable loans and tuition grants to attract better law enforcement officers.

July brought four new bills to the statute books. On July 7, the Vocational Rehabilitation Amendments of 1968 passed. Principal provisions authorized grants to the states and allocated about half a billion dollars for funding various program aspects. The National Science Foundation Act Amendments of 1968 came next, authorizing certain types of organizational and management changes. Three weeks later, a proposal sponsored by Allen Ellender of Louisiana received approval to amend Public Law 480. This bill permitted the government to set aside 2 percent of local international currency agreements for international education. Previously, such funds had been earmarked solely for the Fulbright-Hays Act. On the last day of the month, the President signed the Juvenile Delinquency Prevention and Control Act, which modernized criminal justice for teenagers. He made extended comments, maintaining, as in the past, that if environments were controlled fewer problems would be experienced. He said: "Criminals are made, not born. They are made by slums, they are made by bad schools, by bad health, by idleness, and by deprivation." [24]

Work on educational legislation continued in August and September. In August, the student loan insurance programs under the Higher Education Act of 1965 and the National Vocational Student Loan Insurance Act of 1965 were extended in the one bill. Days later, Sea Grant Program appropriations were set, with $6 million allocated for 1969 and $15 million for 1970.

A more significant bill, however, was signed on August 16. The Health Manpower Act of 1968 amended several health titles, generally improving and extending other legislation in relation to the training of medical and health personnel, con-structing new health training and research facilities, and strengthening student loans and scholarship programs in the health area.

The Early Education of Handicapped Children bill passed on the last day of September. It charged the commissioner of education to arrange by grant, contract, or otherwise with public agencies or private nonprofit organizations for the development and execution of experimental preschool and education programs for the handicapped. Funding was modest: $1 million in 1969; $10 million in 1970; and $12 million in 1971.

In October 1968, the age of education drew to a close. Two bills passed on the sixteenth; both were related to a special message to Congress that Johnson had delivered in February. The first, H.R. 18366, amended and expanded vocational legislation. Congress had gone beyond the recommendations of the White House, but the final measure was one which generally fit into the guidelines. The second, S. 3769, extended four major higher education acts and authorized several new programs, including provisions for helping dis-advantaged students to learn, the sharing of library, television, and computer resource facilities, the awarding of fellowships to individuals who planned careers in public service, im-provement of graduate education, clinical experiences for law students, broadening cooperative education, and providing modern equipment for educationally deprived children.

And on the twenty-fourth, the president gave his approval to extend and modify the Manpower Development and Train-ing Act of 1962.

The two bills signed on October 16 brought education to the heights of which Lyndon Johnson dreamed when he became chief executive. He said: "If they would let me climb up there to where those television cameras are, I would like to shout this from the rooftops. We have come here this morning to sign education laws number fifty-nine and sixty since the beginning of this administration."[25] He added: "If I could do anything, I told myself when I became president, . . . I wanted to do one thing: That was to advance education among all of my people. I wanted every human being to have an opportunity to get all the education that he or she could take. Education for every child. Education for every man and woman."[26] He supported education from, as he once said, conception to resurrection—from preschool to Ph.D. He took as much pride in helping little Pancho at four years of age to get a head start as he took in aiding the child's "great-grandfather, an old farmer, age seventy-four, who always—all of his life—wanted to learn to read and to sign his name without making an X."[27]

It had been just four years and ten months to the day since Lyndon Johnson had signed his first piece of education legislation, the Higher Education Facilities Act. He commended those in the audience who had been coming back again and again to build, "brick by brick, law by law, a new and better system of education in America."[28] Counting the laws had some significance, but nobody, he added, "can count the lives that these laws have and will change."[29] In education, as in civil rights, medicine, space, communications, and perhaps welfare, Johnson had achieved unprecedented success. Some programs had worked well, others were mired in the bureaucracy, and a few were too idealistic, but he and the education establishment had broken barriers and made schooling of all types available to people of all races, creeds, and colors here and abroad. This accomplishment is one likely never to be erased by the sands or the winds of time or tide.

In early November, the nation elected its thirty-seventh president of the United States. The Democratic Convention had snubbed the incumbent, but, as events turned out, perhaps it was best that Lyndon Johnson had not planned on attending. Hubert Humphrey had gotten the nod and had carried the banner of the party to the polls. He was opposed by a man as conservative as Humphrey was liberal. And

George Wallace, the fiery segregationist from Alabama, had obtained enough Democratic votes to sway, by no more than the width of a hair, the election to Nixon. At last, the suspense was over. It is likely that Johnson never had a second thought about his refusal to run again. Vietnam, the revolt of college students, and the assassination of Robert Kennedy made the election of a successor something of a relief. Johnson and Nixon met at the White House on November 11, and informal arrangements for the transfer of power began.

The Thanksgiving and Christmas holidays of 1968 brought some sanity to an otherwise insane year. A successful Apollo space shot, the release of some Cambodian prisoners, the return of the *Pueblo* crew, quiet dinners with friends such as the Humphreys, and testimonial gatherings brought to LBJ a degree of tranquility he had not known in the past ten months. Moreover, both of Lyndon and Lady Bird's daughters were now married. Luci had wedded Patrick J. Nugent on August 6, 1966, and she and her husband now had a child, Patrick Lyndon Nugent. Lynda married Chuck Robb on December 7, 1967. Their first child would be named Lucinda Desha Robb. The doting grandfather relished the idea of spending more time with his growing family.

On December 27, the president addressed the World Organization of Teaching Professions in the cabinet room. He was presented a bound leather book containing the sixty pieces of education legislation passed during his administration. The occasion brought some reflections, and it also signified that another rite of passage was near. Johnson's initial thoughts on planning for his future were not very realistic, considering the fast pace of his life since he had left Texas. He spoke of three retirement objectives: spending some time with Lady Bird, reading books that had been given him for Christmas, and then engaging in some teaching and writing. He expanded on the last category, saying that a great deal "of my time is going to be spent with young people. I am going to try to inspire them, stimulate and create in them a desire to be teachers or preachers, or public servants, because I think you can get a satisfaction in those endeavors that you can't find in many others." [30]

One more major speech had to be given, the now familiar State of the Union, scheduled for January 14, 1969. The president declined several invitations to present it in person, but then he finally gave in to the congressional leadership and delivered his farewell in person. Perhaps he wanted to be coaxed, for the room he spoke in had more pleasant memories than the Oval Office itself. "Most all of my life as a public official" he said, "has been spent here in this building. For thirty-eight years . . . I have known these halls, and I have known most of the men pretty well who walked them." [31] He thanked many, including former presidents and the current leadership, but privately perhaps the face and figure of Sam Rayburn and that of Franklin Roosevelt evoked the most sentiment. He urged that Congress give its support to Richard Nixon, whose burdens would be many without increasing them for the sake of narrow personal or partisan advantage. Then he said simply and softly: "Now, it is time to leave. I hope it may be said, a hundred years from now, that by working together we helped to make our country more just for all of its people, as well as to insure and guarantee the blessings of liberty for all of our posterity." [32]

In January, a number of parting tributes to Johnson were printed in the *Congressional Record*. Most of them were uttered by former fellow legislators or members of the administration. One stated that the president was a good man who tried too much too soon. Another admired LBJ's attempt to get a vast program of social and economic adjustment in a time of prosperity. A third believed that former courtiers had scorned and journalists had destroyed the reputation of a man who had given his best to the office he held. William Proxmire of Wisconsin, not one to praise indiscriminately, ranked Johnson as one of the great presidents. He said that

seldom in the long history of our great Republic have we had in the presidency a man who had the remarkable combination of attributes that Lyndon Baines Johnson has. He combined in the presidency great passion for the causes he believed in, tremendous energy, immense resourcefulness, one of the shrewdest and keenest minds the White House has known, and unparalleled skill to get what he wanted from Congress—a skill that was aided by his sometimes larger-than-life powers of persuasion. Few men have taken up the burdens of the presidency with such awesome credentials. [33]

Other accolades came at a nonpartisan testimonial dinner held in New York City on January 13, 1969. The distinguished author James MacGregor Burns said that he would remember Johnson as the "first president to recognize fully that our basic social ills are so rooted in encrusted attitudes and stubborn social structures that no single solution or dramatic crusade will solve them . . ." [34] Wilbur Cohen felt that his boss had been responsible for more progressive social legislation than any other president of the United States. Roger Stevens, chairman of the National Council of the Arts, believed that Johnson had done more for the arts and humanities than had been done in the entire previous history of the nation. Even Arizona's Barry Goldwater, a persistent competitor, announced that Lyndon's performance after the assassination of Kennedy, if nothing else, would assure the man a lasting place in history. And Harry Byrd of Virginia complimented the tall Texan because he was courteous, patient, and forgiving of politicians who disagreed with him. He thought Johnson a statesman as well as a gentleman.

John Sparkman of Alabama suggested that the short-run judgment of Lyndon Johnson would not prevail for all time, and that the long-run view would mark him as one of the truly outstanding presidents. A Florida legislator praised Johnson, explaining that he had dispelled the myth that a southerner could not serve in the White House. Edmund Muskie of Maine focused on the Great Society, commenting that Johnson understood and worked in harmony with the pulse of American reform movements. Hawaii's Hiram Fong thought Johnson courageous in tolerating the abuse poured on him during his last three years in office. Connecticut's Abraham Ribicoff regarded the chief executive as a man who had made significant strides in the field of education. And last, Clinton Anderson, a New Mexican who entered the Senate with Johnson in 1948, spoke the mind of many when he said: "The mastery that Lyndon Johnson has displayed in the political arena is legend."[35]

On January 20, 1969, less than a week after the testimonial dinner in New York City, the American presidency changed hands. Under other circumstances, the day might have been a sublime moment when the entire nation paused to pay tribute to an individual who had spent all of his adult life in public service. Instead, the accolades went to the thirty-seventh president of the United States. The morning was hurried: there were quick conferences with the staff and some decisions to be made. Should the president by proclamation set aside a large amount of land for a national park? Who should receive Medals of Freedom? There was also a flurry to see if anything had been forgotten. LBJ's meeting with President-elect Richard M. Nixon proved nondescript. His inaugural address spoke of a new American revolution, and with the coming of the bicentennial celebration in a few years, that theme seemed appropriate. Bands played in Washington and in Austin as Lyndon and Lady Bird made connections to reach the LBJ ranch by evening. "Hail to the Chief," "The Yellow Rose of Texas," and "The Eyes of Texas" were the tunes they remembered afterwards. In the late evening, citizen Johnson stepped into the yard for a minute of solitude and reflection. In a subsequent speech and book he stated that he looked up at the stars and thought of the majesty and splendor of the presidency that night. Now it seemed like a dream. And yet, in this moment he knew he had been there. He had carried the cross of political leadership to the ultimate.

CHAPTER FOURTEEN

Dust to Dust

"The great biographies of this age will not, I think, be about John or Robert Kennedy, glamorous and exciting as they were, but finally like meteors in the night, flashing briefly through our lives, instilling a sense of wonder and awe and then gone, but, I think, about Lyndon Johnson and Robert McNamara. The contradictions of our age and of ourselves are most clearly writ in them, the clash between our idealism and our love of power are writ most largely there. History will, I think, care about Lyndon Johnson. . . ."

—David Halberstam, 1970

L YNDON BAINES JOHNSON was a child of the Southwest. His actions and thoughts evolved as much from his formative years as from the genes he inherited from Sam and Rebekah. The return home to Texas brought Lyndon more peace than he had known since he left the region to become a Washington bureaucrat. The communities he had known as a youth welcomed him back warmly because, outside of Sam Houston, no individual in history had done more for the Lone Star state than the man raised on the banks of the Pedernales River. For over thirty years LBJ pumped funds into the area's educational system, defense plants, roads and riverways, cities, rural electrification, military bases, and space installations, as well as communications, medicine, and recreation facilities.

The region had always provided him with strong support. In the 1964 election, Blanco County, where his boyhood home was located, had voted five to one for Johnson, and even Gillespie County, the site of the Johnson ranch, had voted democratic for the first time in thirty-two years. Perhaps the esteem of the populace is best evidenced by the fact that what was once known as the hill country is now called LBJ country. The transition in Johnson's prestige began when private funds were secured to make the Texas White House and surrounding acreage the Lyndon B. Johnson State Park. His birthplace was remodeled, a statue erected, a visitor's center constructed, and an animal park was placed near it complete with Johnson's voice providing narration on tape. Nearby, another locality created Lady Bird Johnson Park, equipped with a lake, a swimming pool, a picnic area, a golf course, a children's playground, baseball and softball diamonds, and an old-fashioned bandstand for outdoor concerts. Even the highway from Austin to Stonewall and beyond assumed the title of the LBJ highway. A living eulogy had begun.

The person who took up residence at the LBJ ranch was a man markedly different from the tall, erect figure who had taken the presidential oath only five years before. Johnson's hair was grayer, and he let it grow long and flowing, western style. His skin had turned saddle brown, his facial lines were deeper, his gait was slower, and his immense physical frame sagged in the center when he resumed enjoying a once forbidden diet. A scotch highball frequently replaced a Fresca-on-the-rocks. A package of cigarettes found its way once more into his shirt pocket. Tailored suits were replaced by tan leisure outfits. One reporter remarked that the former president had taken on the craggy look of the land where he lived.

Johnson maintained his high energy level, however, and newspapers abounded with rumors. Some said he intended to become a banking executive, a newspaper publisher, a land baron, or that he would head up a law firm, despite the fact that he was not a member of the bar. More than one columnist flatly predicted that he would run for the United States Senate in 1970 or 1972. And one wag, clearly out of touch with the situation, prophesied that the rancher would run for the presidency again in 1974. Leslie Carpenter, a journalist and longtime family friend, believed Johnson to be "no normal man. His friends listen with astonished disbelief when he talks about being idle. He never has been, and those who know him best don't believe he can be. . . ." [1]

He was right. Johnson had some general goals, and he worked toward accomplishing them. But when there was no pressing work to do, he made some. He made frequent inspections of the ranch operations, sometimes to the consternation of Dale Malinchek, the manager. Occasionally he took time to speak to sightseers and to give them a ride in a vintage automobile presented to him by Henry Ford II. Luci and Lynda, their husbands, and their children, were constantly in his mind, and for the first time in Lyndon's married life, he had hours instead of minutes to spend with the lady who had become his bride in San Antonio. Bobby Baker, his former Senate associate, was just out of jail. He visited Johnson and wrote that his former boss had drawn up a list of thirty names of people he wanted to see, suggesting that LBJ wanted to make peace with longtime associates where contact had been lost or strained.

Gradually, the chest pains Johnson experienced while in the Senate came back. A prominent heart surgeon diagnosed that two heart valves were completely clogged and that an operation would pose more problems than it would solve. Another thing which must have preyed on Johnson's mind was that his father had died of heart trouble; and the retired president was older than his father had been when he died. The end could not be too far away. Lyndon now spoke often of his boyhood to his future biographer, Doris Kearns, and to his family and friends. Baker, on his last foray to the ranch, asked him why this preoccupation. LBJ replied:

> I guess it is what old men do. We try to go back. You know I'll probably die just a few miles from where I drew my first

breath. That would have seemed like a horrible prospect to me, back when I was young and ambitious and gonna set the world on fire. But there's comfort in knowing you're gonna go full circle, end up where you started out. I've said before that I want to live my last days where folks know when you're sick and care when you die.[2]

There was also real work to be done. Johnson's last four years were spent in lecturing, writing, and supervising two large projects that will be identified later. His first love was teaching. It was no secret that earlier he had wished to join the faculty of the University of Texas. And no less than forty other colleges and universities, including Yale, Rice, the Massachusetts Institute of Technology, and Texas Christian University, wanted him to lecture or teach. Shortly before Johnson left the Oval Office, the *Dallas Morning News* reported what the outgoing man had in mind. "The president is interested in talking with students not only about the problems of the past forty years, during which he has been in government, but also in explaining the problems of the next forty years."[3] Negotiations, however, broke down. Texas was just not the home of placid, cow-country undergraduates anymore, and the faculty, perhaps remembering past troubles with political appointments, were less than enthusiastic about granting full academic credentials to a person who had not taught for forty years. Johnson resented the lukewarm reception, and his dream of conducting a serene class on government fell by the wayside.

However, there was, to use a favorite Johnson cliché, more than one way "to nail a coonskin on the wall." If he could not teach in the university system, perhaps he could use the media to reach an even larger audience. The media had continued to fascinate Johnson: in fact, his first literary publication as a private citizen was a long essay published in the *Britannica Book of the Year for 1969* and excerpted in the *Reader's Digest*. Bob Hardesty and Harry Middleton, both speechwriters, helped him to prepare the text. In it, Johnson scored journalists for overemphasizing failure and conflict and accused them of rearranging facts to suit their purposes. He did not think it fair that public officials like the president of the United States were blamed for everything from the generation gap to the price of bread. Johnson regretted that he had not tried harder with the press, although he did point out that he had held more news conferences than either Eisenhower or Kennedy. Part of the fault, then, for the credibility gap had to be borne by the media. Johnson compared presidential press coverage to a roller coaster: the highs at the beginning of an administration were unreasonably high and the lows at the end of a term were too low.

In spite of some wariness, Johnson decided to take a chance and tell his story on television. In part, money was an incentive: the remuneration he received is thought to have approximated six figures. He signed a contract in 1969 with Columbia Broadcasting System for a series of interviews on his life and presidency. The one-on-one situation had always been his forte, and Walter Cronkite, who was selected to do the questioning, had a big following. But the result was less than satisfactory, and some misunderstanding developed. Cronkite at times seemed in awe of his subject, and Johnson's attempts to document a few controversial points were less than convincing. Then, too, the editing process created friction. Johnson asked that a section dealing with the findings of the Warren Commission be deleted on the grounds of national security. Cronkite, on the other hand, appears to have erased some of his original questions and substituted others in their place. The lip movements do not always match the word sounds on the remaining tapes. In short, both men's performances left something to be desired.

In November 1971, Johnson delivered the Arthur K. Salomon Lecture to the Graduate School of Business Administration at New York University. He selected an intriguing title for his comments: "America Tomorrow: Will We Hang

Together or Hang Separately?" The theme of the address was that business, labor, and government had to work hand in hand to clear up twentieth-century problems like hunger, illiteracy, disease, unemployment, discrimination, overpopulation, poverty and pollution. The United States did not have the option of retreating into its own shell or hiding its head in the sand, as it had done at the end of World War I. LBJ said: "We are the guardians of what I believe to be the greatest economic system and the greatest government known to man. It is up to us whether we pass on to our children and grandchildren a nation unified in common purpose or torn apart by selfish interest."[4]

LBJ gave his last major speech at a Symposium on Civil Rights held in Austin, Texas. He reiterated his belief that the principal job of government was upholding the welfare, dignity, decency, and integrity of every individual, regardless of ancestry, color, creed, sex, or race. He quoted from an address he had given while vice-president, commemorating the hundredth anniversary of Abraham Lincoln's Emancipation Proclamation: "Until justice is blind to color, until education is unaware of race, until opportunity is unconcerned with the color of men's skins, emancipation will be a proclamation but not a fact. To the extent that the proclamation of emancipation is not fulfilled in fact, to that extent we shall have fallen short of assuring freedom to the free."[5] Both of these lectures were published and reached a fairly wide audience.

LBJ's largest effort in the writing field, however, was the composition—some said the production—of his memoirs. He sold the rights to Holt, Rinehart and Winston. The monetary consideration involved hit the million-dollar mark. It had been decided in advance, partly against Johnson's wishes, that the work would be done in one volume and that it would deal with the presidential period. Anything left to be covered would be brought out in other volumes. The title was appropriate: *The Vantage Point: Perspectives of the Presidency, 1963–1969.* His White House papers were now accessible, and Johnson drew upon them to refresh his memories of his presidency. Doris Kearns, the former White House Fellow now teaching at Harvard University, flew to the LBJ ranch on weekends and holidays to assist with the chapters on economics and civil rights as well as to collect material for a personal volume. Instead of writing in his own folksy manner, Johnson decided to use "Ivy League" words and to defend his Vietnam policies. The result did not quite ring true: most reviewers damned the book as stilted and one-sided. Thus another venture into the public arena ended just short of disaster.

Teaching and writing had not brought the public accolades and vindication that Johnson felt he deserved, so his thirst for recognition turned to another direction. Before he left the presidency, Lady Bird had made a thorough study of the Harry S Truman Library in Independence, Missouri, and shortly after her husband's gall bladder surgery she visited several eastern libraries to see how they were run. The success of these tours cemented a decision he had made earlier—to continue the recent trend of building a complex to house official presidential papers and display memorabilia from visiting heads of foreign governments. The papers of Hoover, Roosevelt, Truman, and Eisenhower were already housed, usually in or near their respective hometowns. And plans for a Kennedy library in Massachusetts were on the drawing board. These libraries offered a little something for everybody: journalists and scholarly researchers could use documents for articles and books; the public could view educational displays and get a feel for a man as well as his era; and finally, these complexes helped to instill respect for past leaders as familiarity often helps to resurrect the good interred in the cemetery. Perhaps these libraries came at an opportune time in America, for newspapers reported that some deposed leaders, such as those in the Soviet Union, were often quarantined after retirement. Presidential libraries signified that respect was due to the men who held the office of president even if the occupant was not popular at the end of his years of service.

Plans for the construction of the Johnson library were well under way prior to the president's retirement. Frank Erwin, a member of the University of Texas Board of Regents, had spearheaded the drive for such an institution and promised the use of state funds if Austin was selected as a site. Johnson himself donated royalties from his book and revenues from the CBS television interviews. A $2-million gift from the Sid Richardson Foundation ensured that the new complex would also house the offices of the Texas State Historical Association, the Archives of the State of Texas, and the Institute for Latin American Affairs.

In addition, the edifice would provide classrooms for the newly founded Lyndon B. Johnson School of Public Affairs. This facility had been a pet project of Johnson's for years. All of his professional life, he had wanted to make it easier for those not from the east to prepare for government service. This school would offer graduate training, including an internship, for men and women who aspired to a career as a public servant at the community, state, or national level. The completed complex encompassed eight city blocks and was located on the campus of the University of Texas, near Memorial Stadium and on a hill that overlooked the whole inner campus.

The creation of the School of Public Affairs was an accomplishment in which Lyndon Johnson took much personal pride. He was excited about the selection of John A. Gronouski to serve as the first dean, and he knew most of the first faculty by sight. Some of them had worked in his administration. Johnson occasionally taught a class, and he almost always attended symposia and conferences sponsored by the school. At one of these, he paused in the middle of his part of the program and swallowed some medication. Newspapermen reported this action in detail, suggesting that Johnson's health might be failing. The incident, however, also meant that the school was more important to him than his personal comfort. Perhaps LBJ's only regret, if he had any at all about the school, was that more graduates were placed in local and state offices than federal agencies. Possibly to improve placement, steps were taken in 1975 so interested students could stay in residence an additional two years to take a law degree in conjunction with the University of Texas School of Law. Nevertheless, mention of the School of Public Affairs in conversation with Johnson usually brought a twinkle to now tired eyes.

Dr. Chester Newland, a thirty-eight-year-old professor, supervised much of the planning for the LBJ library while on leave from the University of Southern California. His appointment was made by the General Services Administration, which agency had been placed in charge of Johnson's 31 million documents until the building was finished. Newland's appointment was announced in October 1969, and Johnson let him know that he wanted the papers of his administration available for use as quickly as possible, especially those on education and civil rights.

The first floor of the library contains a reception desk, an area to sell mementos, and some exhibits. The second floor includes an exhibit area, highlighting displays with the extensive use of audio visual equipment, the most modern of any presidential library. Floor eight houses a documents reading room, offices for the staff, a complex for security people, and a re-creation of the famous Oval Office as it had appeared while Lyndon Johnson was president. The building also contains a photo archives, a two hundred fifty-seat lecture hall, and an auditorium that seats one thousand. The rest of the fifty thousand square feet of usable space stores documents.

Dedication services were held in June 1971. Hubert Humphrey and Barry Goldwater asked that a copy of the dedication ceremonies be placed in the *Congressional Record*. The former served as spokesman for the day. He said that such undertakings were to be commended so that the American people could "understand more fully what Aristotle called the 'master art'—politics, the wisdom of Solomon that is required by a chief executive in balancing the national interest and welfare against sectional, state and local interest."⁶ The presidency of Lyndon Baines Johnson, he added, especially needed study, for he had pioneered in many areas, particularly domestic legislation. Medicine, education, civil rights, air and water pollution, conservation, mass transit, housing, consumer protection, space, and manpower training were examples singled out. Humphrey must have drawn a smile from his co-sponsor when he recalled that Everett Dirksen had once said after a crucial Senate vote on a reform issue: "This isn't the Great Society—it's heaven."⁷

The Lyndon B. Johnson Library and the Lyndon B. Johnson School of Public Affairs were the last great educational efforts of the thirty-sixth president of the United States. These institutions were as much a monument to Texas as to himself. The English poet, Alfred Lord Tennyson, has a line in *Ulysses* that reads, "I am all that I have met." And so it was with LBJ. As chief executive of the United States of America he had gone back to the people and places of his youth to fashion, among other things, a program based on the twin principles of equal opportunity and equal education. If he could start school at four, he wanted others to benefit from Headstart. Since he had profited from time spent between high school and college preparing for advanced studies, he wanted others to have the opportunity to be Upward Bound. His early difficulty in getting a job in California because he was unskilled led to his support for a job corps. He had been fortunate enough to secure a loan from a local banker to finance his education; therefore, he wanted to make available Guaranteed Loans for all college youth. And if children in Cotulla could perform better with teachers who were sensitive to the needs of the poor and disadvantaged minorities, why should the country not have a teacher corps? In short, Johnson believed what was good for him was good for the nation.

The Great Society, therefore, was born not of a brain trust or a task force, but in the heart and mind of a man who lived among the homespun people of Central Texas. These people deserved an edifice in Austin so that their sons and daughters could see one of their own kind had reached great heights, and so that they could aim for the stars as well.

In April 1972, a heart attack mortally wounded Johnson's health. Shortly afterward, Lyndon told an audience who had gathered to watch Lady Bird give beautification awards: "I'm not in the speechmaking business nowadays. I'm following the advice of an old mountain woman who said: 'When I walks, I walks slowly. When I sits, I sits loosely. And when I feel a worry coming on, I just go to sleep.' " [8]

The big sleep followed on January 22, 1973. Lyndon bolted from a nap, fell, and bruised his head. Two aides rushed to his side with oxygen tanks, but it was too late, as was a quick flight to the superior medical services available in San Antonio.

The country paid tribute as the casket lay in state at the LBJ Library, the national Capitol, and the National City Christian Church. Black Jack, a gelding that had previously pulled caissons for Herbert Hoover and John F. Kennedy, performed the same task for Johnson, moving through the streets riderless and with boots reversed in the stirrups. The body came home to Texas in *Air Force One*, renamed the *Spirit of '76*. It was the same plane in which Lyndon Johnson had taken the presidential oath. A cold drizzle stopped just prior to interment in the family plot.

Almost four years had passed since Johnson had left the Oval Office. The day before he died, Richard Nixon announced plans for dismantling the Office of Economic Opportunity. On the day following his death, Johnson's successor told the nation that the long, bitter war in Vietnam had been concluded. He said: "Just yesterday, a great American, who once occupied this office, died. In his life President Johnson endured the vilification of those who sought to portray him as a man of war. But there was nothing he cared about more deeply than achieving a lasting peace in the world."[9] With these words, an era in American history came to a close.

The dismantling of some Great Society programs and the absence of a clear-cut victory in Southeast Asia does not mean that the man buried underneath the sprawling oak trees in the Johnson family plot lived his life in vain. Nor should he be regarded as a tragic figure. He had far more successes than failures in the threescore years granted him. Many of the underprivileged and those who were closest to him recognized his achievements. An elderly black hospital attendant who traveled from New Jersey to Washington in order to be present at the last rites in the nation's capitol spoke for more than herself when she whispered: "I really liked him as president. He got Medicaid for us. He was very good with civil rights."[10] Members of the Johnson family expressed similar sentiments at the gravesite just after the "Battle Hymn of the Republic" had been sung and taps had been played. Lady Bird turned her head and commented: "Oh, didn't he live well?" To which his daughter Lynda added: "And didn't he love all of us? Everybody!"[11] The real tragedy of Lyndon Baines Johnson's life is that the American masses did not understand or openly support a patriot who wanted to serve humanity above all else.

Notes

CHAPTER 1.

1. *New York Times*, May 9, 1966.
2. *LBJ Country* (Fredericksburg, Tex.: Awani Press, 1970), p. 5.
3. *Observer*, July 25, 1965.
4. Untitled speech delivered on Oct. 25, 1964, quoted in "Statements of Lyndon B. Johnson" (Lyndon B. Johnson Library, Austin, Texas).
5. Rebekah Baines Johnson, *A Family Album* (New York: McGraw-Hill, 1965), p. 22.
6. Ibid., p. 28.
7. Ibid., p. 5.
8. Ibid., p. 109.
9. Ibid., p. 29.
10. Rebekah Johnson to LBJ, Aug. 26, 1938, "Family Paper Collection" (Lyndon B. Johnson Library).
11. Sam Houston Johnson (Hank Lopez, ed.), *My Brother Lyndon* (New York: Cawles Book Company, 1969), p. 17.
12. Johnson, *A Family Album*, pp. 17–18.
13. Ibid., p. 19.
14. Johnson, *My Brother Lyndon*, pp. 6–7.
15. *New York Times*, May 8, 1966.
16. I. Shelton, "Lyndon Johnson's Mother," *Saturday Evening Post*, May 8, 1965.
17. Alfred Steinberg, *Sam Johnson's Boy* (New York: Macmillan, 1968), p. 1.

18. Quoted from William C. Pool, Emmie Craddock, and David E. Conrad, *Lyndon Baines Johnson: The Formative Years* (San Marcos, Tex.: Southwest Texas State College Press, 1965), pp. 45–46.

19. Belle Kornitilev, "President Johnson Talks About His Mother and Father," *Parade*, Jan. 5, 1964.

20. Untitled radio address delivered on June 26, 1968, quoted in "Statements."

21. *New York Times*, May 8, 1966.

22. Untitled radio address delivered on June 24, 1948, quoted in "Statements."

23. Untitled radio address delivered on Aug. 26, 1948, quoted in "Statements."

24. Quoted in Steinberg, *Sam Johnson's Boy*, p. 14.

25. *Dallas News*, Jan. 19, 1965.

CHAPTER 2.

1. Untitled radio address delivered on July 7, 1948, quoted in "Statements."

2. *Houston Post*, Oct. 31, 1965.

3. *Austin Statesman*, Jan. 20, 1965.

4. David Halberstam, *The Best and the Brightest* (New York: Random House, 1969), p. 442.

5. Untitled speech delivered on June 19, 1948, quoted in "Statements."

6. I. Shelton, "Lyndon Johnson's Mother," *Saturday Evening Post*, May 8, 1965.

7. Untitled radio speech delivered in Lufkin, Texas, June 24, 1948, quoted in "Statements."

8. *Dallas News*, June 30, 1941.

9. *Texas Magazine*, Feb. 6, 1966, p. 1.

10. "Remarks, Dedication of the Gary Job Corps Center," address delivered on April 10, 1965, quoted in "Statements."

11. Untitled radio address delivered on July 21, 1948, quoted in "Statements."

12. Halberstam, *The Best and the Brightest*, p. 442.

13. Steinberg, *Sam Johnson's Boy*, p. 32.

14. Ibid., p. 34.

15. *Dallas News*, June 30, 1941.

16. Johnson, *Family Album*, p. 20.

17. Pool, *LBJ: The Formative Years*, p. 66.

18. Ibid., pp. 90–91.
19. Ibid.
20. Southwest Texas State Teachers College *College Star*, Sept. 21, 1926.
21. *Dallas News*, June 30, 1941.
22. *Austin Statesman*, May 13, 1965.
23. Harvey Wish, ed., *American Historians: A Selection* (New York: Oxford University Press, 1962), p. 8.
24. *College Star*, June 8, 1927.
25. *Austin American*, n.d., 1940.
26. *Houston Post*, Oct. 1, 1963.
27. Pool, *LBJ: The Formative Years*, p. 27.
28. *Pedagog* (San Marcos: Southwest Texas State Teachers College, 1930), n.p.
29. "Remarks, Southwest Texas State Teachers College, San Marcos, Texas," address delivered on Aug. 24, 1968, quoted in "Statements."
30. *Pedagog*, 1930, p. 150.
31. Ibid., p. 151.
32. "Selected Writings of Lyndon B. Johnson, Student Editor, 1927–1929, *College Star*, Southwest Texas State Teachers College," unpublished manuscript (Lyndon B. Johnson Library).
33. Compiled from the *College Star*, 1927–1929.
34. *College Star*, Aug. 18, 1928.
35. Ibid., April 18, 1929.
36. *Pedagog*, 1930, p. 108.
37. Ibid., p. 83.
38. *College Star*, Nov. 9, 1927.
39. "Remarks, Mexican Education Conference Committee," address delivered on Aug. 9, 1963, quoted in "Statements."
40. *Dallas Herald*, Nov. 7, 1966.
41. "Remarks, White House Conference on Education," address delivered on July 21, 1965, quoted in "Statements."

CHAPTER 3.

1. "Remarks, U.S. Chamber of Commerce," speech delivered on Apr. 27, 1964, quoted in "Statements."
2. Untitled radio address delivered on June 11, 1941, quoted in "Statements."
3. *Dallas News*, June 5, 1954.

4. Pool, *LBJ: The Formative Years*, p. 155.

5. Ibid., p. 158.

6. Malcolm Bardwell, Oral History Interview, Oct. 17, 1968 (Lyndon B. Johnson Library).

7. Edwin William Knippa, Jr., "The Early Political Life of Lyndon Baines Johnson, 1931–1937," master's thesis (San Marcos: Southwest Texas State Teachers College, 1967), p. 19.

8. Ibid., p. 37.

9. "Remarks, Jefferson-Jackson Day Dinner," speech delivered on March 2, 1963, quoted in "Statements."

10. Statement delivered by Claudia A. Johnson on May 5, 1965, quoted in "Clippings of LBJ in Barker History Center" (Lyndon B. Johnson Library).

11. *Austin Statesman*, Jan. 20, 1964.

12. LBJ to Rebekah Johnson, undated, "Family Paper Collection."

13. Rebekah Johnson to Claudia Johnson, Nov. 30, 1934, "Family Paper Collection."

14. Knippa, "Early Political Life of LBJ," p. 40.

15. LBJ to Richard Brown, March 20, 1936, U.S. Government Records, "National Youth Administration" (Lyndon B. Johnson Library).

16. Richard Brown to LBJ, March 20, 1936, "National Youth Administration."

17. Steinberg, *Sam Johnson's Boy*, p. 99.

18. Richard Brown to LBJ, May 6, 1936, "National Youth Administration."

19. LBJ to Aubrey Williams, Aug. 8, 1935, "National Youth Administration."

20. "Special Report of Negro Activities of the National Youth Administration of Texas," March 16, 1936, "National Youth Administration."

21. LBJ to Richard Brown, March 4, 1936, "National Youth Administration."

22. "Report, San Antonio Youth Camp," Jan. 1, 1936, "National Youth Administration."

23. Ibid.

24. *Dallas News*, June 30, 1941.

25. Knippa, "Early Political Life of LBJ," p. 83.

26. Ibid., pp. 83–84.

27. LBJ to Richard Brown, March 18, 1937, "National Youth Administration."

28. *Newsweek*, August 19, 1966.

29. "Remarks on House Floor," address delivered on May 31, 1939, quoted in "Statements."

CHAPTER 4.

1. "The South Will Rise," radio address delivered on Aug. 24, 1938, quoted in "Statements."

2. Ibid.

3. Ibid.

4. Doris Kearns, *Lyndon Johnson and the American Dream* (New York: Harper and Row, 1976), p. 87.

5. *San Marcos Daily News*, March 6, 1937.

6. Steinberg, *Sam Johnson's Boy*, p. 110.

7. *Observer*, July 25, 1965.

8. Knippa, "Early Political Life of LBJ," p. 181.

9. *Dallas News*, May 1, 1937.

10. Ibid., May 27, 1937.

11. Ibid., June 6, 1941.

12. Omar Burleson, Oral History Interview, Oct. 3, 1968 (Lyndon B. Johnson Library).

13. Untitled address delivered on Dec. 1, 1939, quoted in "Statements."

14. Untitled address delivered on April 4, 1946, quoted in "Statements."

15. "Remarks, Teacher of the Year Award," address delivered on April 30, 1968, quoted in "Statements."

16. LBJ to Rebekah Johnson, May 8, 1937, "Family Paper Collection."

17. Ibid., Jan. 20, 1941.

18. Rebekah Johnson to LBJ, Sept. 9, 1937, "Family Paper Collection."

19. Ibid., undated.

20. Ibid., Dec. __, 1939.

21. Ibid., Aug. 26, 1938.

22. Ibid., undated.

23. Ibid., Sept. 5, 1939.

24. *Dallas News*, January ___, 1941.

25. Ibid., April 3, 1941.

26. Ibid., June 7, 1941.

27. Ibid., May 1, 1941.

28. LBJ to Mary Allison Willard, in "Barker Clippings."

29. J. E. Haley, *A Texan Looks at Lyndon* (Canyon, Tex.: Palo Duro Press, 1964), pp. 18–19.

30. *Congressional Record*, April 30, 1941, p. 2.

31. *Dallas News*, April 22, 1941.

32. Kearns, *Lyndon Johnson and the American Dream*, pp. 93–94.

33. *Dallas News*, June 25, 1941.

34. Rebekah Johnson to LBJ, July 1, 1941, "Family Paper Collection."

35. Ibid., July 6, 1941.

36. Ibid., Dec. 12, 1941.

37. Quoted in Martin Caidin and Edward Hymoff, *The Mission* (Philadelphia: Lippincott, 1964), p. 34.

38. Claudia Johnson to Rebekah Johnson, June 14, 1942, "Family Paper Collection."

39. Rebekah Johnson to LBJ, July 15, 1946, "Family Paper Collection."

40. *Dallas News*, Aug. 20, 1946.

CHAPTER 5.

1. Quoted in Steinberg, *Sam Johnson's Boy*, p. 224.

2. William S. White, *The Professional Lyndon B. Johnson* (Boston: Houghton Mifflin, 1964), p. 154.

3. *Congressional Record*, May 7, 1947, p. 4965.

4. *Austin American*, Sept. 30, 1947.

5. *Congressional Record*, April 2, 1948, p. 4066.

6. Ibid., April 14, 1948, p. 4454.

7. Ibid., April 15, 1946, p. 3735.

8. Ibid., Feb. 14, 1946, p. A753.

9. Ibid., March 18, 1948, p. 3111.

10. Ibid., April 1, 1948, p. A2050.

11. Ibid., p. A3231.

12. Ibid., July 29, 1948.

13. Ibid., April 2, 1946, p. 2991.

14. Ibid., July 22, 1947, p. 9718.

15. Ibid., June 4, 1946, p. A3170.

16. Ibid., p. 3171.

17. Quoted in Philip R. Rulon, "Henry Garland Bennett: The Father of the 'Great Adventure' in University-Contracts Abroad," *Red River Valley Historical Review*, vol. 2, no. 2 (Summer 1975), p. 264.

18. Quoted from Kearns, *Lyndon Johnson and the American Dream*, p. 100.

19. Untitled speech delivered on June 7, 1948, quoted in "Statements."

20. "The Challenge of a New Day," speech delivered on May 22, 1948, quoted in "Statements."

21. Press release delivered on June 22, 1948, quoted in "Statements."

22. Untitled radio broadcast delivered on July 2, 1948, quoted in "Statements."

23. Ibid.

24. Untitled radio broadcast delivered on July 12, 1948, quoted in "Statements."

25. Ibid.

26. Untitled radio broadcast delivered by Cecil Evans on July 23, 1948, quoted in "Statements."

27. Untitled radio broadcast delivered on July ?, 1948, quoted in "Statements."

28. Quoted from Russell Kirk and James McClellan, *The Political Principles of Robert A. Taft* (New York: Fleet Press Corp., 1967), p. 141.

29. LBJ to Roland Peters, April 22, 1954, in "Papers of Lyndon B. Johnson" (Lyndon B. Johnson Library). Subsequent references to correspondence will be cited simply as "Papers of LBJ." Unless indicated otherwise, these documents may be found by consulting the appropriate section in the Education Finding Aid on file in the Lyndon B. Johnson Library.

30. "Operation Texas," radio broadcast by Carl Estes, delivered on August ?, 1948, quoted in "Statements."

31. Henry Steele Commager, ed., *Documents of American History*, 7th ed. (New York: Appleton-Century-Crofts, 1963), p. 555.

CHAPTER 6.

1. *Congressional Record*, March 9, 1949, p. 2046.
2. Ibid.
3. Ibid., p. 2048.
4. Ibid.
5. Ibid.
6. Ibid.
7. Ibid.
8. Ibid., Oct. 18, 1949, p. 14,850.
9. Untitled address delivered on Nov. 25, 1945, quoted in "Statements."
10. Ibid.
11. Ibid.
12. Ibid.
13. Ibid.
14. Ibid., March 3, 1950, p. A1590.
15. Ibid., p. 1589.
16. Ibid., July 12, 1950, p. 9988.
17. Ibid.
18. Ibid., Aug. 3, 1950, p. A5611.
19. *Washington Star*, July 20, 1950.
20. *Congressional Record*, Dec. 12, 1950. p. 16,458.
21. Ibid.
22. Ibid.
23. Quoted in the *Congressional Record*, Dec. 18, 1950, p. A7754.
24. *Congressional Record*, Jan. 5, 1951, p. A38.
25. Quoted in Steinberg, *Sam Johnson's Boy*, p. 521.
26. *Congressional Record*, Feb. 27, 1951, p. 1565.
27. Ibid., March 9, 1951, p. 2185.
28. Ibid., March 23, 1953, p. 2256.
29. Ibid.
30. Ibid., Aug. 3, 1953, p. 11,047.
31. Ibid., Aug. 29, 1953, p. 15,454.

CHAPTER 7.

1. Quoted in the *Congressional Record*, May 23, 1955, p. 6753.
2. *Wall Street Journal*, June 10, 1955.
3. Ibid.
4. Ibid.

5. Quoted in the *Congressional Record*, June 29, 1955, p. 9438.
6. *Outlook*, Aug. 16, 1964.
7. *Boston Herald*, July 11, 1955.
8. R. G. Mills to LBJ, June 28, 1952, "LBJ Papers."
9. "We Need Not Lag Behind," address delivered on Nov. 29, 1957, quoted in "Statements."
10. Ibid.
11. Untitled address delivered on May 18, 1954, "LBJ Papers."
12. *Congressional Record*, June 16, 1957, p. 8577.
13. Ibid., pp. 8577–78.
14. Ibid., June 17, 1957, p. 9255.
15. Ibid.
16. Untitled address delivered on Dec. 10, 1957, "LBJ Papers."
17. LBJ to Jo Ann McDonald, January 7, 1958, "LBJ Papers."
18. Dean Acheson to LBJ, December 2, 1959, "LBJ Papers."
19. Quoted in Harry McPherson, *A Political Education* (Boston: Little, Brown, 1972).
20. *Congressional Record*, July 30, 1958, p. 15671.
21. Ibid.
22. Ralph Gwinn to DDE, Dec. 30, 1957, Central Files Official File, OF 111–C–7, Federal Aid to Education (21, Box 549, Eisenhower Papers), (Dwight D. Eisenhower Library, Abilene, Kans.).
23. *Congressional Record*, July 30, 1958, p. 15671.
24. *New York Times*, Aug. 12, 1958.
25. *Congressional Record*, Aug. 13, 1958.
26. LBJ to Mary O. Royds, June 10, 1959, "LBJ Papers."
27. "Insurance by Federal Government of Loans to College Students," speech delivered on Sept. 14, 1959, quoted in "Statements."
28. Untitled address delivered on Oct. 10, 1959, quoted in "Statements."
29. The Bryan *Daily Eagle*, June 9, 1959.
30. "Responsibilities and Roadblocks," address delivered on Nov. 26, 1959, quoted in "Statements."

CHAPTER 8.

1. *Congressional Record*, Jan. 7, 1960, p. 179.
2. Ibid., May 7, 1959, p. 7658.
3. Ibid., p. 7660.

4. *Roll Call*, March 30, 1960.

5. *Congressional Record*, June 2, 1960, p. 11,782.

6. LBJ to George E. Wilkin, Jr., May 4, 1960, "LBJ Papers."

7. Transcript of "Meet the Press" program of July 10, 1960, quoted in "Statements."

8. *Congressional Record*, June 17, 1960, p. 12,974.

9. Ibid., p. 12,974.

10. Quoted in Herbert S. Parmet, *Eisenhower and the American Crusades* (New York: Macmillan, 1972), p. 463.

11. *Los Angeles Times*, July 20, 1960.

12. *Washington Evening Star*, Aug. 8, 1960.

13. "The Hearts of Men," address delivered on Aug 23, 1958, quoted in "Statements."

14. *Congressional Record*, April 20, 1959, pp. 6265–66.

15. Hiram L. Fong to LBJ, Sept. 15, 1961, "LBJ Papers."

16. Untitled address delivered on May 9, 1961, quoted in "Statements."

17. Untitled address delivered on May 13, 1961, quoted in "Statements."

18. Ibid.

19. Untitled address delivered on June 9, 1961, quoted in "Statements."

CHAPTER 9.

1. *Public Papers of the Presidents of the United States*, John F. Kennedy, Jan. 1 to Nov. 22, 1963 (Washington, D.C.: Government Printing Office, 1964), p. 899.

2. Ibid., p. 903.

3. *Congressional Record*, Nov. 27, 1963, p. 22,839.

4. Ibid.

5. Ibid., Jan. 8, 1964, p. 113.

6. Ibid., p. 114.

7. U.S., Congress, Senate, *Tributes to the President and Mrs. Lyndon Baines Johnson*, 91st Cong., 1st sess., doc. 91-7 (Washington, D.C.: Government Printing Office, 1969), p. 102.

8. "Remarks of the President upon Signing the Higher Education Facilities Act of 1963," speech delivered Dec. 16, 1963, quoted in "Statements."

9. Ibid.

10. "Remarks of the President on the Signing of the Vocational Education Act," speech delivered on December 18, 1963, quoted in "Statements."

11. Phillip S. Hughes to LBJ, December 18, 1963, "LBJ Papers."

12. "Remarks of the President on the Signing of the Manpower and Development Training Act of 1963," speech delivered on Dec. 19, 1963, quoted in "Statements."

13. "Remarks of President Lyndon B. Johnson at the signing of the Library Services and Construction Act of 1965," speech delivered on Feb. 11, 1964, quoted in "Statements."

14. Ibid.

15. "Address of the President on Signing the Civil Rights Act of 1964," speech delivered on July 2, 1964, quoted in "Statements."

16. Nicholas Katzenbach to Kermit Gordon, July 1, 1964, "LBJ Papers."

17. U.S., Congress, *Extension of Juvenile Delinquency and Youth Offences Control Act of 1961*, 88th Cong., 1st sess., report 483 (Washington, D.C.: Government Printing Office, 1964), p. 5.

18. Lyndon B. Johnson, *The Vantage Point* (New York: Holt, Rinehart and Winston, 1971), pp. 74–75.

19. *Public Papers of the Presidents of the United States*, Lyndon Johnson, 1963–1964, vol. 2 (Washington, D.C.: Government Printing Office, 1965), p. 375.

20. Ibid., p. 381.

21. Johnson, *Vantage Point*, p. 80.

22. Ibid., p. 81.

23. U.S., Congress, *Economic Opportunity Act of 1964*, 88th Cong., 2nd sess., report 1218 (Washington, D.C.: Government Printing Office, 1964), p. 73.

24. U.S., Congress, House of Representatives, *Economic Opportunity Act*, 88th Cong., 2nd sess., report 1458 (Washington, D.C.: Government Printing Office, 1964), p. 89.

25. Quoted in Kearns, *Lyndon Johnson and the American Dream*, p. 98.

CHAPTER 10.

1. Untitled speech delivered to the Federated Women's Clubs on June 12, 1963, in Milwaukee, Wisconsin, quoted in "Statements."

2. Ibid.

3. Memo, Jack Valenti to Abe Fortas et al., Dec. 9, 1963, "LBJ Papers."

4. Untitled speech delivered to the Non-Partisan Political League on Jan. 28, 1964, quoted in "Statements."

5. Ibid.

6. "Remarks, Treasury Department," speech delivered on Febr. 21, 1964, quoted in "Statements."

7. "Remarks, Democratic Congressional Dinner," speech delivered March 19, 1964, quoted in "Statements."

8. Ibid.

9. "Remarks, Convention of United Auto Workers," speech delivered March 23, 1964, quoted in "Statements."

10. Time, April 10, 1964, p. 23.

11. Ibid.

12. "Remarks, 50th Anniversary of Amalgamated Clothing Workers," speech delivered on May 9, 1964, quoted in "Statements."

13. Memo, Horace Busby to Jack Valenti, circa May 1964, "LBJ Papers."

14. "Remarks of the President at the University of Michigan," speech delivered on May 22, 1964, quoted in "Statements."

15. "Remarks of the President at the University of Texas Commencement," address delivered on May 30, 1964, quoted in "Statements."

16. "Remarks of the President at Swarthmore College Commencement," address delivered on June 8, 1964, quoted in "Statements."

17. Ibid.

18. "Remarks, Meeting of School Superintendents," address delivered on July 30, 1964, quoted in "Statements."

19. "Remarks, State University Presidents," address delivered on Aug. 13, 1964, quoted in "Statements."

20. "200th Anniversary Convocation of Brown University," address delivered on Sept. 28, 1964, quoted in "Statements."

21. "Remarks, Cleveland Convention of Communications Workers of America," address delivered on June 17, 1964, quoted in "Statements."

22. "Remarks, Civic Arena," address delivered on Oct. 27, 1964, quoted in "Statements."

23. *Dallas News,* October 28, 1964.

24. "Remarks, Cabinet Meeting," address delivered on July 2, 1964, quoted in "Statements."

25. Ibid.

26. Ibid.

27. Quoted in Bobby Baker, with Larry King, *Wheeling and Dealing* (New York: W. W. Norton, 1978), p. 265.

28. James Gaither, Oral History Interview, November 19, 1968, p. 1 (Lyndon B. Johnson Library).

29. Robert Michel to Joe Califano, Sept. 17, 1965, "The Papers of Douglass Cater" (Lyndon B. Johnson Library).

30. Memo, "Policy Formation in the Johnson Administration," undated, "The Papers of James Gaither" (Lyndon B. Johnson Library).

31. "Remarks of the President upon Signing S. 3060 National Defense Education Act Amendments," speech delivered on Oct. 16, 1964, quoted in "Statements."

32. Quoted in Johnson, *Vantage Point,* pp. 207–8.

33. Press Release, Nov. 1, 1964, Washington, D.C., "The Papers of Richard Goodwin" (Lyndon B. Johnson Library).

34. Richard Goodwin to Douglass Cater, Dec. 31, 1964, "Cater Papers."

CHAPTER 11.

1. Quoted in Harry Hursh, *The United States Office of Education* (Philadelphia: Chilton Books, 1965), p. 143.

2. Douglass Cater to Lyndon Johnson, April 2, 1965, "Cater Papers."

3. Barnaby C. Keeney to Lyndon Johnson, Jan. 6, 1965, "LBJ Papers."

4. Francis Keppel, Oral History Interview, April 21, 1969 (Lyndon B. Johnson Library).

5. *Public Papers of the Presidents of the United States,* Lyndon B. Johnson, I, Jan. 1 to Mar. 31, 1965 (Washington, D.C.: Government Printing Office, 1965).

6. Ibid., pp. 94–95.

7. Francis Keppel to Jack Valenti, Feb. 26, 1965, "LBJ Papers."

8. Monroe Sweetland to Douglass Cater, April 1, 1965, "Cater Papers."

9. Johnson, *Vantage Point*, p. 208.

10. Ibid., p. 208.

11. "Text of the Remarks of the President upon Signing the Education Bill," address delivered on April 11, 1965, quoted in "Statements."

12. Francis Keppel, Oral History Interview, April 21, 1969.

13. "Remarks of the President at the Signing of the Community Health Center Act Amendments," address delivered on August 4, 1965, quoted in "Statements."

14. "Remarks of the President at the Signing of the Arts and Humanities Bill," address delivered on September 29, 1965, quoted in "Statements."

15. "Remarks of the President at the Swearing-In Ceremony for Barnaby Keaney," address delivered on July 14, 1966, quoted in "Statements."

16. U.S., Congress, House of Representatives, *Higher Education Act of 1965*, 89th Cong., 1st sess., report 621 (Washington, D.C.: Government Printing Office, 1965), p. 78.

17. "Remarks of the President at the Signing of the Higher Education Act," address delivered on Nov. 8, 1965, quoted in "Statements."

18. "Remarks, National Teacher of the Year Award Presentation," address delivered on Apr. 7, 1965, quoted in "Statements."

19. "Remarks, Project Headstart," address delivered on May 18, 1965, quoted in "Statements."

20. "Remarks, National Technical Institute for the Deaf," address delivered on June 8, 1965, quoted in "Statements."

21. *Public Papers of the Presidents of the United States*, Lyndon Johnson, vol. 1, p. 3.

22. Ibid., p. 6.

23. Ibid., p. 8.

24. Ibid., p. 12.

25. "Remarks of the President upon Signing the Cold War G.I. Bill," address delivered on March 3, 1966, quoted in "Statements."

26. "Remarks of the President on Signing S. 3467, the Child Nutrition Act," address delivered on Oct. 11, 1966, quoted in "Statements."

27. Harold Howe to Douglass Cater, Feb. 28, 1966, "LBJ Papers."

28. "Remarks at the Dedication of Woodrow Wilson Hall at Princeton University," address delivered on May 11, 1966, quoted in "Statements."

29. "Remarks, Military Park," address delivered on October 7, 1966, quoted in "Statements."

30. Ibid.

31. Ibid.

32. Joseph Califano to Douglass Cater et al., July 23, 1966, "The Papers of Mike Manatos" (Lyndon B. Johnson Library).

CHAPTER 12.

1. Quoted in Commager, *Documents of American History*, p. 554.

2. *Congressional Quarterly Almanac*, 1966, 22 (Washington, D.C.: Government Printing Office, 1967), p. 391.

3. Kearns, *Lyndon Johnson and the American Dream*, p. 252.

4. Quoted in *Newsweek*, Jan. 20, 1969, p. 18.

5. David F. Trask, *Victory Without Peace: American Foreign Relations in the Twentieth Century* (New York: Wiley, 1968), p. 162.

6. Untitled address delivered to the University of Texas Ex-Students Association on Nov. 11, 1959, quoted in "Statements."

7. "Remarks of the President at the East-West Center," address delivered on Oct. 18, 1966, quoted in "Statements."

8. Ibid.

9. Ibid.

10. "Remarks, Association of School Administrators," address delivered on May 14, 1965, quoted in "Statements."

11. *Public Papers of the Presidents of the United States*, Lyndon Johnson, vol. 1, p. 11.

12. Press Release, March 1966, "LBJ Papers."

13. Quoted from LBJ to Ruth Sheldon Knowles, Jan. 6, 1967, "LBJ Papers."

14. Quoted in Charles Frankel, *High on Foggy Bottom* (New York: Harper and Row, 1968), p. 11.

15. Memo, Joseph Laitin, Sept. 16, 1965, "LBJ Papers."

16. "Remarks at the Smithson Bicentennial Celebration," address delivered on Sept. 16, 1965, quoted in "Statements."

17. Ibid.

18. Ibid.

19. "Remarks, Message on International Education," address delivered on Feb. 2, 1966, quoted in "Statements."

20. "Remarks to Convention of American Association of School Administrators," address delivered on Feb. 16, 1966, quoted in "Statements."

21. LBJ to Francis Keppel, April 7, 1966, "LBJ Papers."

22. Quoted in *Dallas News*, Oct. 10, 1966.

23. Ibid.

24. White House Press Release, March 3, 1966, "LBJ Papers."

25. Ibid.

26. "Remarks of the President of the Conference on World Education," address delivered on Oct. 8, 1967, quoted in "Statements."

27. Ibid.

28. Ibid.

29. Ibid.

30. "The Fifth Freedom," message delivered on February 5, 1968, quoted in "Statements."

CHAPTER 13.

1. Morris K. Udall, "Come Let Us Reason Together," *Congressman's Report*, December 1963, "LBJ Papers."

2. Ibid.

3. Ibid.

4. *Public Papers of the Presidents of the United States*, Lyndon Johnson, vol. 1, p. 2.

5. Ibid., p. 10.

6. Ibid., p. 11.

7. Ibid., p. 12.

8. Ibid., p. 13.

9. Ibid., p. 14.

10. Ibid., p. 9.

11. "Statement of the President on Signing H.R. 11945, An Act to Strengthen the College Work-Study Program," address delivered on Sept. 7, 1967, quoted in "Statements."

12. "Remarks of the President at the Signing of the Public Broadcasting Act," speech delivered on Nov. 7, 1967, quoted in "Statements."

13. "Remarks of the President on Signing H.R. 6430, 'Mental

Retardation Bill,'" speech delivered on Dec. 4, 1967, quoted in "Statements."

14. Interview, "A Conversation with the President," Washington, D.C., Dec. 19, 1967, "LBJ Papers."

15. *Public Papers of the Presidents of the United States*, Lyndon Johnson, vol. 1, p. 25.

16. Ibid., p. 27.

17. Ibid., p. 28.

18. Ibid., p. 29.

19. Ibid., p. 30.

20. Doris Kearns, "The Power and Pathos of LBJ," *New Republic*, March 13, 1979, p. 29.

21. "Statement by the President on Signing H.R. 7819," speech delivered on Jan. 2, 1968, quoted in "Statements."

22. Ibid.

23. Ramsey Clark to LBJ, June 14, 1968, "LBJ Papers."

24. "Remarks of the President at the Signing of H.R. 12120," speech delivered on July 31, 1968, quoted in "Statements."

25. "Remarks, Signing of the Higher Education Act and the Vocational Education Act," speech delivered on October 10, 1968, quoted in "Statements."

26. Ibid.

27. Ibid.

28. Ibid.

29. Ibid.

30. "Remarks of the President to World Organization of Teaching Professions," speech delivered on Dec. 27, 1968, quoted in "Statements."

31. *Public Papers of the Presidents of the United States*, Lyndon Johnson, vol. 2, p. 1270.

32. Ibid.

33. *Tributes to the President and Mrs. Lyndon Baines Johnson in the Congress of the United States*, p. 62.

34. Ibid., p. 3.

35. Ibid., p. 79.

CHAPTER 14.

1. *Houston Chronicle*, Nov. 3, 1968.

2. Baker, *Wheeling and Dealing*, p. 273.

3. *Dallas Morning News*, Oct. 29, 1968.

4. "America Tomorrow: Will We Hang Together or Hang Separately?" address delivered on Nov. 15, 1971, quoted in "Statements."

5. *Ebony*, Feb. 1973, p. 111.

6. *Congressional Record*, June 10, 1971, p. 8796.

7. Ibid.

8. Leo Janus, "'72 Has Not Been Kind to the Ailing LBJ," *Life*, Oct. 27, 1972, p. 75.

9. *Congressional Quarterly*, Jan. 27, 1973, p. 121.

10. *Newsweek*, Feb. 5, 1973, p. 31.

11. Ibid.

Bibliography

Compassionate Samaritan: The Life of Lyndon Baines Johnson is a synthesis of almost two decades of scholarship on the development of the American educational system during the last century. The book's point of view is highly personal and thus it may generate comment and criticism from both academic professionals and informed laymen. In addition to listing the sources actually cited in the text, in the six subdivisions below I provide a convenient skeleton for discussing the materials I employed to construct the narrative.

COLLECTIONS, MANUSCRIPTS, AND
MANUSCRIPT RECORDS

The bulk of the research was conducted in presidential libraries. In the late sixties and early seventies, I became interested in the formation of national educational policy and the exportation of American education abroad following World War II. I made several visits in this connection to the Harry S Truman Library in Independence, Missouri. My notes were published in an essay entitled "Henry Garland Bennett: The Father of the 'Great Adventure' in University-Contracts Abroad," *The Red River Valley Historical Review*, 2, no. 2 (Summer 1975), pp. 254–72. This essay centers on the work of the Truman Administration. Next, I became interested in how Sputnik affected American education, and I traveled to the

331

Dwight D. Eisenhower Library in Abilene, Kansas, to search for some answers. My essay entitled "Education Research Opportunities at the Dwight Eisenhower Library," *Prologue*, 10, no. 4 (Winter 1977), pp. 242–51, surveyed educational concerns during the 1950s. A trip to the Lyndon B. Johnson Library in Austin, Texas, convinced me that LBJ could serve as a vehicle for telling the story of education in the twentieth century. My preliminary work in this regard I described in "Working in a Presidential Library: One Researcher's Point of View," *LBJ Newsletter* (August 1976), pp. 6–7. The footnotes cited in these three manuscripts are a key to the progression of *Compassionate Samaritan*.

My notetaking in Austin was greatly facilitated by an education finder's guide prepared by the archivists of the LBJ Library. This document lists relevant sources in nine crucial areas: "Pre-Presidential Papers," "White House Central Files," "Aides Files," "Reports on Pending Legislation," "Task Force Reports," "Reports on Enrolled Legislation," "Administrative Histories," "Statements of Lyndon B. Johnson," and "Oral Histories." The importance of this guide as a timesaving device cannot be overemphasized, as the LBJ Library contains some forty million pages of manuscript material. I also spent time in the library of the Southwest Texas State University at San Marcos. The staff of this organization has gathered yearbooks, editions of the college newspaper, oral histories, and correspondence that pertain to Lyndon Johnson.

Sources:

"The Papers of Douglass Cater," Lyndon Baines Johnson Library, Austin, Texas.

"The Papers of Dwight David Eisenhower," Dwight D. Eisenhower Library, Abilene, Kans.

"The Papers of Richard Goodwin," Lyndon Baines Johnson Library, Austin, Texas.

"Clippings of LBJ," The Barker History Center, Lyndon Baines Johnson Library, Austin, Texas (on microfilm).

"The Johnson Family Papers," Lyndon Baines Johnson Library, Austin, Texas.

"Selected Writings of Lyndon Baines Johnson, Student Editor, 1927–1929, *The College Star*, Southwest Texas State Teachers College," Lyndon B. Johnson Library, Austin, Texas.

"The Speeches of Lyndon Baines Johnson," Lyndon Baines Johnson Library, Austin, Texas.

"The Statements of Lyndon Baines Johnson," Lyndon Baines Johnson Library, Austin, Texas.

Knippa, Edwin William. "The Early Political Life of Lyndon Baines Johnson, 1931–1937," unpublished Master's Thesis, Southwest Texas State Teachers College, 1967.

"The Papers of Mike Manatos," Lyndon Baines Johnson Library, Austin, Texas.

U.S. GOVERNMENT DOCUMENTS

Fortunately, the LBJ Library has secured and catalogued the federal records of the National Youth Administration as they relate to the Texas NYA. The local records have been destroyed. The presence of these items in one location was helpful in piecing together a crucial part of Johnson's life that heretofore has been largely neglected. The *Congressional Record, Congressional Almanac*, and *Public Papers of the Presidents of the United States* aided in identifying important speeches, summaries of relevant legislation, and the names and dates of service of staff.

Sources:

The Congressional Records of the United States Congress. Washington, D.C.: Government Printing Office, 1937–1961.

Correspondence and Records of the National Youth Administration, 1935–1937. Lyndon Baines Johnson Library, Austin, Texas (Xerox copies).

88th Congress, 2nd Session, House of Representatives. Report No. 1458, *Economic Opportunity Act.* Washington, D.C.: Government Printing Office, 1964.

88th Congress, 2nd Session. Report No. 1218, Economic Act of 1964. Washington, D.C.: Government Printing Office, 1964.

88th Congress, 1st Session. Report No. 483, *Extension of Juvenile Delinquency and Youth Offences Control Act of 1961.* Washington, D.C.: Government Printing Office, 1964.

89th Congress, 1st Session, House of Representatives. Report No. 621, *Higher Education Act of 1965.* Washington, D.C.: Government Printing Office, 1965.

The Public Papers of the Presidents of the United States. Washington, D.C.: Government Printing Office, 1963–1969.

Udall, Morris K. "Come Let Us Reason Together," in *Congressman's Report*, December 1963.

ORAL HISTORIES

I read approximately thirty oral histories, all of which were on deposit in the LBJ Library. Most of these tapes were prepared under the able supervision of Professor Joe Frantz of the University of Texas. These sources provided many details unavailable in traditional historical documents.

Sources:

Bardwell, Malcolm. Oral History Interview of Oct. 17, 1968. Lyndon Baines Johnson Library, Austin, Texas.

Burleson, Omar. Oral History Interview of Oct. 3, 1968. Lyndon Baines Johnson Library, Austin, Texas.

Gaither, James, Oral History Interview of Nov. 19, 1968. Lyndon Baines Johnson Library, Austin, Texas.

Keppel, Francis. Oral History Interview of Apr. 21, 1969, Lyndon Baines Johnson Library, Austin, Texas.

NEWSPAPERS

The Barker History Center in Austin has kept a newspaper clipping file of LBJ's public life that extends back to the early congressional years. These data have been microfilmed and placed on deposit in the LBJ Library. This collection, as did the education finder's guide, saved many laborious hours.

Sources:

The Austin (Texas) *American,* Sept. 30, 1947.

The Austin (Texas) *Statesman,* 1940–1965.

The Boston (Massachusetts) *Herald,* July 11, 1955.

The (Southwest Texas State Teachers College) *College Star,* 1926–1930.

The Dallas (Texas) *Herald,* Nov. 7, 1966.

The Dallas (Texas) *News,* June 30, 1937–1968.

The Houston (Texas) *Chronicle,* Nov. 3, 1968.

The Houston (Texas) *Post,* Oct. 31, 1965.

The Los Angeles (California) *Times*, July 20, 1960.
The New York (New York) *Times*, 1958–1966.
The San Marcos (Texas) *Daily News*, Mar. 6, 1937.
The Wall Street Journal, July 20, 1950.
The Washington (District of Columbia) *Star*, July 20, 1950.
The Washington (District of Columbia) *Evening Star*, Aug. 8, 1960.

ARTICLES

No doubt the hundreds of essays and articles published in popular periodicals and professional journals are reflected in the final narrative. Most of these items are available in any good public or university library.

Sources:

Janus, Leo. "'72 Has Not Been Kind to the Ailing LBJ," *Life*, Oct. 27, 1972.
Kearns, Doris. "The Power and the Pathos of LBJ," *New Republic*, March 13, 1979.
Kornitilev, Belle. "President Johnson Talks About His Mother and Father," *Parade*, Jan. 5, 1964.
Newsweek, Aug. 15, 1966.
Rulon, Philip R. "Henry Garland Bennett: The Father of the 'Great Adventure' in University-Contracts Abroad." *Red River Valley Historical Review*, 2, no. 1 (Summer 1975).
Shelton, I. "Lyndon Johnson's Mother," *Saturday Evening Post*, May 8, 1965.

BOOKS

The LBJ Library has a specialized book collection numbering twenty-five thousand volumes that pertain to the public and private life of Lyndon B. Johnson. I searched these volumes and then added some other personal selections as well. I owe a very heavy debt to five volumes in particular. The charming essays in Rebekah Johnson's *A Family Album* were instrumental in ascertaining the roots of the thirty-sixth president of the United States. Almost daily, I consulted William C. Pool, Emmie Craddock, and David E. Conrad's *Lyndon Baines Johnson: The Formative Years*. This book is a model of its kind. The most detailed biography of LBJ so far is

Alfred Steinberg's *Sam Johnson's Boy: A Close-up of the President from Texas*. I found the chronology of much value. Unfortunately, however, the author has a strong bias that seeps through almost every page. No present or future biographer can afford to ignore an insightful volume entitled *Lyndon Johnson and the American Dream*, drafted by Doris Kearns. Her tome is a pioneering effort. Last, Lady Bird Johnson's *A White House Diary* proved most helpful in ascertaining the comings and goings of her late husband from 1963 to 1969. It is unfortunate that this skilled journalist has not written more.

Sources:

Baker, Bobby, with Larry King. *Wheeling and Dealing*. New York: W. W. Norton, 1978.

Caidin, Martin, and Hymoff, Edward. *The Mission*. Philadelphia: J. B. Lippincott, 1964.

Commager, Henry S., ed. *Documents of American History*, 7th ed. New York: Appleton-Century-Crofts, 1963.

Frankel, Charles. *High on Foggy Bottom*. New York: Harper and Row, 1968.

Halberstam, David. *The Best and the Brightest*. New York: Random House, 1969.

Haley, J. E. *A Texan Looks at Lyndon*. Canyon, Tex.: Palo Duro Press, 1964.

Johnson, Lyndon B. *The Vantage Point*. New York: Holt, Rinehart and Winston, 1971.

Johnson, Rebekah Baines. *A Family Album*. New York: McGraw-Hill, 1965.

Johnson, Sam Houston (Hawk Lopez, ed.). *My Brother Lyndon*. New York: Cowles, 1969.

Kearns, Doris. *Lyndon Johnson and the American Dream*. New York: Harper and Row, 1976.

Kirk, Russell, and McClellan, James. *The Political Principles of Robert A. Taft*. New York: Fleet Press, 1967.

LBJ Country. Fredericksburg, Tex. Awani Press, 1970.

McPherson, Harry. *A Political Education*. Boston: Little, Brown, 1972.

Parmet, Herbert S. *Eisenhower and the American Crusades*. New York: Macmillan, 1972.

The Pedagog. San Marcos, Texas: Southwest Texas State Teachers College, 1927–1931.

Pool, William C., Craddock, Emmie, and Conrad, David E. *Lyndon Baines Johnson: The Formative Years,* San Marcos, Tex.: Southwest Texas State Teachers College Press, 1965.

Steinberg, Alfred. *Sam Johnson's Boy.* New York: Macmillan, 1968.

Trask, David F. *Victory Without Peace: American Foreign Relations in the Twentieth Century.* New York: John Wiley, 1968.

Wish, Harvey, ed. *American Historians: A Selection.* New York: Oxford University Press, 1962.

Index

Abell, Bess, 194
Acheson, Dean, 138, 140
Agriculture, support by LBJ, 92
Alamo Purchase Bill, 10
Allen, Robert S., 77
Allied Health Professions Personnel Training, 242
Alsop, Stewart, 130
American Association of School Administrators, 115
Anderson, Clinton, 105, 132
Anderson, Samuel E., Lt. Col., 83
Appalachian Regional Development Act, 227–28, 283
Armed Forces Committee, 90, 121
Arts and Humanities, National Foundation on the, 233–34, 292
Atomic Energy, Joint Senate and House Committee on, 90–91
Avery, C.N., 68
Ayes, William H., 235

Bailey, Joseph Weldon, 13, 44–45
Bailey, Stephen, 225, 229
Baines, Mrs. George Wilson, Sr. (LBJ's great-grandmother, née Melissa Ann Butler), 12
Baines, George Wilson, Sr. (LBJ's great-grandfather), 11–12
Baines, Mrs. Joseph Wilson, Jr. (LBJ's grandmother, née Ruth Ament Huffman), 12
Baines, Joseph Wilson, Jr. (LBJ's grandfather), 11, 12, 13

Baines, Rebekah. See Johnson, Mrs. Samuel Ealy, Jr.
Baines, Mrs. Thomas (LBJ's great-great-grandmother, née Mary McCoy), 11
Baines, Rev. Thomas, (LBJ's great-great-grandfather), 11
Baker, Bobby, 125
Bankhead, William B., 71
Bardwell, Malcolm, 47
Bay of Pigs, 251
Bell, David, 262
Bennet, Henry Garland, 95, 161
Bestor, Arthur, 143
Birdwell, Sherman, 54, 62
Black, Justice Hugo, 104
Blanco Blitz. See Johnson, Lyndon Baines
Blanton, Dr. John, 15
Boehn, Frederick M., 195
Boehringer, Eugenia, 49
Bowles, Chester, 153
Bowman, Edward, 26
Brademas, John, 225, 231, 264
Branch, March, 58
Branscomb, Harvie, 155, 263
Braude, Max A., 257
Breckinridge, John W., 9
Brett, General George H., 83
Bridges, Styles, 116
Briggs, Thomas, 33
Brigman, Percy T., 29
Brodie (music teacher), 25
Bronk, Detlov, 141
Brown, George, 132
Brown, Herman, 132

Brown, Richard, 55
Brownlee, Houghton, 68
Brown v. The Topeka Board of Education, 129, 134–35, 184
Bryan, William Jennings, 13, 25
Buchanan, James P., 62, 67
Bundy, McGeorge, 178, 194
Bunton, Lucius, 9
Bunton, Robert Holmes, 8
Burleson, Omar, 72
Burnett, Judge Will, 69
Burns, John A., 164
Busby, Horace, Jr., 100–101, 105, 194, 199, 208
Byrd, Harry, 139

Calhoun, John, 111
Califano, Joseph A., 194, 195, 215, 244–45
Carey, Hugh, 231, 242
Carmichael, William D., 214
Carpenter, Elizabeth S., 194
Carpenter, Leslie, 105
Casparis, Johnny, 26
Castro, Fidel, 251
Cater, S. Douglass, 194, 195, 229, 231, 256, 261, 262, 264, 267, 269, 270
Celebrezze, Anthony, 216, 224, 230
Celler, Emanuel, 231
Chapman, Oscar, 153
Chapman, Virgil, 116
Child Nutrition Act, 241
Christian, George E., 194
Civilian Conservation Corps., 52, 58
Civil rights
  after JFK, 175, 183–85
  and LBJ, 159
  in 1948, 108, 109–13
Civil Rights Act of 1964, purpose and scope of, 183–85
Civil Rights Bill of 1964, 229
Clapp, Margaret, 263
Clark, Albert, 131
Clay, Henry, 111
Clements, Earle, 124
Cloture Rule (Rule 22), as anti-filibuster measure, 109–13
Code of the West, 8
Coffey, Matthew B., 195
Cohen, Wilbur, 214, 224, 229, 230
Cold War, 133, 135, 280–81

College Star, 36–38
Colquitt, Oscar, 23
Communism
  as campaign issue, 78–80, 103, 104
  and China, 115–16
  growth of, 92–93, 95
  and Tonkin Resolution, 248–49.
  See also Vietnam War
Compton Commission, 121
Comstock, E. B., 100
Conant, James, 142
Congress, "Little," 48
Connally, John, 105, 153
Connally, Thomas, 47, 111, 125
Conner, J. O., 58
Conrad, David E., 29
Containment, in Korea, 119
Corporation for Public Broadcasting, 283–84
Creative federalism, 208
Crider, Otto, 27
Crider, Tom, 27
Cronkite, Walter, 305
Cubberley, Ellwood Patterson, 33
Culbertson, Charlie, 13

Daley, Richard J., 189
Daniels, Price, 125
Daughters of the American Revolution, 9
Davis, Carol, 40
Davis, Russell, 257
Davis, W. L., 58
Deadrich, Katie, 20–21, 230
Deaf, National Technical Institute for the, 232, 234
Deason, Willard, 54–55
Defense, national
  budget, 116–20, 251–52
  and LBJ, 113, 115–16, 117, 135
  and Senate Bill 1, 120–21
Desha, Mary, 9
Desha, Governor, 9
Dewey, John, 30–31, 43
Dickson, B., 100
Dies, Martin, 78, 96
Dillon, Douglas, 140
Dirksen, Everett, 184–85
Disarmament, and Open Curtain speech, 135–36
Doolittle, General James, 145
Dougherty, Dudley, 126

Douglas, Helen Gahagan, 103
Douglas, Paul, 105
Drewry, Pat, 77
Duggan, Ervin S., 195
Dulles, John Foster, 135–36, 139, 140
Dungon, Ralph, 193
Dutton, Fred, 211

Early Education of Handicapped Children bill, 294
East-West Center, 160–66, 253–54
Economic Opportunity Act (EOA), 178, 234, 284
  as reform legislation, 185–92
Education
  and beginnings of accountability, 113–14, 129–30, 137, 141, 143
  for blacks, under NYA, 58–59
  changing character of, 43
  de facto and *de jure* segregation in, 129, 134–35
  and defense, 120–21, 135, 137, 145
  effect of Open Curtain speech on, 135–36
  federal aid to, 97–100, 101–2, 104–5, 130, 133, 135–36, 137–40, 145, 167, 229, 234
  formula for federal aid to, 230
  golden age of, 32–33
  under Great Society, 208–10, 212–13, 226–33
  importance of, in Texas, 6, 9–10, 21, 24
  international, 160–66, 168, 253, 256–66, 267, 270
  LBJ's editorials on, 39
  legislation, 154–55, 179–83, 185–88, 216–20, 225, 233, 239, 240, 241–42, 244–45, 263, 269, 282–85, 291–94, 295
  in loco parentis and, 32
  loyalty oaths in, 129, 138
  and NDEA, 137–40, 141–43, 156–57, 217, 218–19, 242
  overspecialization in, 114–16
  science needs in, 130, 134–36, 140–42
  student loans for, 143–44, 155–57, 159–60, 218, 242
  task force on, 216, 229
  television and, 257–58, 269–74
  as thrust of NYA, 57, 59–61
  for veterans and families, 92
  See also South Vietnam
Education, U.S. Office of, 139, 142, 180
  increased role of, 157, 185–86, 223–24, 225, 232, 243–44, 265
  See also Education, legislation
Education, White House Conference on, 137
Education and Labor, House of Representatives Committee on, 137
Education Beyond the High School, President's Committee on, 137
Edwards, India, 153
Eisenhower, Dwight D., 88, 122–23, 133, 140, 149, 158, 161, 221, 248, 279
  and education, 137, 139, 142–43
Elementary and Secondary Education Act, 228–29, 231, 234, 236, 292
Eliot, Charles William, 43
Ellis, Manton, 37
Equal Employment Opportunity, President's Committee on, 169–70
Ervin, Sam, 180
Evans, Cecil, 34–36, 80, 100, 235
Evans, Hiram Wesley, 35
Evans, Louise, 131

Fair Deal, 105, 108, 113, 122
Fair Employment Practices Commission, 109
Farley, Big Jim, 69
Feldman, Myer, 194
Federal City College, 243
Federal Communication Commission, and radio Station KTBC, 88–89
Federal Emergency Relief Administration, 52–53
Ferguson, Jim "Pa," 23–24
Fischer, John, 263
FitzGerald, Frances, 256
Fleeson, Doris, 117
Fletcher, Tom, 189–90, 192
Fogarty, John, 211, 225
Folsom, Marion B., 139
Fong, Hiram, 165, 298–99
Ford, William, 234
Foreign affairs, 90–91, 105
  and LBJ, 160–61, 238–39
  in 1948, 49, 108
  See also South Vietnam; Vietnam War

Foreign Service Academy, 144–45
Fortas, Abraham, 169–70, 199
Frankel, Charles, 260, 261, 262, 264, 269, 270
Franklin, John Hope, 263
Freeman, Roger, 139
Frelinghuysen, 191
Friday, William C., 215
Fulbright, J. William, 111, 160, 256, 260, 261, 264, 268, 269
Furness, Betty, 194

Gaither, James C., 195, 215
Galbraith, John Kenneth, 260
Gallaudet College, 232, 242
Gardner, Herman, 164
Gardner, John W., 214, 215, 224, 226, 256, 258, 260, 261, 262
Gardner Commission, 216
Garner, John Nance (Cactus Jack), 47, 48
George, Walter, 111
Gilchrist, Gib, 59
Glidden, Stella, 25
Goldman, Eric, 194, 199, 200, 203, 210
Goldstein, Ernest, 194
Goldwater, Barry, 123, 180, 200, 221, 309
Goodwin, Richard, 192, 193, 208, 221
Gordon, Kermit, 178
Gorham, William, 214
Government, LBJ definition of, 209
Graham, Elmer, 40
Great Society
    as label, 198–200, 202, 203
    scope of, 200, 208–10, 238–39
    speech, 203–8
    task forces on, 211–16
    See also Education
Green, Alter, 84
Green, Edith, 225, 235, 242
Greene, H.M., 34, 40
Gronouski, John A., 308
Gulf of Tonkin Resolution. See Tonkin Resolution
Gwinn, Ralph W., 138–40

Halberstam, David, 24–25
Haley, J. Evetts, 89
Hallack, Charles, 153
Harbin, Estelle, 48
Hardesty, Bob, 304, 305

Harris, Merton, 68, 70
Harris, Seymour E., 155
Hawaii, as international education center, 164–66
Hawes, Gene R., 180
Haworth, Leland J., 262
Hayden, Carl, 113
Headstart, Project, 236–37
Health, 233, 234, 242
Health Professions Educational Assistance Act, 218, 234
Heller, Walter, 178, 188
Herling, John, 154
Herter, Christian, 165
Higher Education Act of 1965, 234–35
Higher Education Amendments, 242
Higher Education Facilities Act, The, 179–81
Hill, Grover, 79
Hill, Lister, 111, 140–41
Hobby, Oveta Culp, 256
Hofstadter, Richard, 143
Holland, Elmer J., 182
Hollers, Judge Hardy, 95
Hoover, Herbert, 190, 279, 311
Hopkins, Harry, 79
Hopkins, Wally K., 45–46
Hornig, Donald F., 194
Houston, Sam, High School, 44–46
Howe, Harold, II, 225, 263, 264
Hughes, Judge Sarah, 174
Hughes, Philip S., 182
Humphrey, Hubert H., 105, 131, 140, 158, 196, 290, 309
Hunt, Lester, 116
Hurst, Dr. John Willis, 132

Indians, American, 236
Ink, Dwight Albert, 214, 225, 231–32
Ink Commission, 225, 231
Internal Revenue Service (IRS), and educational deductions, 180
International Education Act (IEA), 241–42, 263–66, 267–68, 269
Ireland, John, 12
Irish Mafia, 151

Jackson, Andrew, 25
Jackson, Bob, 48
Jacobsen, E. Jake, 194
Jasper, Herbert, 225

Javits, Jacob, 244
Jenkins, Walter W., 105, 193
Jim Crow Laws, effect on NYA, 58–59
Job Corps, 187, 192
Johnson, George (LBJ's uncle), 44–45
Johnson, James Polk, 23
Johnson, Mrs. Jesse Thomas (LBJ's great-grandmother, née Lucy Webb Barnett), 8
Johnson, Jesse Thomas (LBJ's great-grandfather) 7–8
Johnson, Josefa Hermine (LBJ's sister) 16, 23
Johnson, Lady Bird (Claudia Alta Taylor), 67, 81, 189, 193, 196, 201, 202, 211, 296, 299, 302, 312
   marriage, 49–52
   See also Johnson, Lyndon Baines
Johnson, Lucia Hoffman (LBJ's sister), 16, 23
Johnson, Lucy Baines (Mrs. Patrick J. Nugent), 88, 296, 303
Johnson, Lynda Bird (Mrs. Chuck Robb), 88, 296, 303
Johnson, Lyndon Baines (LBJ)
   administrative skills, 35–36, 48, 54–56, 58
   and the Alpha and Omega Club (White Star), 40, 48
   birth and early years, 15–20, 23
   campaigns, 67–70, 77–82, 95–106, 125–27
   as congressional aide, 46–49, 52
   Congressional committees served by, 71–72, 90–91
   as congressman, 71–77, 82–86, 89, 91–95, 104–5
   and early editorial titles, 37–38, 40
   education, 20–21, 24–26, 29–36
   educational career, 33–35, 40–41, 44–46
   environmental influences, 4, 25, 27–29, 32, 34
   and Far East, 83, 85
   foreign affairs and, 90–91, 105, 115–17
   health, 74–75, 96, 127, 132–33, 233, 303–4, 308, 311
   and journalism, 12–13, 34, 36–39
   Library and School of Public Affairs, 307–10
   as lieutenant commander, 82–85

   loyalty and, 52, 54, 158–59
   March 1968 speech, 288–90
   maternal lineage of, 11–13
   military support by, 91–92
   organizational background, college, 35–36
   parental influences, 17–19, 25–26, 29, 31, 35, 50–52
   paternal lineage of, 7–11
   as president, 1963–1964, 175–76
   as presidential pedagogue, 236–37
   religious background, 8, 11–12, 40
   retirement, 269–97, 302–3, 304, 305–6
   on Robert Taft, 101–3
   as Senate majority leader, 127, 131, 133–39, 140–46, 152–53, 154–57, 160
   as Senate minority leader, 123–26
   as Senate whip, 120–21
   staffs, 105, 125, 177–78, 193–95, 244
   State of the Union addresses, 221–22, 237–38, 279–82, 286–88, 297
   State Park, 302
   on Truman Committee, 116–20
   and use of public support, 55–56, 69, 79–80
   as vice president, 158, 165, 166–71
   See also Baines; Education; Presidential election; Vietnam War
Johnson, Rebekah Luruth (LBJ's sister), 16, 23, 44, 52
Johnson, Sam Houston (LBJ's brother), 15, 16, 23, 44, 52, 75–76, 105
Johnson, Mrs. Samuel Ealy, Jr. (LBJ's mother, née Rebekah Baines)
   death, 141
   importance of family line to, 7, 11
   and LBJ, 25–26, 29–39, 75–76, 81
   on LBJ's marriage, 50–52
   marriage, 12–14, 23–24
Johnson, Samuel Ealy, Jr. (LBJ's father) 7, 9–11, 12–13, 14–15, 23–24, 28, 41–42, 46, 67, 70, 75
   See also Johnson, Lyndon Baines
Johnson, Mrs. Samuel Ealy, Sr. (LBJ's grandmother, née Eliza Bunton), 8–9
Johnson, Samuel Ealy, Sr. (LBJ's grandfather), 7–8, 16, 17, 23
Johnson, "Skeeter" (no relation to LBJ), 125
Johnson, Tom, 195

Johnson City Windmill, 97–98
Jones, James R., 194, 195
Josephs, Devereux Colt, 137
Juvenile Delinquency and Youth Offenses Control Act, 185, 232

Kearns, Doris, 291, 303, 307
Keele, Kate, 15
Keeney, Barnaby, 152, 210, 225, 234
Kefauver, Estes, 105, 116
Kellam, Jesse, 54, 61–62, 235
Kennedy, Edward (Ted), 151
Kennedy, John F. (JFK), 138, 150, 200, 248, 251, 278, 311
  and 1960 campaign, 151–52, 153, 154, 157–59, 166
  as president, 166–71
  programs after death, 174–75, 184–85
Kennedy, Robert, 151, 188, 267, 288
Kennon, George, 119
Kenny, General George C., 83
Kent, Frank, 131
Keppel, Francis, 225, 226, 229, 230, 231, 256, 262, 267
Kerr, Clark, 164
Kerr, Robert, 105
King, Charles, 95
Kintner, Robert E., 194
Kleberg, Richard E., 46–49, 52, 236
Knippa, William, 57, 61–62
Knowland, William, 123, 125
Knowles, Ruth Sheldon, 260
Komer, Robert W., 194
Korean conflict, 116–20
Krock, Arthur, 131
Krushchev, Nikita, 135–36, 152
KTBC radio station, 88–89

LaFollette, Bob, 43
Laitin, Joseph, 261
Landrum, Phillip, 188
Lasker, Mary, 155
Lasswell, Harold, 27–28
Latimer, George, 45
Lawrence, David, 151, 194
Lee, H. Rex, 271
Leonhart, William, 194
Levinson, Lawrence, 195
Library Services and Construction Act, 183, 241, 284
Lindig, Otto, 24

Lindquist, Clarence B., 134
Linen, James A., III, 263
Lippmann, Walter, 131, 159, 200
Loney, Chester, 20
Long, Huey, 82
Long, Russell, 105
Loomis, Henry, 225
Lovell, James A., Jr., 194
Lund, F. Edward, 155
Lynch, Vernon, 37

MacArthur, General Douglas, 83
McCarthy, Eugene, 288
McCarthy, Joseph, 125
McClelland, John, 269
McCormack, John, 77, 188
McElroy, Dorothy, 49
McElroy, Neil, 137
McFarland, Ernest, 120, 123
McGill, Ralph, 159
McGovern, George S., 154
McHunt, Joseph, 214
McInerney, General T.A., 131
McNamara, Robert, 178, 251
MacPhail, Donald B., 270
McPherson, Harry C., Jr., 138, 194, 195, 263, 292
Macy, John W., Jr., 215
Magnuson, Warren, 283
Maguire, Charles M., 195
Malinshek, Dale, 303
Manatos, Michael, 193, 194, 244
Mann, Gerald, 78
Mann, Horace, 6
Manpower Development and Training Act, 182–83, 232, 243, 294
Mansfield, Mike, 141, 152, 188
Marine Resources Education and Research Act, 241
Markman, Sherwin, 195
Marks, Leonard, 262, 270
Marshall, George, 119
Marshall Plan, 90, 95
Martin, Clarence, 17
Martin, Joseph, 90
Marvel, William, 263
Maverick, Maury, 55, 59, 71
Meade, Edward J., 257, 258
Medicare bill, 233
Mental Retardation Facilities and Community Health Centers Construction Act, 284

Michel, Robert H., 215
Middleton, Harry, 304–5
Miles, Rufus E., Jr., 226
Military-industrial complex, 88
Miller, Paul A., 215, 270
Model Secondary School for the Deaf Act, 241
Montgomery, Robert, 54
Montoya, Joseph, 282
Moon, Rexford G., 155
Morse, John F., 155
Morse, Wayne, 119–20, 126, 180, 183, 225, 230, 244, 255, 261, 264, 267
Mosse, Richard, 195
Moyers, Bill, 194, 199, 208, 211, 212
Moyes, W. J., 45, 99
Mundt, Karl, 138
Murphy, Charles S., 194
Murray, James, 141
Musial, Stan, 194
Muskie, Edmund, 298
Mutual Security Agency (MSA), 161–62, 164

National Council on the Arts, 217
National Defense Education Act (NDEA), purpose and passage of, 137–40, 141–43, 156–57, 181
National Security Training Corps, 120–21
National Teacher Corps, 235
National Youth Administration (NYA), 53, 62–63, 74. *See also* Texas National Youth Administration
NDEA. *See* National Defense Education Act (NDEA)
Neff, Pat, 45, 49
Nelson, Richard, 199
New Deal, and LBJ, 49, 52, 67, 70–71
New England Transcendentalists, 6
New Frontier, 152, 171
after JFK, 175
Newland, Dr. Chester, 309
Nichols, Thomas, 235
Nixon, Richard M., 103, 123, 150, 153, 166, 213, 221, 265, 290, 299, 311
Nolle, Dean A. H., 31
North Vietnam. *See* Vietnam War
Nurses Training Act of 1964, 217–18
NYA. *See* National Youth Administration
Nye Commission, 85–86

Nye, Gerald, 85

O'Brien, Lawrence, 151, 178, 189, 231
O'Daniel, Governor W. Lee, 78, 81
Odegaard, Charles, 263
O'Donnell, Kenneth P., 193
Oganovic, Nicholas, 225
Omnibus Crime Control and Safe Streets Act, 292
O'Neill, Mike, 224
Open Curtain speech, 135–36, 152
Operation Breadbasket, 93
Opportunity House, 44

Parks, roadside, under TNYA, 59
Parr, George, 104
Patman, Wright, 10, 18, 28, 47
Peace Corps, 167, 248, 270
Pearson, Drew, 77, 233
Pedagog, 37
Peddy, George, 96, 100, 101
Pedernales Electric Power Project, 34
Pell, Claiborne, 233
Perkins, Carl, 181, 225, 228, 231
Peterson, Esther, 194
Phillips, David Graham, 107
Porter, Jack, 104
Postwar Military Policy, Select Committee on, 90
Postwar Policy Committee of the House of Representatives, 121
Poverty
in Cotulla, 41–42
in Far East, 83
war on, 175–76, 178, 188-89, 200–201, 236–37
See also Economic Opportunity Act; Education; South Vietnam
Powell, Adam Clayton, 225, 231
Preparedness Investigating Subcommittee of the Senate Armed Forces Committee, 116, 137, 141
Presidential elections
of 1960, 150–54, 157–59, 165, 166
of 1964, 220–21
of 1968, 295–96
Price, T.A., 72
Pringle, Henry S., 119
Progressivism, 23
Project Echo, 152
Public Broadcasting Act, 274
Public Health Service Act, 234

Pucinski, Roman, 241
Pusey, Nathan, 155

Quinn, William, 165

Randolph, Jennings, 267, 283
Ransom, Harry, 263
Rather, Dan, 285
Rather, Mary, 105
Rayburn, Sam, 10, 47, 68, 72, 77, 89–90, 127, 153, 157
Reed, Thomas, 111
Reed, Wayne, 225
Reedy, George E., 194, 199
Reston, James, 140
Reynolds, Frank, 285
Rhoads, Joseph, 58
Rice, Joseph Mayer, 43
Rickover, Hyman, 143, 145
Robers, Charles M., 99–100
Roberts, Juanita Duggan, 132, 194
Roberts, Kenneth A., 217
Robinson, Joseph, 111
Roche, John P., 194
Rockefeller, Nelson, 220
Rogers, Paul, 241–42
Rooney, John, 264
Roosevelt, Eleanor (Mrs. Franklin D.), 55
Roosevelt, Franklin Delano, 44, 52, 55, 62–63, 200, 248, 279
    death of, 90
    inaugural address by, 49
Rosen, Harold, 269
Rosenblatt, Peter R., 195
Ross, Ayres K., 68
Ross, Kittie Clyde, 26, 29
Ross, Stanford G., 195
Rostow, Walt W., 194
Roundtree, Payne, 27
Rowen, Henry R., 263
Rudder, James Earl, 257, 258
Rural Electrification Administration, 72, 77
Rusk, Dean, 178, 214, 251, 262
Russell, Richard, 109, 113, 131

Sakai, Sabura, 84
Salinger, Pieere, 193
Saltonstall, Leverett, 116
Sandburg, Carl, 234
Sanders, Harold Barefoot, Jr., 194

Scherer, Ray, 285
Schlesinger, Arthur, Jr., 193
Schultz, George P., 215
Schultze, Charles L., 214
Sheldon, Charles M., 43
Shelton, Polk, 68
Shelton, R. H., 100
Sheppard, Morris, 47
Shivers, Allan, 125
Shriver, Sargent, 88, 178, 189, 263
Silber, John R., 237
Smathers, George, 131
Smith, Adam, 203
Smith, Courtney, 155
Smith, "Judge" Howard, 188
Smith, Stanley S., 68
Smith, Stephen, 151
Smithson, James, 262
Snyder, John L., 182
Sorensen, Theodore, 151, 193, 194
South Vietnam
    modernization policies in, 252–54, 255, 256–62, 266
    task force, 256, 257, 262, 264
    See also Vietnam War
Southwest Texas State Teachers College (STSTC)
    Alpha and Omega Club, 40
    Harris-Blair Club, 40
    influence on LBJ, 29–32, 35–36
    journalism at, 36–37
    LBJ as alumnus, 65–67
    Schoolmaster's Club, 39–40
    Press Club, 39
Space Council, NASA and LBJ, 169
Sparkman, John, 298
Staggers, Harley, 242
Steinberg, Alfred, 192
Stevens, Robert L., 194
Stevenson, Adlai, 122, 150, 153, 157
Stevenson, Coke, 96–97, 100, 103, 126
Stewart, William H., 256
Stone, Sam, 68
Student Loan Insurance Bill (S. 2710) 155–57, 159–60
Summy, Otho, 27
Surplus Property Act of 1944, 91–92
Sweetland, Monroe, 229
Symington, Stuart, 153, 157

Tabor, John, 108
Taft, Robert, 97, 113, 123, 125, 167